MOVING THROUGH ADOLESCENCE: DEVELOPMENTAL TRAJECTORIES OF AFRICAN AMERICAN AND EUROPEAN AMERICAN YOUTH

Leslie Morrison Gutman, University College London
Stephen C. Peck, University of Michigan
Oksana Malanchuk, University of Michigan
Arnold J. Sameroff, University of Michigan
Jacquelynne S. Eccles, University of California, Irvine

WITH COMMENTARY BY

Judith G. Smetana

Patricia J. Bauer
Series Editor

MONOGRAPHS OF THE SOCIETY FOR RESEARCH IN CHILD DEVELOPMENT

Serial No. 327, Vol. 82, No. 4, 2017

WILEY

Boston, Massachusetts   *Oxford, United Kingdom*

MOVING THROUGH ADOLESCENCE: DEVELOPMENTAL TRAJECTORIES OF AFRICAN AMERICAN AND EUROPEAN AMERICAN YOUTH

CONTENTS

I. INTRODUCTION: MOVING THROUGH ADOLESCENCE: DEVELOPMENTAL   7
TRAJECTORIES OF AFRICAN AMERICAN AND EUROPEAN AMERICAN YOUTH
Leslie Morrison Gutman, Stephen C. Peck, Oksana Malanchuk, Arnold J. Sameroff,
and Jacquelynne S. Eccles

II. METHOD   29
Leslie Morrison Gutman, Stephen C. Peck, Oksana Malanchuk, Arnold J. Sameroff,
and Jacquelynne S. Eccles

III. PRELIMINARY ANALYSES AND ANALYTIC PLAN   54
Leslie Morrison Gutman, Stephen C. Peck, Oksana Malanchuk, Arnold J. Sameroff,
and Jacquelynne S. Eccles

IV. PSYCHOLOGICAL WELL-BEING   70
Leslie Morrison Gutman, Stephen C. Peck, Oksana Malanchuk, Arnold J. Sameroff,
and Jacquelynne S. Eccles

V. R/E IDENTITY AND DISCRIMINATION   83
Leslie Morrison Gutman, Stephen C. Peck, Oksana Malanchuk, Arnold J. Sameroff,
and Jacquelynne S. Eccles

VI. ACADEMIC FUNCTIONING   95
Leslie Morrison Gutman, Stephen C. Peck, Oksana Malanchuk, Arnold J. Sameroff,
and Jacquelynne S. Eccles

VII. PROBLEM BEHAVIORS   106
Leslie Morrison Gutman, Stephen C. Peck, Oksana Malanchuk, Arnold J. Sameroff,
and Jacquelynne S. Eccles

VIII. FAMILY CHARACTERISTICS   114
Leslie Morrison Gutman, Stephen C. Peck, Oksana Malanchuk, Arnold J. Sameroff,
and Jacquelynne S. Eccles

IX. PEER CHARACTERISTICS   124
Leslie Morrison Gutman, Stephen C. Peck, Oksana Malanchuk, Arnold J. Sameroff,
and Jacquelynne S. Eccles

X. INTEGRATIVE SUMMARY   133
Leslie Morrison Gutman, Stephen C. Peck, Oksana Malanchuk, Arnold J. Sameroff,
and Jacquelynne S. Eccles

REFERENCES   143

ACKNOWLEDGMENTS   166

COMMENTARY

COMMENTARY ON "MOVING THROUGH ADOLESCENCE: DEVELOPMENTAL   167
TRAJECTORIES OF AFRICAN AMERICAN AND EUROPEAN AMERICAN YOUTH"
Judith G. Smetana

CONTRIBUTORS   178

STATEMENT OF EDITORIAL POLICY   180

SUBJECT INDEX   182

I. INTRODUCTION: MOVING THROUGH ADOLESCENCE: DEVELOPMENTAL TRAJECTORIES OF AFRICAN AMERICAN AND EUROPEAN AMERICAN YOUTH

Leslie Morrison Gutman, Stephen C. Peck, Oksana Malanchuk, Arnold J. Sameroff, and Jacquelynne S. Eccles

This article is part of the issue "Moving Through Adolescence: Developmental Trajectories of African American and European American Youth" Gutman, Peck, Malanchuk, Sameroff, and Eccles (Issue Authors). For a full listing of articles in this issue, see: http://onlinelibrary.wiley.com/doi/10.1111/mono.v82.4/issuetoc.

ABSTRACT In this monograph, we investigate the developmental trajectories of a predominantly middle-class, community-based sample of European American and African American adolescents growing up in urban, suburban, and rural areas in Maryland, United States. Within risk-protection and positive youth development frameworks, we selected developmental measures based on the normative tasks of adolescence and the most widely studied indicators in the three major contexts of development: families, peer groups, and schools. Using hierarchical linear growth models, we estimated adolescents' growth trajectories from ages 12 to 20 with variation accounted for by socioeconomic status (SES), gender, race/ethnicity, and the gender by race/ethnicity interaction. In general, the results indicate that: (a) periods of greatest risk and positive development depended on the time frame and outcome being examined and (b) on average, these adolescents demonstrated much stronger evidence of positive than problematic development, even at their most vulnerable times. Absolute levels of their engagement in healthy behaviors, supportive relationships with parents and friends, and positive self-perceptions and psychological well-being were much higher than their reported angry and depressive feelings, engagement in risky behaviors, and negative relationships with parents and peers. We did not find evidence to support the idea that adolescence is a time of heightened risk. Rather, on average, these adolescents experienced relatively stable and developmentally healthy trajectories for a wide range of characteristics, behaviors, and relationships, with slight increases or decreases at different points in development that varied according to domain. Developmental trajectories differed minimally by SES but in some expected ways by gender and race/ethnicity, although these latter differences were not very marked. Overall, most of the young people navigated through their adolescence and arrived at young adulthood with good mental and physical health, positive

Corresponding author: Leslie Morrison Gutman, Department of Clinical, Educational and Health Psychology, University College London, 1-19 Torrington Place, London WC1E 7HB, email: l.gutman@ucl.ac.uk
DOI: 10.1111/mono.12327

relationships with their parents and peers, and high aspirations and expectations for what their future lives might hold.

Adolescence is a critical period for the development and consolidation of behaviors, values, aspirations, and attitudes that impact current and future options and outcomes. Adolescence is also a time filled with changing risk and protective factors operating at both the individual and social/contextual levels. Many teenagers have reported engaging in increasing levels of risky behaviors such as drinking alcohol, smoking cigarettes, and taking drugs from early to late adolescence (cf., Johnston, O'Malley, Bachman, & Schulenberg, 2011) and experiencing an overall decline in achievement and motivation over the junior high and high school years (cf., Wigfield, Byrnes, & Eccles, 2006). At the same time, adolescents have reported rising levels of self-esteem (Greene & Way, 2005), more egalitarian and less conflictual interactions with parents, and increasingly close and supportive friendships (De Goede, Branje, & Meeus, 2009; Rubin, Bukowski, & Laursen, 2011).

Given that adolescence is a period of such rapid change, it is a perfect time to study changes in the beliefs, behaviors, and relationships that are associated with the challenges and opportunities during this stage of life. Media portrayals suggest that many youth are getting caught up in risky behaviors and relationships as they pass from early to late adolescence (e.g., http://www.nytimes.com/2014/06/29/opinion/sunday/why-teenagers-act-crazy.html?_r=0) and, as a consequence, experiencing major mental and physical health problems. Is this the case? A longitudinal examination of adolescents' beliefs, behaviors, emotional functioning, and relationships is needed to answer this question. Determining whether these trajectories vary by gender, race/ethnicity, or their intersection, as well as socioeconomic status (SES), will tell us whether the answer varies by major social groups in the United States. Together, these results will help us understand the nature of the risks our adolescents face as they develop and provide insights into how we might better support their healthy development.

A comprehensive, integrated description of such normative changes from early to late adolescence is sorely lacking. Such a systematic effort is highly regarded as one of the main goals in the developmental science of adolescence (Baltes, Reese, & Nesselroade, 1977; Lerner, 2007) and is considered the primary basis of formulating developmental models in context (Bronfenbrenner, 2009; Eccles et al., 1993; Lerner, 2007; Magnusson, 1985, 2003). The need is especially marked for racial/ethnic (R/E) minority adolescents, who remain underrepresented in studies of normative development. One reason for this research gap is the dearth of longitudinal data documenting developmental changes from early to late adolescence for R/E minority youth from a wide range of socioeconomic backgrounds (Hagen, Nelson, & Velissaris, 2004). Such an investigation would provide a much-needed portrait of African American and European American youth during a formative and unique period of development.

Drawing upon the Maryland Adolescent Development in Context Study (MADICS), we sought to fill this knowledge gap through a wide-ranging description of changes in aspects of risky and positive youth development from each of the major domains of adolescent development including psychological well-being, R/E identity, academic functioning, problem behaviors, and family and peer characteristics. In keeping with a long tradition in developmental psychology of providing an "as accurate as possible" narrative of changes across important periods of development, we estimated the growth trajectories of the most commonly studied indicators of functioning for a locally representative sample of African American and European American youth from early through late adolescence. We adopted a unified but parsimonious approach to describing developmental pathways in both intrapersonal and interpersonal spheres, thus bringing together in one document a wide-ranging picture of adolescence for a sample of young people in the United States.

Our study provides a unique contribution to the literature, as few longitudinal datasets include both African American and European American adolescents from a broad and comparable range of socioeconomic backgrounds that span from 12 to 20 years of age. Until quite recently, most studies comparing African American and European American youth have confounded race/ethnicity and family SES. This sample was purposively selected to overcome this limitation by studying African American and European American adolescents growing up in families with as comparable social class statuses as possible given the context of the United States, attending the same school system, and living in the same geographical region.

THEORETICAL FRAMEWORK

In order to understand healthy adolescent development, it is essential to consider both the adolescent and the social-ecological context within which development occurs (Bronfenbrenner & Morris, 1998; Eccles et al., 1993; Furstenberg, Cook, Eccles, Elder, & Sameroff, 1999; Lerner, 2007). Many characteristics of both adolescents and their developmental context can be conceptualized strategically in terms of risk and protective factors. The science of prevention (Coie et al., 1993) highlights the importance of identifying risk factors to prevent the occurrence of problem behaviors before they become less amenable to change (Catalano et al., 2012; Hawkins, Catalano, & Miller, 1992; Welsh & Farrington, 2007) and recognizing the positive factors that promote healthy development or mitigate problem behaviors (Gootman & Eccles, 2002; Lösel & Farrington, 2012). In order to effectively minimize risk and boost protection at the right time for various adolescents, it is necessary to chart the developmental trajectories of characteristics, behaviors, and contexts associated with risk and protective factors from early to late adolescence, examining variations in different groups of youth. As it stands, studies that have examined these pathways in adolescence have focused on a narrow set of behaviors and contexts (e.g., Kim, Oesterle, Catalano, & Hawkins, 2015; Van Der Put et al., 2011). A comprehensive assessment of how these characteristics, behaviors, and contexts typically change during adolescence—and whether these changes vary according to adolescents' family status, SES, gender, race/ethnicity, and the intersection of gender and race/ethnicity—will provide important information regarding the optimal timing of risk prevention and enhanced protection for different groups of adolescents.

Exactly what are risk and protective factors? Are they different from each other or are they the opposite ends of similar factors? Family climate, for example, can be a major risk factor, where hostile, but can also be conceived of as a protective factor for youth who live in a supportive family context. Are these just the opposite ends of a continuum of negative to positive family context? Or, is it useful to make clear distinctions between what are conceptualized as risk factors versus protective factors? Sameroff and Gutman (2004) argued that the answer to this latter question is, "yes," if our goal is to create interventions designed to reduce risk and increase protection. Based on the common conceptualization of risk factors as those factors that increase the likelihood of risk, and protective factors as those that facilitate healthy development, they concluded it is useful to distinguish the two. Unfortunately, connotative meanings are frequently overlapping, and denotative meanings are often conflicting (Gutman, Sameroff, & Cole, 2003).

In its earliest conception, the term "protective factor" was reserved for only those factors that counteract the effects of risk (Garmezy, Masten, & Tellegen, 1984; Rutter, 1987). However, many researchers have used the term protective factor to refer to all potentially positive influences regardless of the individual's risk levels. In order to lessen the imprecision of the use of the term protective, Sameroff (2000) proposed that when a variable has a positive but non-interactive direct effect it should be labeled as *promotive* to contrast it with a *protective* variable; whereas the term *protective* should be reserved for those variables that protect those at risk. Some researchers also refer to promotive factors as *developmental assets* because they are assumed to facilitate healthy development regardless of the presence or absence of risk (Ford & Lerner, 1992). In short, both conceptually and empirically, the terms promotive factors and developmental assets overlap considerably (Schwartz, Pantin, Coatsworth, & Szapocznik, 2007).

In this study, we focused on two key perspectives for understanding, predicting, and intervening in adolescent development; namely, resilience and positive youth development. Although these two perspectives are both rooted in the notion of plasticity, where individual development can be

10

redirected by changing the nature of the individual-context relationship (Schwartz et al., 2007), they differ in their implications for the study of adolescent development. Resilience research focuses on relatively successful development, despite experiencing major adversity, and elucidates the role of protective factors in buffering the negative effects of risk. Positive youth development, in contrast, emphasizes that positive developmental trajectories are the result of mutually beneficial relationships between the individual and aspects of their context that promote healthy development (Benson, Scales, Hamilton, & Sesma, 2006; Lerner, 2005, 2007). Lerner and his coworkers (see Lerner, 2007) identified five characteristics of positive youth development that they labeled as the Five Cs: confidence, competence, character, caring, and connection. These Cs include positive psychosocial and relational constructs such as self-esteem, academic competence, interpersonal skills, and connections to family, friends, and community.

These two approaches have complementary strengths and weaknesses. Resilience, for example, acknowledges the negative effects of risk but tends to neglect indicators of positive development; in contrast, positive youth development highlights the strengths inherent in young people but overlooks the role of risk factors and the possibility of negative outcomes in development. Bringing together these two frameworks provides a more holistic approach to understanding optimal adolescent development (Kia-Keating, Dowdy, Morgan, & Noam, 2011; Schwartz et al., 2007). This goal guided our selection of the developmental measures of adolescence included in this monograph. We examined a broad set of characteristics, behaviors, and social contexts related to the major developmental tasks of adolescence; namely, identity formation, the maintenance of psychological well-being during a turbulent period of development, the completion of schooling and training for the transition into adulthood, the exploration of behaviors associated with adulthood, the shift in relationships within one's family and peer groups, and coping with living in a socially stratified culture.

As a first step, we differentiated characteristics, behaviors, and contexts that should be viewed as risky versus protective. To achieve this goal, we were mindful of the extent to which any particular characteristic, behavior, or context might serve as either a risk or protective factor and could vary as a function of race/ethnicity, gender, SES, and developmental stage. For instance, although having controlling parents might be considered a risk factor for middle-class European American adolescents, it might be a protective factor in African American families living in high-risk neighborhoods, especially during early adolescence (Smetana, Campione-Barr, & Daddis, 2004). Furthermore, what might be deemed as risky or protective at one point in time may not be risky or protective at another. For example, first alcohol use between the ages of 11 and 14 constitutes a heightened risk for progression to later alcohol disorders, whereas first alcohol use at age 19 and older is associated with a very low risk of developing disorders (DeWit, Adlaf, Offord, & Ogborne, 2000). Although we discuss these nuances where pertinent, we distinguished factors that are considered risky and lead to worse outcomes from factors that are typically viewed as positive and facilitate healthy development for most adolescents.

The classification of our constructs as either risky or protective was based on previous empirical research detailed below in the subsections for each domain. We did not distinguish between promotive and protective factors in our categorization, given their extensive overlap in positive spheres of development (Schwartz et al., 2007). However, it is important to point out that, for given youth at specific times in development, these positive factors may take on promotive or protective effects, depending on the characteristics of the youth and the outcome in question. With these categories in mind, risk factors assessed in our study include: suffering from poor psychological well-being, facing high levels of R/E discrimination, engaging in problem behaviors, experiencing controlling parents and negative parent–adolescent relationships, and having a lot of friends engaged in risky behaviors. Promotive/protective factors include: good psychological well-being; developing a positive R/E identity; holding high educational and occupational aspirations and educational expectations; possessing positive academic self-beliefs, values, and motivation; and enjoying positive parent and peer relationships, communication, and support.

ADOLESCENT DEVELOPMENT

The developmental period from early to late adolescence is distinctive in its multitude of concurrent changes across various contexts and dimensions (Eccles et al., 1993). Adolescents' assessment and construction of both themselves and their surroundings are typically assumed to shift markedly as a result of changes in the social contexts that adolescents inhabit, the social norms to which adolescents are expected to respond, biologically programmed brain maturation, socially mediated cognitive growth, and the nature of social relationships (Eccles et al., 1993). These biological and social forces are likely to influence the course of adolescents' trajectories. As a result, the phase of life between early to late adolescence is an ideal period to examine trajectories of developmental change, as reflected in their intra-individual and interpersonal worlds. As noted earlier, we considered multiple domains, each of which represents a significant context of adolescent development.

Within each of these domains, a summary of previous findings regarding normative longitudinal trajectories and how these might vary according to sociodemographic characteristics is presented below. In particular, the following points were addressed: (a) why this domain is important to study in adolescence; (b) what the research says about how the measures we studied reflect either risk, promotive, or protective factors; (c) what the longitudinal trajectories look like; and (d) how they differ by gender and race/ethnicity. Where pertinent, we include our hypotheses about what we expect to find, given the current literature.

PSYCHOLOGICAL WELL-BEING

Adolescence is a particularly important period for investigating trajectories of psychological well-being. Given the myriad of physical and social changes facing adolescents, changes and stability in psychological functioning signify how youth are managing during this developmental stage (Eccles et al., 1993). In general, most youth manage to navigate through adolescence with relatively high and stable self-esteem (Birkeland, Melkevik, Holsen & Wold, 2012) and feelings of resiliency (Vecchione, Alessandri, Barbaranelli & Gerbino, 2010). At the same time, however, approximately one in four or five adolescents meet the criteria for a mental health disorder with severe impairment across their lifetime (Merikangas et al., 2010). The majority of mental health problems emerge during adolescence (Hudson, Hiripi, Pope, & Kessler, 2007; Merikangas et al., 2010)—including mood disorders, behavioral problems, and eating pathology—underscoring the need for prevention and early intervention during this developmental stage (Cohen et al., 1993; Kim-Cohen et al., 2006; Lewinsohn, Hops, Roberts, Seeley, & Andrew, 1993). In our study, we examined a number of risk factors related to psychological well-being: anger, depressive affect, eating disorders, and expectations of negative life chances, as well as two promotive/protective factors: self-esteem and resiliency. It is important to note that resiliency here does not refer to the theoretical framework of resilience. Rather, resiliency here refers to the psychological ability to adapt to challenges and new situations. Thus it is somewhat analogous to the currently popular concept of grit (Duckworth, Peterson, Matthews, & Kelly, 2007).

Numerous studies have documented the risk, promotive, and protective effects of adolescents' psychological functioning on a wide range of outcomes. Negative indicators of psychological functioning in childhood and adolescence predict mental health problems in adulthood as well as a number of deleterious outcomes, including antisocial behavior, poor social relationships, alcoholism, and substance abuse (Card, Stucky, Sawalani, & Little, 2008; McLeod, Horwood, & Fergusson, 2016; Measelle, Stice, & Hogansen, 2006). In terms of promotive effects, having high self-esteem predicts long-term success and well-being in a number of domains including work, relationships, and mental and physical health (Orth & Robins, 2014); in contrast, low self-esteem predicts poor physical and mental health, low economic prospects, and high levels of criminal behavior in adulthood (Orth, Robins, & Robert, 2008; Trzesniewski et al., 2006). Resiliency has been shown to predict less alcohol use in adolescence (Wong et al., 2006). Together, these findings suggest that boosting these positive factors in adolescence may both promote healthy development and protect against adverse outcomes, equally concurrently and in the future.

Longitudinal studies have generally shown either stability or increases in both positive and negative aspects of psychological well-being during adolescence, although there are variations depending on the specific indicator examined. For example, previous studies have found a pattern of increasing depressive symptoms from early to middle adolescence (Cole et al., 2002; Garber, Keiley, & Martin, 2002) and declining levels of depression and anger in late adolescence and early adulthood (Galambos, Barker, & Krahn, 2006; Galambos & Krahn, 2008; Ge, Natsuaki, & Conger, 2006). Eating disorders have been shown to increase steadily during adolescence, peaking in early adulthood (Hudson et al., 2007; Measelle et al., 2006). An increase in self-esteem has also been demonstrated during adolescence (Erol & Orth, 2011; Orth & Robins, 2014) and emerging adulthood (Galambos et al., 2006). Resiliency, on the other hand, has been shown to remain stable across adolescence (Vecchione et al., 2010). However, few studies have examined multiple trajectories of psychological well-being across the entire period of adolescence. Given the available findings, we expected an initial increase in the levels of depression, anger, eating disorders, and self-esteem in early adolescence followed by declines in depression and anger but continued increases in self-esteem and eating disorders during late adolescence. We had no predictions for expectations of negative future life events because this has rarely been studied, and we expected our indicator of resiliency to remain stable.

In terms of gender differences, female adolescents generally evidence worsening trajectories on several indicators of psychological well-being compared to male adolescents; for example, females are more likely than males to report increasing levels of depression (Cole et al., 2002; Garber et al., 2002). Although some studies have also shown stereotypic gender differences for self-esteem (Baldwin & Hoffmann, 2002; Block & Robins, 1993; Zimmerman, Copeland, Shope, & Dielman, 1997), others have found no differences in the developmental trajectories of self-esteem between males and females (Erol & Orth, 2011). The prevalence of eating disorders is also greater for female than for male adolescents (Smink, Hoeken, & Hoek, 2012), with an increase in girls' eating pathology from early to late adolescence (Measelle et al., 2006), peaking around age 18–21 (Hudson et al., 2007). Although boys generally report higher levels of aggression compared to girls (Card et al., 2008), there is little evidence of gender differences in the

14

developmental trajectories of aggression (Brody et al., 2003; Kim, Kamphuis, Orpinas, & Kelder, 2010). Therefore, we hypothesized that gender differences would be evident for most of our indicators, with females showing lower and deteriorating psychological well-being compared to males. For anger and expectations of negative chances, we expected that males would have higher levels but similar trajectories compared to females.

There is much less research examining these psychological functioning trajectories for racially/ethnically diverse adolescents, particularly those that untangle the effects of race/ethnicity, gender, and SES. On the one hand, African American adolescents report higher levels of self-esteem (Bachman, O'Malley, Freedman-Doan, Trzesniewski, & Donnellan 2011) and sharper increases from early adolescence to adulthood (Erol & Orth, 2011) compared to European American youth. On the other hand, some studies show African American adolescents reporting higher levels of depression compared to European American adolescents (Adkins, Wang, & Elder, 2009; Gore & Aseltine, 2003), with persistent R/E differences in parallel trajectories that did not converge from adolescence to young adulthood (Brown, Meadows, & Elder, 2007). Furthermore, earlier research indicated that much of the R/E gap in depression is explained by SES differences (Adkins et al., 2007). Thus, we hypothesized that African American adolescents would show a greater increase in self-esteem from early to late adolescence than would European American adolescents but that the rate of change in depressive symptoms would be similar for both. As there is a dearth of research examining R/E differences in the adolescent trajectories for our other measures of psychological well-being, we made no predictions for these other indicators.

R/E IDENTITY AND DISCRIMINATION

The development of psychosocial identity is considered a critical task of adolescence (Erikson, 1950). Adolescence is a pivotal period in which to examine changes in identity as it is a time when abstract reasoning abilities increase and the exploration of one's identities becomes salient. Nevertheless, there has been surprisingly little longitudinal research on R/E identity development, until most recently (French, Seidman, Allen, & Aber, 2006). In response to previous calls to examine the development of ethnically diverse children and adolescents (Garcia-Coll et al., 1996; McLoyd, 1990; McLoyd & Steinberg, 1998; Phinney, 1990), there has been a substantial increase in the attention to ways in which one's race/ethnicity affects human development (Eccles, Wong, & Peck, 2006). Some of this work has focused on content and processes associated with R/E identity formation (e.g., Phinney & Ong, 2007; Seaton, Scottham, & Sellers, 2006; Sellers et al., 1998). Other scholars have focused explicitly on the impact of discrimination on various aspects of mental health and school engagement (e.g., Ogbu, 2003; Wong, Eccles & Sameroff, 2003). Finally, others have examined R/E identity and socialization within the contexts of family and friendships (e.g., Hughes et al., 2006; Kao & Joyner, 2004; Parke & Buriel, 1998; Quillian & Campbell, 2003). Although studies are beginning to examine adolescents' construction of, and experiences related to, their race/ethnicity, developmental research is still needed to document changes in these beliefs and identities from early to late adolescence for African American and European American males and females (Côte, 2009; Eccles & Roeser, 2011). In this monograph, we examined R/E importance and involvement, R/E friendship networks, and experiences of R/E discrimination.

Research into resilience has highlighted the importance of R/E identity as a protective factor, particularly for African American adolescents exposed to adverse circumstances (Caldwell et al., 2004; Miller & MacIntosh, 1999; Sellers, Copeland-Linder, Martin, & Lewis, 2006; Tynes, Umana-Taylor, Rose, Lin, & Anderson, 2012; Williams, Aiyer, Durkee, & Tolan, 2014; Wong et al., 2003). These studies have demonstrated that having a strong, positive connection to one's R/E group buffers the impact of multiple stressors, including R/E discrimination, on a range of outcomes. Research has also shown that having same R/E friendships is associated with more positive outcomes (Schneider, Dixon, & Udvari, 2007), whereas having cross R/E friendships is associated with lower well-being and more conflictual friendships, especially for African American adolescents (McGill, Way, & Hughes, 2012). However, there is evidence that cross R/E friendships have a promotive effect: Having cross R/E friends has been associated with lower perceived vulnerability (Graham, Munniksma, & Juvonen, 2014) and declines in relational victimization (Kawabata & Crick, 2011). For R/E discrimination, a multitude of recent studies has documented the adverse impact of these experiences on African American adolescents, in terms of both undermining their academic achievement and exacting a heavy toll on their psychological and physical health (e.g., Brody et al., 2014; Caldwell, Kohn-Wood, Schmeelk-Cone, Chavous, & Zimmerman, 2004; Cooper, Brown, Metzger, Clinton, & Guthrie, 2013; Greene, Way, & Pahl, 2006; Harris-Britt, Valrie, Kurtz-Costes, & Rowley, 2007; Huynh & Fuligni, 2010; Seaton, Neblett, Upton, Hammond, & Sellers, 2011; Smith-Bynum, Lambert, English, & Ialongo, 2014; Wang & Huguley, 2012; Williams, Neighbors, & Jackson, 2003; Wong et al., 2003).

In terms of longitudinal trajectories, studies of diverse R/E samples have shown that R/E identity increases in early and middle adolescence, with R/E group-esteem increasing in both early and middle adolescence and R/E identity exploration increasing in middle adolescence (French et al., 2006) and into the college years, in terms of both R/E identity exploration and commitment (Syed & Azmitia, 2009). In one study of urban, low-income African American adolescents, Pahl and Way (2006) reported a quadratic pattern in the exploration of one's R/E identity for African Americans from middle to late adolescence, with the peak rates of exploration occurring in middle adolescence followed by declines in the salience of identity exploration. In another longitudinal study of African American adolescents, however, there was no evidence of developmental changes in R/E centrality, which measures the extent to which race/ethnicity is a defining characteristic for the individual, or in private regard, which measures how individuals personally feel about their race/ethnicity (Seaton, Yip, & Sellers, 2009). Given the little available longitudinal evidence, we tentatively expected increases in R/E involvement and importance with a peak occurring in middle adolescence.

Regarding R/E friendships, research has shown that same R/E friendships tend to be more stable compared to cross R/E friendships (Aboud, Mendelson, & Purdy, 2003; Rude & Herda, 2010). Some research has shown that R/E friendships peak in early adolescence and then remain stable throughout high school (Shrum, Check, & MacD, 1988). However, studies examining cross race/ethnicity friendships have shown a decline over time, especially after the transition to high school (Aboud & Janani, 2007; Epstein, 1986). We therefore hypothesized similar trajectories for our measures of same and cross R/E friendships.

For age-related changes in perceived R/E discrimination, there is somewhat inconsistent evidence. In Greene et al.'s (2006) study of African American adolescents, perceived rates of R/E discrimination by both adults and peers increased across the high school years. In Seaton et al.'s (2009) longitudinal examination of African American adolescents aged 14–18, perceived R/E discrimination decreased slightly during middle adolescence and then increased in late adolescence. Other studies have shown that there are several distinct longitudinal patterns of change in perceived R/E discrimination (Brody et al., 2014; Niwa, Way, & Hughes, 2014). For example, Brody and colleagues (2014) found two longitudinal classes of perceived discrimination for African American adolescents from 16 to 18 years: (1) high, stable and (2) low, increasing. Although relatively little research exists documenting these processes through the entire adolescent period, available findings suggest that increasing levels of perceptions of discrimination may be expected for African American adolescents.

There is little longitudinal research examining gender differences in these constructs for either African American or European American adolescents. In two of the only studies examining gender differences in trajectories of perceived R/E discrimination for African American adolescents, males not only reported more R/E discrimination than females as they aged, the negative consequences of perceived R/E discrimination were stronger for males than for females (Smith-Bynum et al., 2014; Wang & Huguley, 2012). Given the scarcity of research, we made no predictions about

17

gender differences in the trajectories of R/E identity or friendships but expected that African American males would report a greater rate of increase in perceived R/E discrimination compared to African American females.

In terms of R/E differences in the longitudinal pathways of these constructs, much of the research has focused on R/E minorities. In one of the two studies of both African American and European American youth, various aspects of R/E identity increased from early to middle adolescence for both groups, but the increases were stronger for African American adolescents (French et al., 2006). In another study, African American adolescents started college with higher levels of R/E identity exploration and commitment compared to European American adolescents, but there were no R/E differences in their linear slopes (Syed & Azmitia, 2009). As our study explored the R/E identity of African American adolescents only, we did not entertain any predictions for group differences in the trajectories. There is also little work comparing the longitudinal trajectories of R/E friendships and discrimination between African American and European American adolescents. Here, we have the available data to examine R/E differences but did not have any specific predictions regarding whether such differences would be evident.

ACADEMIC FUNCTIONING

Schools represent one of the most important social contexts for adolescents, influencing many aspects of their development (Wigfield et al., 2006). Adolescents not only spend most of their waking hours in school or in the pursuit of school-related activities, they must also navigate the various academic, social, and institutional demands of the school environment. Schools are where most adolescents interact with nonfamilial adults, socialize with their peers, encounter intellectual challenges, engage in extracurricular activities, and adjust to institutional culture (Eccles & Roeser, 2011; Elmore, 2009). Although some adolescents flourish in the school environment, most more or less manage to make it, and still others feel alienated and disengaged from school leading to subsequent school failure and dropout (Cohen & Smerdon, 2009). Factors that differentiate adolescents' school experiences include not only their academic achievement but also students' academic self-related beliefs and attitudes and their engagement in, and identification with, school (Eccles & Roeser, 2011). In this monograph, we examined indicators of adolescents' academic functioning such as academic achievement and their aspirations and expectations, motivational beliefs, and positive school identification.

The riskiest times for poor academic functioning are during and immediately following the transitions from elementary school to middle school and then again from middle school to high school. In accordance with stage-environment fit theory (Eccles & Midgley, 1989), youth confront changes in the organizational, social, and instructional processes of the school, which may not meet their developing needs as adolescents. The transition to high school, in particular, has been shown to be the riskiest time for subsequent academic failure and school dropout (Cohen & Smerdon, 2009), especially for disadvantaged students (Finn, 1989). Research has emphasized the importance of boosting academic achievement, academic competence, and school engagement to prevent these negative school outcomes (Casillas et al., 2012; Eccles et al., 1993; Gootman & Eccles, 2002; Wang & Dishion, 2012; Wang & Fredricks, 2014). There are also numerous studies highlighting the importance of academic functioning to prevent subsequent negative outcomes including substance abuse, engagement in problematic behaviors, and psychological problems (e.g., Bradley & Greene, 2013; Henry, Knight, & Thornberry, 2012; Verboom, Sijtsema, Verhulst, Penninx, & Ormel, 2014) and to promote positive well-being and educational success (e.g., Stiglbauer, Gnambs, Gamsjäger, & Batinic, 2013; Wang & Eccles, 2012).

There is substantial evidence that many students experience declines in academic-related outcomes and performance across both middle school and senior high school (Eccles & Midgley, 1989; Gottfried, Fleming, & Gottfried, 2001; Gutman, 2006; Wigfield et al., 2006). Evidence also indicates that academic task- and self-related beliefs (e.g., see De Fraine, Van Damme, & Onghena, 2007; Eccles et al., 1993; Gniewosz, Eccles, & Noack, 2012) and school engagement and identification, on average, decrease across adolescence (Roeser & Eccles, 1998; Wang & Dishion, 2012). In light of these findings, we expected to find similar declines in most of our measures of academic functioning. For educational expectations, however, Mello (2008) found a decrease in educational expectations from age 14 to 16, followed by an increase until age 20, and then a decrease from ages 20 to 26. For occupational expectations, Mello (2009) found an increase from 14 to 18 years and then a slight decline to age 26. We thus predicted that educational expectations, on average, would decline, whereas occupational aspirations would increase from early to mid-adolescence, although these trends may either reverse or stabilize in later adolescence.

Regarding gender differences, studies have typically shown that female adolescents outperform male adolescents in academic performance during middle school, high school, and university (Voyer & Voyer, 2014). Female adolescents also have higher educational and occupational aspirations and expectations and school motivation, but lower levels of academic self-concept, compared to their male peers (Gutman & Schoon, 2012; Huang, 2012; Mello, 2008; Schoon, Martin, & Ross, 2007). In terms of race/ethnicity, African American adolescents usually report higher educational and occupational aspirations and more engagement in their school work than do European

Americans (Johnson, Crosnoe, & Elder, 2001), yet the Black–White achievement gap still persists in American schools (Kao & Thompson, 2003; Magnuson & Waldfogel, 2008).

There is a dearth of research examining gender and R/E differences in academic functioning from early to late adolescence, particularly in diverse samples with similar distributions of SES. Mello (2008, 2009), in a study of educational and occupational expectations from adolescence to young adulthood, reported that gendered and R/E patterns were generally stable across this developmental period. Furthermore, studies of African American adolescents have shown similar declines in academic-related outcomes and performance as those shown in European American adolescents (Gutman & Midgley, 2000; Roderick, 2003). Given this, we hypothesized that there would be mean-level differences according to gender and race/ethnicity but that these gaps would not diverge from early to late adolescence, with the exception of academic self-concept. Research has shown that females report a sharper decline in academic self-concept compared to males in a sample of Dutch adolescents (De Fraine et al., 2007), whereas males report a steeper decline compared to females in a sample of African American adolescents (Dotterer, Lowe, & McHale, 2014). Therefore, we postulated that there would be a significant interaction between gender and race/ethnicity for this particular construct.

PROBLEM BEHAVIORS

Adolescence is a particularly vulnerable period for engagement in problem behavior and experimentation with various substances. For some adolescents, the teen years are the years of peak involvement in problematic behaviors, with early and rapid increases in such behaviors during the early and middle adolescent years and then marked declines in late adolescence and adulthood. There has been a great deal of renewed concern over the role that brain maturation may play in some adolescents' participation in risky behaviors (Steinberg, 2005). This research suggests that heightened risk-taking during adolescence may be normative, biologically driven and, perhaps, inevitable (Steinberg, 2008). Others suggest that such changes are rare and just as likely to reflect the socially constructed stresses associated with adolescence in modern societies (Eccles et al., 1993; Lerner, 2007). However, regardless of the cause, adolescents' maturing brains are vulnerable to the physical effects of using alcohol, nicotine, and drugs and, thus, these behaviors are quite risky during this period of development (Clark, Thatcher, & Tapert, 2008; Crews, He, & Hodge, 2007). Cognitive deficits resulting from alcohol and drug use in childhood and adolescence have potentially harmful consequences for subsequent academic, social, psychological, and occupational functioning in adulthood (Squeglia, Jacobus, & Tapert, 2009). Thus, in this monograph, we examined trajectories of substance use (i.e., cigarette, alcohol, and marijuana use) associated with biological risk, problematic behaviors at school that put academic achievement at risk, and illegal behaviors associated with delinquency.

Early onset of these types of problematic behaviors are among the most commonly identified risk factors for subsequent problems in adulthood (Windle & Windle, 2012). The potential for developing lifetime substance abuse and dependence is substantially greater when an individual's first exposure to alcohol, nicotine, or illicit drugs occurs during adolescence rather than in adulthood (Breslau, Kilbey, & Andreski, 1993; Grant & Dawson, 1997). The earlier that an individual begins using nicotine, alcohol, or other drugs, the higher their risk of meeting the clinical criteria for substance use disorders later in adulthood (Steinberg, 2008). There has also been considerable research conducted on childhood-onset and adolescent-onset antisocial behaviors as significant predictors of mental health and substance abuse disorders and criminality in adulthood (Lynam, Caspi, Moffitt, Loeber, & Stouthamer-Loeber, 2007; Moffitt, Caspi, Harrington, & Milne, 2002). Consequently, these early-onset problem behaviors are often the focus of prevention programs to delay or prevent their initiation (Kandel & Yamaguchi, 2002; Spoth, Trudeau, Guyll, Shin, & Redmond, 2009).

Most longitudinal studies have shown that average levels of engagement in problem behaviors increase during adolescence and then decrease in adulthood. The average rate of alcohol and cigarette use has been found to increase steadily from early to late adolescence (Lloyd-Richardson, Papandonatos, Kazura, Stanton, & Niaura, 2002). Average levels of engagement in aggressive and criminal activities also have been shown to increase from early to mid-adolescence but then level off (Hirschi & Gottfredson, 1983; Moffitt, 1993), peaking around age 17 (Piquero, 2007). Given these previous findings, we hypothesized that frequency of engagement in these types of problem behaviors would increase from early to late adolescence, although some of these behaviors may stabilize in late adolescence. However, given the low rates of these types of behaviors at all ages (see http://www.monitoringthefuture.org/), we predicted that the overall rates would be low.

Problem behaviors may also vary across the gender and race/ethnicity of the adolescent (see Chassin, Hussong, & Beltran, 2009). For example, European American and male adolescents typically report higher levels, and faster rates of increase, of alcohol, cigarette, and substance use than do African American and female adolescents (Bray, Adams, Getz, & Baer, 2001; Chen & Jacobson, 2012; Wallace et al., 2002; Webb, Bray, Adam, & Getz, 2002). Thus, we expected that males and European Americans would both engage in more substance use and show faster rates of increase in their use from early to late adolescence than would females and African Americans. Although adolescent males consistently report higher levels of engagement in delinquent behaviors than do female adolescents, studies have revealed few gender and R/E differences in either the shape or the patterns of these trajectories (Bongers, Koot, Van Der Ende, & Verhulst, 2004; Lynne-Landsman, Graber, Nichols, & Botvin, 2011; Miller, Malone, Dodge, & Conduct Problems Prevention Research Group, 2010). In line with these findings, we hypothesized that although males would report higher levels of engaging in delinquent behaviors and having school problems than would females, the slopes of these trajectories would be similar for all groups.

FAMILY CHARACTERISTICS

One of the salient developmental tasks confronting adolescents is establishing themselves as autonomous beings (Eccles et al., 1993; Erikson, 1959; Smetana, 2000; Steinberg, 1990). As children in the United States mature, their relationships with their parents evolve from being hierarchical and dependent to becoming more egalitarian and independent and, ultimately, to the adolescents taking primary responsibility for their own lives (Smollar & Youniss, 1989). These changes may lead adolescents to question their parents' authority and push for more decision-making power with their parents while also spending more time with their peers and progressively less time with their parents (Laursen, Coy, & Collins, 1998). These developmental changes may precipitate disruptions in the parent–adolescent relationship, including heightened conflict and diminished support and closeness, that may continue until these relationships and roles are renegotiated (Collins, 1995). This set of findings and beliefs has fueled the idea that youth turn from their parents and families to their peer groups during adolescence. But is this true? Other studies suggest that parents continue to matter a great deal to their adolescent children throughout adolescence and adulthood (Collins & Laursen, 2004; DeVore & Ginsburg, 2005; Steinberg, 2001). In this monograph, we included indicators of risky parenting—such as intrusive, strict, and negative parenting—and promotive/protective parenting, such as family social support, communication, and positive identification with parents.

Family characteristics can operate as risk, promotive, and protective factors for adolescents (Deković, 1999; Fergus & Zimmerman, 2005; Gutman, Sameroff, & Eccles, 2002; Masten, 2001). Positive parenting practices both delay the likelihood of engaging in risky behavior and reduce an increase in their continued engagement. These parenting practices also predict higher levels of healthy development, particularly among adolescents living in very risky neighborhoods (DeVore & Ginsburg, 2005). Authoritative parenting—which is characterized by a high degree of parental warmth and support, consistent limit setting, open communication, and high levels of supervision—predicts a number of positive developmental outcomes in adolescence (DeVore & Ginsburg, 2005; Juang & Silbereisen, 2002; Steinberg, Mounts, Lamborn, & Dornbusch, 1991) and reduced levels of engagement in negative outcomes such as drug use (Montgomery et al., 2008). In contrast, harsh, controlling parenting is associated with adolescent depression, anxiety, and externalizing behaviors, even after controlling for the effects of other parenting measures (Bender et al., 2007). Adolescents who have warm and close relationships with their parents are better adjusted (Attar-Schwartz, 2015; Gutman & Eccles, 2007) and engage in less risky behaviors associated with cigarette, alcohol, and drug use (Gutman, Eccles, Peck, & Malanchuk, 2011; Resnick et al., 1997; Tilson et al., 2004).

Many scholars have reported that children undergo a stressful period with their parents during adolescence (Eccles et al., 1993; Smetana, 1988, 1989; Steinberg, 2001). Parent-adolescent conflict often peaks during early adolescence; the emotional intensity of this relationship increases during middle adolescence and then stabilizes (Laursen et al., 1998). Parental control, on the other hand, declines from early to late adolescence and youth tend to provide their parents with less knowledge about their whereabouts, activities, and peer relationships as they grow older (Keijsers & Poulin, 2013; Wang, Dishion, Stormshak, & Willett, 2011). As youth progress through adolescence to young adulthood, interactions with parents generally become more egalitarian and less conflictual (De Goede et al., 2009; Rubin et al., 2011). Based on these findings, we predicted that our measures of perceived parental control would peak in early adolescence and then decline, stabilizing in late adolescence.

Researchers have also documented that feelings of support, emotional closeness, and time spent with parents generally decline during adolescence (Conger & Ge, 1999; Larson, Richards, Moneta, Holmbeck, & Duckett, 1996; Meeus, Iedema, Maassen, & Engels, 2005; Steinberg, 1988; Wang et al., 2011). Most notably, there have been documented declines in supportive parenting from early to mid-adolescence, followed by stability in young adulthood (Shanahan, McHale, Crouter, & Osgood, 2007). We thus predicted that our measures of supportive parenting would follow a similar trajectory.

In terms of gender differences, females typically report closer relationships with their parents than do males (Geuzaine, Debry, & Liesens, 2000; Gilligan, 1982; Gilligan, Lyons, & Hammer, 1990). However, there is less evidence that gender moderates developmental trajectories of parent–adolescent relationships more generally (Laursen & Collins, 2004). In a study of adolescents' perceptions of their relationship with their parents, for example, there were no gender differences in the patterns of developmental change for perceived parental conflict and parental power (i.e., relative power and dominance of parents) from early to late adolescence (De Goede et al., 2009). Parental support, warmth, and closeness also showed similar declines from early to middle adolescence for both males and females (De Goede et al., 2009; Kim et al., 2015; Wang et al., 2011). However, from middle to late adolescence, females reported an increase in parental support and closeness; in contrast, males reported a decrease in parental closeness and no change in perceived parental support during this period (De Goede et al. 2009; Kim et al. 2015). Another recent study found that, following a decline in communication during early adolescence for both genders, females reported more intense parent–adolescent communication from middle to late adolescence, whereas adolescent males reported stable, low levels of parent–adolescent communication from middle adolescence onward (Keijsers & Poulin, 2013). Thus, we predicted more positive slopes in parent–adolescent relationships for females than for males from middle to late adolescence only.

Previous research indicates that normative patterns of relinquishing parental control during adolescence may differ across race/ethnicity, with adolescents from European American families reporting lower levels of, and more rapid declines in, parental control compared to adolescents from African American families (e.g., Dornbusch, Ritter, Leiderman, Roberts, & Fraleigh, 1987; Smetana et al., 2004; Steinberg et al., 1991). Smetana et al. (2004) suggested that parental control is more normative during early adolescence in African American middle-class families than in European American middle-class families and may protect African American adolescents from the pervasive risks of racism and prejudice. In addition, strict parental control and emphasis on obedience among some lower-income R/E minority families may be an adaptive strategy to protect teenagers from the dangers of the neighborhood in which they live (Furstenberg et al., 1999). If so, then the African American versus European American differences found in some studies might reflect group differences in the likelihood of living in risky neighborhoods. In this monograph, we have the opportunity to look at these trajectories for African American and European American adolescents living in the same neighborhoods.

However, regardless of one's neighborhood of residence and one's normative levels of parental controls, both theory and research suggest that European American and African American parents come to allow greater decision-making opportunities and reduce their controlling strategies as their adolescent children mature (Gutman & Eccles, 2007). These findings suggest that the gradual transformation from a hierarchical relationship to a more egalitarian one during the adolescent years is a normative process for most families, regardless of race/ethnicity. Less is known about variations in closeness according to race/ethnicity or SES background, especially regarding different norms and cultural forms of family relationships and

24

obligations (Laursen & Collins, 2009). However, cultural comparisons show that greater diversity often exists within rather than between these groups (Harkness & Super, 2002). As such, similar developmental trajectories for indicators of family relationships have been found in R/E minority families (e.g., Fuligni, 1998; Choe, Stoddard, & Zimmerman, 2014), despite the fact that African American adolescents tend to report more positive feelings toward their parents than do European American adolescents (Gutman & Eccles, 2007). We thus hypothesized that although mean-level differences might be evident in measures of parental control and closeness, the patterns of developmental change would be quite similar between African American and European American adolescents.

PEER CHARACTERISTICS

Much attention has been focused on the heightened importance of peers during adolescence. As adolescents mature, they gain increasing independence from their parents and become closer to their peer group. During adolescence, youth are increasingly likely to turn to their friends as sources of support (Değirmencioğlu, Urberg, Tolson, & Richard, 1998; Levitt, Guacci-Franco, & Levitt, 1993; Wilkinson, 2004). At times, this increase in peer focus may undermine parental influence (Steinberg, 2001). Research has suggested that the preference for peers peaks in early to middle adolescence and then gradually declines in late adolescence (Rubin et al., 2011; Steinberg & Silverberg, 1986). By late adolescence, most adolescents have developed a healthy balance between their parents and their peers, relying on both for support (Fuligni, Eccles, Barber, & Clements, 2001). These changes render adolescence an ideal time to study longitudinal trajectories of peer characteristics and relationships. Here, we examined the trajectories of both peer risk factors, including negative friendships and friends' endorsement of drug use, as well as promotive and protective aspects of peer relationships, including communication, support, and positive friendships.

Scholars have shown that peers can operate either as risk or protective factors in relation to adolescent development (Dodge, Dishion, & Langsford, 2006; Hartup, 1996; Wang & Dishion, 2012). On the one hand, adolescents who associate with riskier peers have more opportunities to take part in risky behaviors, receive more positive reinforcement for engaging in such behavior, and are more likely to engage in problem behavior in the future compared to their peers who associate with less risky friends (Dishion, 2000; Goldstein, Davis-Kean, & Eccles 2005; Patterson, Dishion, & Yoerger, 2000). Having friends who approve of drug use has also been shown to predict higher rates of cigarette, alcohol, and marijuana use (Mason, Menis, Linker, Bares, & Zaharakis, 2014).

25

On the other hand, friends also provide necessary support and communication for adolescents. Having positive peer support has been linked to a number of positive outcomes, including academic achievement. Adolescents who had friends who liked school or did well in school had fewer academic problems compared to those whose friends were less academically oriented (Crosnoe, Cavanagh, & Elder, 2003), and adolescents who had supportive friends were more engaged in school compared to those who had less supportive friends (Li & Lerner, 2011). Peer support has also been shown to be a protective factor in supporting the academic achievement of high-risk African American adolescents (Gutman et al., 2003). Positive peer characteristics, including peer support and high quality friendships, have further been found to buffer adolescents from negative outcomes, such as depression (Costello, Swendsen, Rose, & Dierker, 2008; Gutman & Sameroff, 2004) and peer victimization (Goldbaum, Craig, Pepler, & Connolly, 2003).

Although many studies have examined the correlates and consequences of adolescents' peer relationships, a dearth of longitudinal research has investigated the developmental trajectories of peer characteristics themselves (Lansford, Dodge, Fontaine, Bates, & Pettit, 2014). In those few exceptions, studies have shown that friendships become increasingly closer and supportive from early to late adolescence (De Goede et al., 2009; Rubin et al., 2011; Way & Greene, 2006), although friendship quality has been found to decline from late adolescence (Lansford et al., 2014). Given the general increase in the importance of peers during this period, we predicted an increase in the extent of communication with one's peers as well as perceived peer closeness and support, which may stabilize or decline approaching late adolescence.

There is also some longitudinal evidence that being affiliated with deviant peers increases from early to middle adolescence (Simons-Morton & Chen, 2009; Wang & Dishion, 2012). This seems very likely given that that average rates of engagement in risky behaviors increase over adolescence. Thus, we predicted that, on average, adolescents would report having more friends who engaged in risky behaviors and endorsed the use of drugs from early to middle adolescence, which again may stabilize or decline in late adolescence, but we expected that these rates would be relatively low.

Studies have also found that the quality of friendships varies by adolescents' gender. For example, adolescent females consistently report having more friendship support, greater communication with their friends, and more prosocial friends compared to adolescent males (see Fuligni, Hughes, & Way, 2009; Kim et al., 2015; Rose & Rudolph, 2006, for reviews). Longitudinal research on friendship quality for male and female adolescents from different R/E groups is extremely limited, with most longitudinal studies focusing on younger children over brief periods of time or middle class, European American adolescents (Fuligni et al., 2009). However, studies focusing on racially/ethnically diverse youth have also shown similar improvements in friendship support during adolescence, with males reporting a sharper increase in the perceptions of the quality of their same-sex, closest friendships compared to females (Way & Green, 2006). Given the lack of evidence, however, we did not make any predictions about gender or R/E differences in the developmental trajectories of peer characteristics in our sample.

CURRENT STUDY

Using hierarchical linear modeling (HLM), our first goal was to describe the developmental trajectories of a population of African American and European American adolescents living on the Eastern Seaboard of the United States at the turn of the 21st century. Using risk-protection and positive youth development frameworks, we selected developmental measures based on the normative tasks of adolescence and the most widely studied indicators in the three major contexts of development—families, peer groups, and schools. Our second goal was to investigate whether these trajectories varied by parents' marital status and SES and adolescents' race/ethnicity, gender, and the intersection of their race/ethnicity and gender.

To satisfy the systematic investigation of adolescent trajectories, we retained the same covariates within each model for purposes of comparison. With an economically diverse but socioeconomically comparable sample of African American and European American adolescents, we examined growth curve trajectories within each domain of functioning and how they varied according to adolescents' gender and race/ethnicity, parents' SES and marital status, and the interaction between adolescents' gender and race/ethnicity. Considering that little research has been devoted to interactions among demographic variables (Schwartz, Montgomery, & Briones, 2006), understanding the longitudinal trajectories of intra-individual processes particularly related to diversity including gender, race/ethnicity, and the intersection between the two, can greatly enhance our understanding of adolescent development (Smetana et al., 2006).

The youth came from a county near Washington, DC, in which the socioeconomic backgrounds of the African American and European American families were more similarly distributed than in most other counties in the United States. This county was selected purposefully in order to control for differences in the kinds of social and physical experiences that are commonly associated with social class and thus often confound comparisons between African American and European American youth. This choice does not mean that we believe that socioeconomic conditions are unimportant to our understanding of R/E differences in human development. Quite the contrary, we believe that such conditions are so important and so poorly understood that one cannot easily look at the generalizability of developmental trajectories across African American and European American youth in samples that confound R/E differences with family SES differences. Admittedly, it is unfeasible to achieve absolute comparability in this culture at this historical period between various subgroups within the larger population of youth in the United States; thus, it was also important to investigate the effects of key sociodemographic variables including parents' SES and marital status. Nevertheless, this constraint on selecting the community in which to conduct this study made obtaining equivalently representative samples of other R/E groups within the United States impossible.

Regarding the organization of our monograph, Chapter II describes the sample, procedures, and measures of the study in more detail. Chapter III provides some preliminary analyses and an overview of our analytic plan. Chapters IV–IX report the results for each domain. Within each of these chapters, we describe the trajectories of each measure, in turn, allowing a short discussion of individual findings. We conclude each of these chapters with a summary and discussion of the findings, taken as a whole, in relation to our predictions, for the particular domain in question. Where appropriate, we highlight how these findings relate to those shown in previous chapters. Lastly, Chapter X provides a comprehensive view of the developmental trajectories for the domains taken together; first examining these findings through the lens of risk, promotion, and protection at each stage of adolescent development and then identifying similarities and differences in the mean levels and/or slopes of these trajectories according to adolescents' gender, race/ethnicity, and their interaction as well as parents' SES and marital status. This chapter also includes discussions of the limitations of our study and potential future research. We end with overarching conclusions about our findings.

II: METHOD

Leslie Morrison Gutman, Stephen C. Peck, Oksana Malanchuk,
Arnold J. Sameroff, and Jacquelynne S. Eccles

This article is part of the issue "Moving through Adolescence: Developmental Trajectories of African American and European American Youth" Gutman, Peck, Malanchuk, Sameroff, and Eccles (Issue Authors). For a full listing of articles in this issue, see: http://onlinelibrary.wiley.com/doi/10.1111/mono.v82.4/issuetoc.

PARTICIPANTS

The participants were part of the Maryland Adolescent Development in Context Study (MADICS)—a study originally designed and funded by the MacArthur Research Network on Successful Adolescent Development among Youth Living in High Risk Settings (chaired by Richard Jessor; members included Albert Bandura, James Comer, Tom Cook, Delbert Elliott, Jacquelynne Eccles, Glen Elder, Frank Furstenberg, Robert Haggerty, Beatrix Hamburg, Norman Garmezy, Arnold Sameroff, Marta Tienda, and William J. Wilson) and subsequently funded by the National Institute of Child Health and Human Development, the National Institute on Aging, the W. T. Grant Foundation, and the Spencer Foundation. This project was headed up by Jacquelynne S. Eccles and Arnold J. Sameroff.

MADICS is a longitudinal study of adolescents, their families, and their wider social contexts (e.g., schools) in Prince George's County, Maryland. Prince George's County is a geographically large county near

---

Corresponding author: Leslie Morrison Gutman, Department of Clinical, Educational and Health Psychology, University College London, 1-19 Torrington Place, London WC1E 7HB, email: l.gutman@ucl.ac.uk

DOI: 10.1111/mono.12328

Washington, D.C. The county is quite diverse. Areas closest to the city are more densely populated, more urban, and less affluent. Most other areas are suburban with the exception of a large rural and sparsely populated area in the southeast. The county was selected for the study because it was the premier middle class African American county in the country, and the SES distribution was as close as possible between the African American and European American sub-populations. According to the U.S. Bureau of the Census, in 1990 when this study began, 51% of the residents in the county were African American, 43% were European American, 4% were Latino, and 4% were Asian. Median household incomes were $41,265 for African Americans and $46,822 for European Americans, with the corresponding national averages being $18,676 and $31,231. Therefore, the county represents a relatively affluent population of both African American and European American families, and its R/E income differential was less than that of the nation at large. Beginning in 1970, the county experienced considerable White flight. By 1990, 170,000 Whites had moved out of the county and were replaced by an approximately similar number of African Americans. Even so, only one of the 173 census tracts in the county had an average household income under $20,000, and none had a poverty rate of more than 30% in 1990. Nevertheless, none of the census tracks is as wealthy as can be found in adjacent counties in both Maryland and Virginia.

MADICS began as part of a larger longitudinal, evaluation study: the Study of Adolescents in Multiple Contexts (SAMC; Cook, Herman, Phillips, & Settersten, 2002). The two longitudinal studies differed slightly in their focus and method of data collection. However, because the data were collected collaboratively, extensive information is available about the adolescents and their families. The county had 25 middle schools, 23 of which participated in the study. In 1990, SAMC invited all entering 7th-grade students in 23 of the county's 25 schools to participate in their study. In 1990–1992, they administered questionnaires in schools to students whose parents gave their consent at the beginning of 7th-grade and at the end of the adolescents' 8th-grade. These questionnaires asked for information about the adolescents' perceptions of their families, their friends, and their own psychological attitudes and behaviors.

Of the approximately 5,000 adolescents in the second SAMC cohort (1991), 1,482 adolescents and their families also participated in the MADICS project. In the fall of 1991, a brief description of the study was sent home with each 7th grader in the county. This data collection coincided with the first wave of data collection on this cohort of SAMC. Families who were interested in learning more about the study were asked to sign and return a form giving the study staff permission to contact them. Of all the families, 1,700 agreed to be contacted about the study. There were 1,500 families randomly selected to participate based on a stratified sampling procedure designed to get proportional representations of families from each of the 23 middle schools.

MADICS participants have now been assessed at eight time points ranging from early adolescence (7th grade) through young adulthood (Waves 7 and 8 were collected when the participants were 29–32 years old). We focus here on four of these waves of data: Wave 1 collected in the fall 1991 when the target adolescents were in seventh grade (i.e., the first year of junior high school); Wave 3 collected in the summer and fall of 1993 when the adolescents were making the transition to high school; Wave 4 collected in 1996 when most of the adolescents were in 11th grade; and Wave 5 collected in 1998 about 1 year after most of the adolescents had graduated from high school. Wave 2 was a telephone interview for parents and youth that focused mainly on their summer activities after the 7th grade. Waves 6–8 did not include similar family relation measures as had the earlier waves and therefore were not included in our analyses for this monograph.

In this study, only data from the African American and European American target adolescents from Wave 1 ($n = 1329$), Wave 3 ($n = 948$), Wave 4 ($n = 940$), and Wave 5 ($n = 778$) were used. The R/E composition of the families corresponded roughly to the R/E composition of the county at large; 60% African Americans, 30% European Americans, and 10% of other R/E backgrounds. Of the 10% of "other" R/E backgrounds, 4% identified themselves as biracial (which included African/European American, Latino/European American, African American/Latino, and Asian/European American), 2% identified as Latino, 1% as Asian, and 3% in some other way. Participants from the "other" R/E groups were diverse yet too small in number to be included in our analyses.

The African American families had slightly lower mean levels of income (between $40,000 and $44,999 in 1990) and years of education ($M = 14.16$, $SD = 2.44$) than the income (between $45,000 and $49,999) and years of education ($M = 15.11$, $SD = 2.90$) of the European American families. The mean-level difference in SES (based on a composite of standardized income, education, and occupation scores) for the European American families ($M = 0.23$, $SD = 0.77$) and African American families ($M = -0.16$, $SD = 0.82$) was statistically significant, $F(1, 1325) = 70.93$, $p < .001$. For this reason, SES was included as a covariate. Nevertheless, it is important to note that this difference is much smaller than national averages because of the unique characteristics of the county.

The two R/E groups also differed in the nature of their families. The African American youth were more likely than the European-American youth to live in single-parent households in which the mother had never married (9% vs. 1%). In contrast, the European American youth were more likely than the African American youth to live in a family in which the mother and father

31

had been married to each other for their child's entire life (68% vs. 46%). Thus, we have included covariates for both of these kinds of family compositions.

MISSING DATA

The longitudinal data used in MADICS can be described as a complex pattern of complete and missing data. There are two basic kinds of missing data: data provided by participants at some waves but not at other waves (including partial data provided at any given wave), and data that are missing because participants discontinue providing data at all subsequent waves. Attrition refers only to the latter case, is difficult to estimate, and requires some corrective strategies that differ from those pertaining to other forms of missing data. As described below, despite the fact that the participants who dropped completely out of the study tended to be male and lower SES compared to those who remained in the study ($n = 118$ from Wave 1), we nevertheless retained a sufficient number of participants from the full range of our primary developmental outcomes to adequately address questions about the effects of gender and race/ethnicity; this continues to be one of the greatest strengths of this data set.

Defined conservatively, we retained over 70% of the original sample of 1,482 participants at Waves 3 and 4. These retention percentages, when viewed in the context of our entire study, are actually 89% and 81%, respectively, as some of the participants who appeared to drop out of the study at Wave 3 or Wave 4 returned to the sample in Wave 4 or Wave 5. At Wave 5, we obtained data from 62% of the Wave 1 sample of target adolescents. To ascertain whether the adolescents who only participated at Wave 1 ($n = 118$) differed from the adolescents who participated in all four waves ($n = 567$) in terms of their demographic characteristics and Wave 1 measures, a series of crosstab analyses and t-tests were conducted. Significant differences emerged between the two groups only on gender, SES, and Wave 1 Occupational Aspirations. Proportions and means indicated that participants who remained in the study for all four waves were more likely to be female, have higher SES, and report higher occupational aspirations at Wave 1 than those who dropped out of the study after Wave 1. However, the percentages of females and males were equally divided until Wave 5 when 57% of the sample was female.

In evaluating these patterns of attrition, it is important to keep in mind that the "effects of attrition on study conclusions in a general sense are not nearly as severe as commonly feared" (Graham, 2009, p. 567). Specifically, attrition alone tells us little about the quality of the data in question; rather, it is the specific *type* of attrition that can be problematic (Graham, 2009;

32

Little & Rubin, 1987; Schafer & Graham, 2002). Attrition that does not vary systematically in relation to study variables is referred to as missing completely at random—this type of missingness is considered ignorable because, despite the loss of power, the retained sample is equally representative of the original sample. Attrition that is predicted by study independent variables is referred to as missing at random and is also considered ignorable as this type of missingness is easily dealt with using multiple imputation or model-based approaches to parameter estimation. Attrition that is predicted by study outcome variables is often referred to as missing not at random and is the only type of missing data that is non-ignorable. Notably, longitudinal data that include Wave 1 measures of subsequently missing outcome variables (as in our case) can be treated as missing at random (Graham, 2009).

Based on generally accepted criteria (e.g., Graham, 2009), these patterns of missing data can be described as missing at random, in that missingness is predicted by observed data; namely, adolescents' gender and family SES. One of the advantages of HLM is its ability to handle missing data (Byrk & Raudenbusch, 1992). Because multilevel models do not assume equal numbers of observations or fixed time points, respondents with missing data are not problematic (Hox, 2000). As outlined by Zaidman-Zait and Zumbo (2013), data patterns characterized as missing at random can be correctly handled in HLM using full maximum likelihood estimation. Thus, we conducted HLM models on respondents who had data available at three or more time points, and we included the relevant variables that predicted missingness in the models.

PROCEDURE

An in-home interview format was used in Waves 1, 3, and 4. In each family, the primary caregiver and target adolescent were interviewed and given a self-administered questionnaire to complete. As often as possible, the race/ethnicity of the interviewer was matched to the race/ethnicity of the primary caregiver. Interviewers were from the local area and were mostly women. The MADICS staff trained all interviewers in a 3-day workshop. Interviewers were paid on a per-interview basis. To ensure that interviewers were following the interview protocol accurately, 15% of families were randomly selected and re-contacted by the study staff to verify that the interview had taken place, that all of the questions had been asked, and that the interviewer had behaved professionally while in the family's home. These verification calls revealed no problems with the interview staff.

33

The interviewer phoned the household and asked to speak with the parent identified by the school, generally the mother. After describing the study and obtaining his or her agreement to participate, the interviewer asked this adult, "Out of the people living in this household, what is the name of the person who has the most responsibility for and knows the most about (the target adolescent)?" The person named in response to this question was identified as the primary caregiver. The majority of the primary caregivers were either the mothers (86%) or fathers (7%) of the target adolescents; however, primary caregivers also included grandparents and other relatives. Although not all of the primary caregivers were parents of the target adolescents, the terms parent and primary caregiver are used interchangeably in this monograph.

Following the initial phone contact, the remainder of the interviewing process took place in the home of the family. The primary caregiver and target adolescent were asked to complete two booklets: one using a face-to-face structured interview format and one using a self-administered format. During the first portion of the interview, the adolescent completed his or her self-administered booklet in a quiet, private place, while the interviewer administered the face-to-face portion to the parent. During the second portion of the interview, the parent completed his or her self-administered booklet in a quiet, private place, while the interviewer administered the face-to-face portion to the adolescent. A card containing all relevant response scales was provided to the respondent for the face-to-face interviews. Interviewers referred respondents to this card rather than reading each response scale. Interviewers were also instructed to read all the questions exactly as written in the books and not to define words or interpret questions for the respondents. Each face-to-face interview took approximately 1 hour, and each self-administered booklet took approximately 30 minutes to complete. Primary caregivers and target youth were offered $20 each to participate in Waves 1, 3, and 4. For Wave 5, adolescents were mailed three self-administered booklets: a general booklet, one focused on their romantic relationships, and one on their work experience. Each booklet took approximately 65 minutes to complete. Target youth received $35 for their time.

MEASURES

This section provides the origin and a brief description of each construct in the domains of psychological well-being, R/E identity and discrimination, academic functioning, problem behaviors, family characteristics, and peer characteristics. Table 1 provides a full description of the scale items and their

TABLE 1

SCALE ITEMS AND RESPONSE VALUES ACCORDING TO DOMAIN

Psychological Well-Being

Self-esteem
3 items

How often do you wish you were different than you are?*
How often would you like to change lots of things about you if you could?*
How often are you pretty sure about yourself?

Response values — 1 = Almost never, 2 = Once in a while, 3 = Sometimes, 4 = Often, 5 = Almost always

Resiliency
4 items

How often are you very good at figuring out problems and planning how to solve them?
How often are you very good at carrying out the plans you make for solving problems?
How often are you very good at bouncing back quickly from bad experiences?
How often are you good at learning from your mistakes?

Response values — 1 = Almost never, 2 = Once in a while, 3 = Sometimes, 4 = Often, 5 = Almost always

Anger
3 items

During the last month (including today), how often have you felt so angry you wanted to smash or break something?
During the last month (including today), how often have you felt you couldn't control your temper?
During the last month (including today), how often have you felt so upset you wanted to hit or hurt someone?

Response values — 1 = Almost never, 2 = Once in a while, 3 = Sometimes, 4 = Often, 5 = Almost Always

Depressive affect
6 items

In the past two weeks, how often have you had these feelings?
I am sad ... 1 = Once in a while, 2 = Many times, 3 = All the time
I feel like ... 1 = Nothing will ever work out for me, 2 = I am not sure if things will work out for me, 3 = Things will work out for me O.K.*
I am worthless ... 1 = All the time, 2 = Many times, 3 = Once in a while*
I feel like ... 1 = I hate myself, 2 = I do not like myself, 3 = I like myself*
I feel like crying ... 1 = Everyday, 2 = Many days, 3 = Once in a while*
Things bother me ... 1 = All the time, 2 = Many times, 3 = Once in a while*

Eating disorders
9 items

How often do you do the following things:
I think about dieting.
I feel extremely guilty after overeating.
I am terrified of gaining weight.
If I gain a pound, I worry that I will keep going.

(Continued)

TABLE 1. (*Continued*)

Psychological Well-Being

	I eat when I am feeling sad or upset.
	I have gone on eating binges where I felt that I could not stop.
	I eat moderately in front of others and stuff myself when they are gone.
	I have thought of trying to vomit in order to lose weight.
	I make myself throw up after eating. (W1 only)
Response values	1 = Never, 2 = Rarely, 3 = Sometimes, 4 = Often, 5 = Usually, 6 = Often

Expected negative life chances
5 items
What do you think the chances are that you will...
Have a drinking problem?
Get in trouble with the police?
Get involved in gang activity?
Often skip school?
Start having sex too young?

Response values   1 = Very low, 2 = Low, 3 = In the middle, 4 = High, 5 = Very high,
6 = Already happened

R/E Identity and Discrimination

R/E importance
3 items
How important is your racial or ethnic background to the daily life of your family?
How important is it for you to know about your racial or ethnic background?
How proud are you of your racial or ethnic background?

Response
values   1 = Not at all, 2 = A little, 3 = Somewhat, 4 = Very

R/E behavioral involvement
3 items
How often do you study the traditions or history of people with your racial background?
How often do you participate in community activities with people of your racial background?
How often do you celebrate any special days connected to your racial background?

Response
values   1 = Almost never, 2 = Rarely, 3 = Occasionally, 4 = Frequently, 5 = Almost always

Same R/E friends
1 item
For African American adolescents:
How many of the friends you spend most of your time with are black?
For European American adolescents:
How many of the friends you spend most of your time with are white?

Response
values   1 = None of them, 2 = A few of them, 3 = About half of them, 4 = Most of them, 5 = All of them

Cross R/E friends
1 item
For African American adolescents:
How many of the friends you spend most of your time with are white?

For European American adolescents:
How many of the friends you spend most of your time with are black?

Response values   1 = None of them, 2 = A few of them, 3 = About half of them, 4 = Most of them, 5 = All of them

Expected R/E discrimination

2 items   How much do you think discrimination because of your race might keep you from getting the amount of education you want?

How much do you think discrimination because of your race might keep you from getting the job you want?

Response values   1 = Not at all, 2 = A little, 3 = Some, 4 = Quite a bit, 5 = A lot

R/E John Henryism

2 items   Because of your race, no matter how hard you work, you will always have to work harder than others to prove yourself.

Because of your race, it is important that you do better than other kids at [work or] school in order to get ahead.

Response values   1 = Strongly disagree, 2 = Disagree, 3 = Agree, 4 = Strongly agree

Parents' worries about R/E discrimination

2 items   How much do your parents worry that you will be discriminated against at school because of your race?

How much do your parents worry that you will be discriminated against at work when you grow up because of your race?

Response values   1 = Not at all, 2 = A little, 3 = Some, 4 = Quite a bit, 5 = A lot

---

Academic Functioning

GPA

1 item   On your semester report card last year, how many. . .

Response values   4 = A's did you get?
3 = B's did you get?
2 = C's did you get?
1 = D's did you get?
0 = F's did you get?

Educational aspirations

1 item   If you could do exactly what you wanted, how far would you like to go in school?

Response values   W1–W3: 1 = 8th grade or less, 2 = 9–11th grade, 3 = Graduate from high school, 4 = Post-high school vocational or technical training, 5 = Some college, 6 = Graduate from a business college or a two-year college with associate degree, 7 = Graduate from a 4-year college, 8 = Get a master's degree or a teaching credential, 9 = Get a law degree, a Ph.D., or a medical doctor's degree. W4: 1 = 11th grade or less 2 = Graduate from high school, 3 = Post-high school vocational or technical training, 4 = Some college, 5 = Graduate from a business college or a two-year college with associate degree, 6 = Graduate from a 4-year college, 7 = Get a master's degree or a teaching credential, 8 = Get a law degree, a Ph.D., or a medical doctor's degree. The Wave 4 response values were recoded so that they ranged from 2 to 9 to match the values used in previous waves.

37

Educational expectations

1 item

We can't always do what we want most to do. How far do you think you actually will go in school?

Response values

W1–W3: 1 = 8th grade or less, 2 = 9–11th grade, 3 = Graduate from high school, 4 = Post-high school vocational or technical training, 5 = Some college, 6 = Graduate from a business college or a two-year college with associate degree, 7 = Graduate from a 4-year college, 8 = Get a master's degree or a teaching credential, 9 = Get a law degree, a Ph.D., or a medical doctor's degree. W4: 1 = 11th grade or less 2 = Graduate from high school, 3 = Post-high school vocational or technical training, 4 = Some college, 5 = Graduate from a business college or a two-year college with associate degree, 6 = Graduate from a 4-year college, 7 = Get a master's degree or a teaching credential, 8 = Get a law degree, a Ph.D., or a medical doctor's degree. The Wave 4 response values were recoded so that they ranged from 2 to 9 to match the values used in previous waves.

Occupational aspirations

1 item

If you could have any job you wanted, what kind of job would you most like to have when you are grown up?

Response values

(1 = counter attendant, dishwasher; 100 = physician, surgeon).

Academic importance

2 items

How important is Math?

How important are other school subjects?

Response values

1 = Much less important to me than other things... 7 = Much more important to me than other things

Academic self-concept

4 items

How well do you do in Math? 1 = Much worse than other kids... 7 = Much better than other kids

How well do you do in other school subjects? 1 = Much worse than other kids... 7 = Much better than other kids

How good are you in Math? 1 = Not good at all... 7 = Very good

How good are you in other school subjects? 1 = Not good at all... 7 = Very good

Positive school identification

3 items

In your school, the academic program is very good.

In general, you like school a lot.

You would recommend to other kids that they go to your school.

Response values

1 = Strongly disagree, 2 = Disagree, 3 = Neither agree nor disagree, 4 = Agree, 5 = Strongly agree

---

Problem Behaviors

School problems

4 items

In the past year ...

How often have you cheated on tests or exams?

How often have you skipped class without a valid excuse?

How often have you been sent to the principal's office?

How often have you brought alcohol or drugs to school?

Response values 0 = Never, 1 = 1–9 times, 2 = 10 or more times

Cigarette use
  1 item   How many cigarettes have you smoked in the past 30 days?
  Response values 1 = None, 2 = Less than 1 a day, 3 = 1–5 a day, 4 = About a half a pack a
                   day, 5 = About a pack a day, 6 = 1 and ½ packs a day, 7 = 2 or more
                   packs a day

Delinquent behaviors
  6 items   In the past (W1 = year; W3, W4, W5 = 6 months), how often have you ...
                   Hit someone for what they said/did?
                   Lied to your parents?
                   Stolen from a store?
                   Been involved in a gang fight?
                   Damaged public or private property for fun?
                   Stolen a motor vehicle?
  Response values 0 = Never, 1 = 1–9 times, 2 = 10 or more times

Alcohol use
  1 item   How often have you had an alcoholic drink in the past 30 days?
  Response values 0 = None, 1 = Rarely, 2 = 2–3 times per month, 3 = Once a week,
                   4 = More than once a week

Marijuana use
  1 item   How often have you smoked marijuana in the past 30 days?
  Response values 0 = None, 1 = Rarely, 2 = 2–3 times per month, 3 = Once a week,
                   4 = More than once a week

Family Characteristics

Intrusive parenting
  5 items   Now, thinking about your parent, how often do the following things
                   happen?
                   Your parent is always telling you what to do and how to act.
                   Your parent asks you too many questions about where you've been or what
                   you've been doing.
                   Your parent treats you more like a kid than like an adult.
                   Your parent doesn't like it when you question (his/her) decisions and rules.
                   Your parent thinks you have no right to get angry at (him/her).
  Response
  values   1 = Almost never, 2 = Rarely, 3 = Occasionally, 4 = Frequently, 5 = Almost
                   always

Negative interactions with parent

---

  4 items   During the past month, how often did your parent...
                   Hit, push, grab or shove you?
                   Criticize you or your ideas?
                   Put his or her needs ahead of your needs?
                   Yell at you?
  Response
  values   1 = Never, 2 = Once or twice, 3 = 3 or 4 times, 4 = A couple of times a week,
                   5 = Almost every day

Strict parenting
  2 items   When you break one of your parent(s)' important rules, how often do they
                   ...
                   Ground you?
                   Take away some privilege?

Response	W1: 1 = Almost never, 2 = Once in a while, 3 = Sometimes, 4 = Often,
values	5 = Almost always
	W3: 1 = Almost never, 2 = Not too often, 3 = About half the time, 4 = Fairly
	often, 5 = Almost every day
	W4: 1 = Almost never, 2 = Not too often, 3 = About half the time, 4 = Often,
	5 = Almost always

Family social support

3 items   How often do your family members support each other?

How often do your family members care about what happens to each other?

How often can your family members turn to each other for support in times of crisis?

Response values   1 = Almost never, 2 = Rarely, 3 = Sometimes, 4 = Often, 5 = Almost always

Parent-adolescent communication

2 items   How often do the following things happen?

You talk with your parents about your plans for the future.

You talk to your parents about how things are going with your friends.

Response values   1 = Almost never, 2 = Less than once a month, 3 = 1–3 times a month, 4 = About once a week, 5 = A few times a week, 6 = Almost every day

Positive identification with parent

4 items   How much do you want to be like the kind of person your parent is when you are an adult?

How often do you and your parent do things together that you enjoy?

How much do you respect your (parent)?

How close do you feel to your parent?

Response values   1 = Not at all, 2 = Just a little, 3 = Quite a bit, 4 = A lot

---

Peer Characteristics

Peer communication

4 items   How often do the following things happen?

You and your friends talk about how things are going in your life.

You talk to your friends about how things are going with your parents.

You talk with your friends about your plans for the future.

You talk with your friends about problems you are having in school.

Response values   1 = Almost never, 2 = Less than once a month, 3 = 1–3 times a month, 4 = About once a week, 5 = A few times a week, 6 = Almost every day

Peer support

3 items   When you have a social/personal problem at school, how often can you depend on friends to help you out?

When you have a social/personal problem at school, how often can you depend on other students to help you out?

When you're having trouble on schoolwork, how often do you go to your friends for help?

Response values   1 = Almost never, 2 = Not too often, 3 = About half the time, 4 = Fairly often, 5 = Almost always

Positive peers

4 items   How many of the friends you spend most of your time with …

Plan to go to college?

Like to discuss schoolwork/intellectual things with you?

Think it is important to work hard on schoolwork?

Do well in school?

Response values   1 = None of them, 2 = A few of them, 3 = About half of them, 4 = Most of them, 5 = All of them

Negative peers

4 items   How many of the friends you spend most of your time with . . .

Are in youth or street gangs?

Cheat on school tests?

Have stolen something worth more than $50?

Put pressure on you to use drugs?

Response values   1 = None of them, 2 = A few of them, 3 = About half of them, 4 = Most of them, 5 = All of them

Peer drug norms

2 items   How cool or uncool would your friends think you were if you . . .

Drank beer, wine, or liquor?

Used pot, marijuana, or other illegal drugs?

Response values   1 = Very uncool, 2 = Somewhat uncool, 3 = Neither cool nor uncool, 4 = Somewhat cool, 5 = Very cool

---

*Item reversed.

response scales, and Table 2 shows the scale characteristics including the mean, standard deviation, sample size, and alpha for each wave.

Many of the items used to construct the scales described below were modified versions of items developed for other large-scale longitudinal studies; the specific studies are mentioned below in relation to each construct. Scale construction was guided by theoretical concerns and confirmed by exploratory and confirmatory factor analyses. Rather than combining all available items into a single analysis, these analyses were conducted using subsets of items classified into domains (e.g., R/E identity, family, peers, and school). For each full scale, we used items included at every wave to create *matched scales*. For example, if the full scale for a given construct included nine items, but three of those items varied across the relevant waves, we used only the six items that were identical across all waves to create the matched scale. Consequently, all descriptive statistics and growth curve analyses reported in this monograph were based on the matched scales.

Regarding item non-response: because we assume that all the items for a given scale are equally representative of the scale construct, we calculated scale scores for participants who had complete data on at least 66% of the items composing a given scale. Each item was reversed-scored, where relevant, such that higher scores correspond to the construct name. In addition, in the few cases where response scales differed across items for a given scale, response values were recoded to a common range of values (as discussed where describing the relevant construct). In order to preserve the meaning of the response values for purposes of interpreting the growth curves, no items were standardized prior to creating scale scores.

TABLE 2

SCALE CHARACTERISTICS: MEAN, *SD*, SAMPLE SIZE, AND ALPHA

Psychological Well-Being

Scale name	Wave	Mean	SD	N	Alpha
Self-esteem	1	3.60	.95	1,322	.80
	3	3.88	.90	941	.73
	4	3.82	.90	938	.75
	5	3.65	1.00	754	.77
Resiliency	1	3.60	.80	1,318	.74
	3	3.83	.64	941	.68
	4	3.96	.66	912	.73
	5	3.84	.73	755	.72
Anger	1	2.24	.93	1,322	.75
	3	2.34	1.08	941	.87
	4	2.17	1.02	868	.87
	5	1.93	.96	754	.87
Depressive affect	1	Scale does not exist			
	3	1.29	.40	934	.80
	4	1.54	.28	885	.77
	5	1.29	.39	681	.82
Eating disorders	1	Scale does not exist			
	3	1.96	1.01	921	.87
	4	1.87	.96	891	.89
	5	1.85	.96	764	.86
Expected negative life chances	1	1.38	.71	1,270	.71
	3	1.52	.58	930	.77
	4	1.62	.80	896	.67
	5	Scale does not exist			

R/E Identity and Discrimination

Scale Name	Wave	Mean	SD	N	Alpha
R/E importance	1	Scale does not exist			
	3	3.54	.54	615	.63
	4	3.40	.55	534	.75
	5	3.31	.67	454	.75
R/E behavioral involvement	1	Scale does not exist			
	3	2.90	.86	615	.67
	4	2.92	.90	506	.71
	5	2.62	.92	403	.75
Same R/E friends	1	3.78	.91	1,323	One item
	3	4.07	.87	937	One item
	4	4.06	.89	818	One item
	5	4.04	.89	684	One item

(Continued)

TABLE 2. (*Continued*)

R/E Identity and Discrimination

Scale Name	Wave	Mean	SD	N	Alpha
Cross R/E friends	1	2.25	.83	1,323	One item
	3	2.03	.85	938	One item
	4	1.92	.82	816	One item
	5	1.84	.80	684	One item
Expected R/E discrimination	1	Scale does not exist			
	3	1.72	.84	941	.74
	4	1.81	.85	944	.67
	5	1.78	.90	742	.80
R/E John Henryism	1	Scale does not exist			
	3	2.18	.93	934	.83
	4	2.10	.87	812	.87
	5	2.44	.98	740	.92
Parents' worries about R/E discrimination	1	Scale does not exist			
	3	1.97	1.08	937	.81
	4	1.83	.95	894	.78
	5	1.67	.94	671	.85

Academic Functioning

Scale Name	Wave	Mean	SD	N	Alpha
Grade point average (GPA)	1	3.13	.58	1,177	–
	3	3.11	.63	922	–
	4	2.90	.73	816	–
	5	Scale does not exist			
Educational aspirations	1	7.63	1.56	1,323	One item
	3	7.82	1.37	942	One item
	4	6.67	1.48	848	One item
	5	Scale does not exist			
Educational expectations	1	6.81	1.17	1,318	One item
	3	7.04	1.56	941	One item
	4	5.91	1.62	846	One item
	5	Scale does not exist			
Occupational aspirations	1	81.88	21.42	1,175	One item
	3	80.92	20.33	881	One item
	4	81.02	19.10	802	One item
	5	80.07	18.22	627	One item
Academic importance	1	5.51	1.27	1309	.81
	3	5.14	1.29	939	.81
	4	4.90	1.38	820	.79
	5	Scale does not exist			
Academic self-concept	1	5.36	1.07	1,305	.78
	3	5.23	1.13	935	.82
	4	5.03	1.10	898	.79
	5	4.82	1.15	693	.78

(*Continued*)

TABLE 2. (*Continued*)

Academic Functioning

Scale Name	Wave	Mean	SD	N	Alpha
Positive school identification	1	3.48	.75	1,321	.61
	3	3.30	.81	939	.64
	4	3.41	.80	816	.64
	5		Scale does not exist		

Problem Behaviors

Scale Name	Wave	Mean	SD	N	Alpha
School problems	1	.25	.28	1,328	Count
	3	.41	.37	1,185	Count
	4	.44	.41	948	Count
	5		Scale does not exist		
Cigarette use	1	1.12	.64	1,176	One item
	3	1.22	.78	1,011	One item
	4	1.59	1.16	928	One item
	5	1.74	1.33	681	One item
Delinquent behaviors	1	1.61	.60	1,194	Count
	3	1.72	.70	1,016	Count
	4	1.42	.53	940	Count
	5	1.34	.42	696	Count
Alcohol use	1	.34	.64	1,020	One item
	3	.50	.86	988	One item
	4	.74	.94	939	One item
	5	1.39	1.07	691	One item
Marijuana use	1	.60	.45	755	One item
	3	.18	.68	702	One item
	4	.62	1.20	938	One item
	5	.86	1.36	693	One item

Family Characteristics

Scale Name	Wave	Mean	SD	N	Alpha
Intrusive parenting	1		Scale does not exist		
	3	2.78	.85	941	.73
	4	2.77	.92	940	.79
	5	2.50	1.09	665	.86
Negative interactions with parent	1	1.89	.65	1,321	.65
	3	1.77	.61	943	.61
	4	1.70	.60	942	.60
	5	1.79	.71	666	.67
Strict parenting	1	3.06	1.17	1,317	.74

(*Continued*)

TABLE 2. *(Continued)*

Family Characteristics					
Scale Name	Wave	Mean	*SD*	*N*	Alpha
	3	2.90	1.12	942	.80
	4	2.60	1.20	894	.83
	5	Scale does not exist			
Family social support	1	Scale does not exist			
	3	4.25	.78	942	.77
	4	4.22	.79	894	.81
	5	4.37	.77	693	.83
Parent–adolescent communication	1	3.75	1.32	1,324	.72
	3	3.57	1.41	943	.68
	4	3.55	1.38	893	.74
	5	3.67	1.44	666	.86
Positive identification with parent	1	3.37	.51	1,323	.67
	3	3.18	.59	943	.75
	4	3.11	.62	938	.74
	5	3.04	.66	667	.82

Peer Characteristics					
Scale Name	Wave	Mean	*SD*	*N*	Alpha
Peer communication	1	Scale does not exist			
	3	3.58	1.37	942	.82
	4	3.94	1.04	863	.85
	5	3.90	1.27	689	.85
Peer support	1	3.02	.96	1316	.73
	3	2.99	.85	942	.63
	4	3.06	.83	791	.59
	5	Scale does not exist			
Positive peers	1	3.47	.76	1323	.68
	3	3.37	.69	939	.69
	4	3.40	.79	820	.79
	5	3.17	.99	682	.80
Negative peers	1	1.17	.30	1323	.54
	3	1.49	.63	939	.75
	4	1.61	.59	895	.66
	5	Scale does not exist			
Peer drug norms	1	1.41	.78	1320	.63
	3	1.97	1.05	938	.80
	4	2.56	1.05	895	.82
	5	Scale does not exist			

COVARIATES

Gender

This was contrast-coded as a dichotomous variable (males $= -0.5$; females $= +0.5$).

Race/Ethnicity

This was an open-ended question asked at all of the waves so that the resulting categories are subjective self-identifications: "What is your race or ethnicity, for example Black, White, Asian, Latino or something else?" There was some shifting in identification in a very small number of cases, and they were coded at their most consistent response. Race/ethnicity was contrast-coded as a dichotomous variable (African Americans $= -0.5$; European Americans $= +0.5$).

Socioeconomic Status (SES)

SES was a composite scale created from information provided by the primary caregiver at the 7th grade visit (Wave 1). The composite score was a mean of the following standardized scores (using the full sample): the highest level of education of either parent (0–20, with 20 being doctorate or M.D.), the highest occupational status of either parent (0–99, with doctor being 99) based on Nam and Powers (1983), and the family income based on annual income categories (1–16, with 16 being more than $75,000).

Parents' Marital Status

This was obtained from a question asking primary caregivers their current marital status (Wave 1). From this question, we derived two variables: *married, intact families* and *single, never married families.* Married, intact families included only those families who had never been separated, divorced, or widowed with both the primary and secondary caregivers (married $= 1$; else $= 0$). Single, never married families included only those families whose primary caregiver had never been married (single, never married $= 1$; else $= 0$).

Self-Esteem

This scale was based on Harter's (1985) concept of self-worth. It has been shown to have good internal consistency (i.e., measurement reliability) and predictive and face validity in many studies (Cogburn, Chavous, & Griffin, 2011; Colarossi & Eccles, 2003; Garrett & Eccles, 2009; Goldstein, Malanchuk, Davis-Kean, & Eccles, 2007; Gutman & Eccles, 2007; Ludden & Eccles, 2007).

Resiliency

This scale was developed for the Philadelphia Family Management Study (Furstenberg, Cook, Eccles, Elder, & Sameroff, 1999) to measure adolescents' ability to adapt to challenges and new situations. It was shown to have good predictive and face validity (Furstenberg et al., 1999) and reliability (Wong et al., 2003).

Anger

This scale was adapted from Derogatis's (1996) Symptom Check List—90 to measure adolescents' angry feelings. It was shown to have good reliability and predictive and face validity in Derogatis (1996).

Depressive Affect

This scale was adapted from the Children's Depression Inventory (Kovacs, 1992). It has been shown to have good reliability and predictive and face validity in many studies (Cogburn et al., 2011; Colarossi & Eccles, 2003; Goldstein et al., 2011; Gutman & Eccles, 2007; Ludden & Eccles, 2007).

Eating Disorders

This scale was adapted from the Eating Disorder Inventory (EDI) for Anorexia Nervosa and Bulimia (Garner, Olmstead, & Polivy, 1983), which measures psychological and behavioral traits common in anorexia nervosa and bulimia. The EDI is not a diagnostic tool but, rather, a preliminary screening instrument. It was shown to have good reliability and predictive and face validity in many studies (e.g., Tangney, Baumeister, & Boone, 2004; Stice, 2002).

Expected Negative Life Chances

The scale was adapted from other standard life expectancy scales and expanded for this study by the PIs (Eccles and Sameroff). It has excellent face validity and very good reliability.

R/E Importance

This scale was created for MADICS based on the work of Cross (1991) and Crocker and Luhtanen (1990) to measure the personal importance of one's race/ethnicity. For Wave 3, European American adolescents were not asked these questions; therefore, these scales were constructed only for African American adolescents in this monograph. It has good face validity as well as good reliability (Chatman, Malanchuk, & Eccles, 2001; Tang, McLoyd, & Hallman, 2016).

R/E Behavioral Involvement

This scale was developed for MADICS to assess adolescents' involvement in activities related to their R/E background based on open-ended interviews and the work of Cross (1991). For Wave 3, European American adolescents were not asked these questions; therefore, these scales were constructed only for African American adolescents.

Same R/E Friends

This measure was developed for MADICS, assessing adolescents' proportion of same R/E friends. It is similar to items used to assess friends' characteristics on national survey studies (Chatman et al., 2001). This measure was calculated using two questions that asked about the proportion of African American and European American friends. For European American adolescents, we used the question about their proportion of European American friends, whereas the reverse was true for African American adolescents.

Cross R/E Friends

This measure was developed for MADICS, assessing adolescents' proportion of other R/E friends. It is similar to items used to assess friends' characteristics on national survey studies (Chatman et al., 2001). This measure was calculated using two questions asking about the proportion of African American and European American friends. For African American adolescents, we used the question about their proportion of European American friends, whereas the reverse was true for European American adolescents. We did not assess whether the adolescents had friends who were from another R/E group.

Expected R/E Discrimination

This scale was developed for MADICS to measure adolescents' expectations of discrimination affecting their educational and employment opportunities and was based on the types of items used to assess expected future discrimination in national survey studies (Eccles et al., 2006; Peck, Brodish, Malanchuk, Banerjee, & Eccles, 2014).

R/E John Henryism

This scale was developed for MADICS based on the concept of "*prolonged, high effort coping* with difficult psychosocial stressors" (James, 1994, p. 166). It has good face validity and is similar in format to these kinds of items on national survey studies (Chatman et al., 2001; Tang et al., 2016).

Perceived Parents' Worries About R/E Discrimination

This scale was developed for MADICS to assess adolescents' perceptions of their parents' worries about R/E discrimination based on open-ended interviews and the work of Cross (1991).

ACADEMIC FUNCTIONING

Grade Point Average (GPA)

This was a series of questions that was asked about their school grades for that year. It is similar to questions asked on national surveys to measure GPA. Responses were then converted into a GPA.

Educational Aspirations

This was taken from the National Educational Longitudinal Study of 1988 (NELS) to measure the young person's hopes for future education.

Educational Expectations

This was taken from NELS 1988 to assess adolescents' realistic expectations for future education.

Occupational Aspirations

This measured the adolescents' hopes for their future career. Open-ended answers were coded using Nam and Powers (1983); scores ranged from 1 = "dishwasher; counter attendant" to 99 = "surgeon; physician".

Academic Importance

This scale was derived from measures developed for Michigan Study of Adolescent Life Transitions (MSALT; Eccles et al., 1993) assessing the importance adolescents ascribed to math and other school subjects. It has excellent face validity, predictive validity, and reliability (Durik, Vida, & Eccles, 2006; Eccles & Wigfield, 1995; Simpkins, Davis-Kean, & Eccles, 2006).

Academic Self-Concept

This scale was based on scales developed for MSALT (Eccles et al., 1993) and measures adolescents' perceptions of their ability in school subjects. It has excellent face validity, predictive validity, and reliability (Archambault, Eccles, & Vida, 2010; Bouchey, Shoulberg, Jodl, & Eccles, 2010; Denissen, Zarret, & Eccles, 2007; Diemer, Marchand, McKellar, & Malanchuk, 2016; Durik et al., 2006; Eccles & Wigfield, 1995).

Positive School Identification

The construct of school identification measured students' sense of school belonging and valuing of education by using items from the (MSALT; Eccles et al., 1993), items from the work of Mickelson (1990), and items from the Philadelphia Study (Furstenberg, Cook, Eccles, Elder, & Sameroff, 1999).

PROBLEM BEHAVIORS

School Problems

This scale was based on the work of Elliott, Huizinga, and Menard (1989) and consisted of a count of items asking about their problems in school (Harris, 2008; Wong et al., 2003).

Cigarette Use

This was derived from the Monitoring the Future studies (O'Malley, Bachman, & Johnston, 1987), asking about how often they smoked a cigarette. It has been shown to have good predictive and face validity (Gutman et al., 2011; Ludden & Eccles, 2007).

Delinquent Behaviors

This was a count of items asking about adolescents' engagement in delinquent behaviors based on the work of Elliott, Huizinga, and Menard

(1989). It has been shown to have good reliability and predictive and face validity (Gutman & Eccles, 2007; Ludden & Eccles, 2007).

Alcohol Use

This was based on Monitoring the Future (O'Malley et al., 1987), asking about how often they had an alcoholic drink. It has been shown to have good predictive and face validity (Gutman et al., 2011; Ludden & Eccles, 2007).

Marijuana Use

This was based on a single item from Monitoring the Future (O'Malley et al., 1987) asking how often they smoked marijuana. It has been shown to have good predictive and face validity (Ludden & Eccles, 2007).

FAMILY CHARACTERISTICS

Intrusive Parenting

This scale was based on ideas associated with Baumrind's (1991) parenting styles as well as the more recent work on controlling parenting by Barber (2002).

Negative Interactions With Parent

This scale was adapted from the Iowa Youth and Family Study (Conger, Ge, Elder, Lorenz, & Simons, 1994; Conger et al., 1991) and assessed problematic parent-adolescent relationships. It has been shown to have good reliability and predictive and face validity in many studies (Eccles, Early, Fraser, Belansky, & McCarthy, 1997; Gutman & Eccles, 1999, 2007; Gutman et al., 2011).

Strict Parenting

This scale was based on ideas associated with Baumrind's parenting styles (Baumrind, 1991), asking adolescents about their parents' discipline strategies when they break one of their parents' important rules.

Family Social Supports

This scale was from the Philadelphia Family Management Study (Furstenberg et al., 1999), assessing the adolescents' perception of the supportive nature of their family relationships. It has been shown to have good predictive and face validity (Colarossi & Eccles, 2003).

Parent–Adolescent Communication

This scale was based on MSALT (Eccles et al., 1993) and measured how often adolescents talk with their parents. It has been shown to have good predictive and face validity (Tang et al., 2016).

Positive Identification With Parent

This scale was adapted from the Iowa Youth and Family Study (Conger et al., 1991, 1994) assessing the closeness of the parent–adolescent relationship. It has been shown to have good reliability and predictive and face validity in many studies (Gutman & Eccles, 2007; Gutman et al., 2011; Jodl, Michael, Malanchuk, & Eccles, 2001; Risch, Jodl, & Eccles, 2004).

PEER CHARACTERISTICS

Peer Communication

This scale was developed for MSALT (Eccles et al., 1993) and assessed how often the adolescent talked with their friends. It has been shown to have good predictive and face validity (Fuligni & Eccles, 1993).

Peer Support

This scale was developed for MSALT (Eccles et al., 1993) and asked about how often they can depend on their friends for support. It has been shown to have good reliability and predictive and face validity (Colarossi & Eccles, 2000; Gutman et al., 2002).

Positive Peers

This scale was developed for MADICS and consisted of items asking how many of their friends are academically oriented. It has been shown to have good reliability and predictive and face validity in many studies (Eccles et al., 1997; Fredricks & Eccles, 2010; Garret & Eccles, 2009; Harris, 2008; Ludden & Eccles, 2007).

Negative Peers

This scale was developed for MADICS and asked how many of their friends engage in delinquent behaviors. It has been shown to have good reliability and predictive and face validity in many studies (Eccles et al., 1997; Garrett & Eccles, 2009; Goldstein et al., 2007; Ludden & Eccles, 2007).

Peer Drug Norms

This scale was developed for MADICS, asking about their friends' norms concerning the use of alcohol and drugs. It has been shown to have good predictive and face validity (Eccles et al., 1997).

III: PRELIMINARY ANALYSES AND ANALYTIC PLAN

Leslie Morrison Gutman, Stephen C. Peck, Oksana Malanchuk, Arnold J. Sameroff, and Jacquelynne S. Eccles

This article is part of the issue "Moving through Adolescence: Developmental Trajectories of African American and European American Youth" Gutman, Peck, Malanchuk, Sameroff, and Eccles (Issue Authors). For a full listing of articles in this issue, see: http://onlinelibrary.wiley.com/doi/10.1111/mono.v82.4/issuetoc.

In this chapter, we describe our preliminary analyses and analytic plan. The preliminary analyses were focused on several aspects of construct validity. We first distinguish between *construct invariance and measurement invariance* as two different approaches to establishing that our scales mean the same thing to adolescents categorized as African American or European American and female or male. We then consider the extent to which (a) correlations between the same construct assessed at different points in time provide evidence of *convergent validity* and (b) correlations between a given construct and theoretically similar and dissimilar construct provide evidence of convergent and *discriminant validity*, respectively. Given that our assessment of construct invariance (described below) revealed some differences in the magnitude and direction of correlations for the R/E discrimination measures across the four R/E and gender groups, we next describe our analysis of measurement invariance for these measures. Finally, we provide an overview of the HLM analyses that were used to examine the growth curve trajectories in Chapters IV through IX and describe how the results are presented in tables and figures.

Corresponding author: Leslie Morrison Gutman, Department of Clinical, Educational and Health Psychology, University College London, 1-19 Torrington Place, London WC1E 7HB, email: l.gutman@ucl.ac.uk
DOI: 10.1111/mono.12329

PRELIMINARY ANALYSES

In this section, we explore the extent to which our measures relate similarly to each other both within and across time for our four groups. In order to accomplish this goal, we appealed to Nesselroade et al.'s (2007) distinction between specific item content and the abstract meaning of the corresponding measures. Nesselroade and colleagues (e.g., Nesselroade et al., 2007; Nesselroade, Gerstorf, Hardy, & Ram, 2009; Nesselroade & Molenaar, 2010; Zhang, Browne, & Nesselroade, 2011) have argued that using factor-loading patterns (or other aspects of measurement models, such as item means) as the basis for invariance claims may be putting the invariance emphasis at the wrong level of abstraction; that is, "a rigidly standardized measurement framework at the observable level may not be the most appropriate and compelling way to proceed with the assessment of abstract constructs" (Zhang et al., 2011, p. 198). The primary reason for this concern seems to be that, as scientists who study developmental processes, they are familiar with the challenge of studying abstract, dynamic processes (e.g., autonomy) that challenge simple measurement procedures. For example, expressions of autonomy are expected to vary across developmental time such that the same behavior (e.g., getting dressed alone, getting to school alone) may be less useful for understanding autonomy at different ages, even though the abstract concept of autonomy remains the same. As a strategy for maintaining focus on the abstract psychological concept under study, they suggested allowing some item responses to vary across individuals and focusing more on the relations among the abstract concepts (e.g., correlations among factors). Although we did not conduct the statistical tests for assessing construct invariance described by Nesselroade and colleagues, we used their conceptual distinction between specific item content and the abstract meaning of the corresponding measures to guide our examination of the extent to which the patterns of correlations among our domain-specific measures support our assumption that the meaning of the measures used in this study are sufficiently similar to allow meaningful interpretation of growth, and differences in growth, across groups.

Correlational Analyses

For the correlational analyses, we focused on addressing two major questions: (a) do the patterns of correlations of the same construct with itself across waves, and the patterns of correlations of different constructs within and across domains, provide evidence of convergent and discriminant validity as well as support our decisions about which scales to aggregate to a more general level and which to keep separate? and (b) are the patterns of these correlations within and across domains similar enough across the R/E by gender groups to justify our assumption that the scales have comparable meanings across the four groups?

To address these questions, we conducted two sets of correlational analyses. First, we examined correlations within each domain across waves for each R/E and gender group, separately. These tables are presented online as Supporting Information (see Supporting Information Tables S1–S12). Second, we examined the associations across domains within each wave for each R/E and gender group. Tables 3 and 4 present the Wave 3 correlational matrices for African American males and females and European American males and females, respectively. The correlations within Waves 1, 4, and 5 for each R/E and gender group are presented online as Supporting Information (see Supporting Information Tables S13–S18).

Regarding the first question, most of the correlations between different waves of the same measure were significant (Cohen, 1988). According to Cohen, correlation coefficients in the order of .10 are "small," those of .30 are "medium," and those of .50 are "large" in terms of magnitude of effect sizes (see pp. 77–81). Given that the majority of relevant correlations were medium in magnitude, these patterns support our assumption that the scales, by and large, showed convergent validity across time. Within Wave 3, constructs within domains were generally correlated more highly than constructs across domains, supporting both convergent and discriminate validity. Across domains, measures of positive adolescent characteristics and contexts were generally positively associated with each other, and the same was true for relations among negative characteristics, demonstrating the convergent validity of these measures. However, the strength of the correlations between similarly negative or positive measures within the same domain and measures in other domains often differed, supporting our decision to examine trajectories of distinct constructs within domains as opposed to higher-order constructs that could be constructed for other purposes. Regarding the second question, the associations between different measures within and across domains were quite similar across the four subgroups for most, but not all, of the measures. We next describe these patterns in more detail.

For *psychological well-being*, the correlations across waves of the same construct were generally medium to large in magnitude, showing convergent validity across time (see Supporting Information Tables S1 and S2). Within Wave 3, measures of psychological well-being generally had medium to large associations with each other in the expected direction with the exception of negative chances, demonstrating convergent validity (see Tables 3 and 4). On the other hand, measures of psychological well-being had associations with R/E discrimination measures that were small in magnitude, showing discriminant validity. Furthermore, the strength of the associations between Wave 3 measures of psychological well-being and those from other domains differed depending on the measure in question. For example, there were

TABLE 3

Correlations Among Wave 3 Measures for African American Adolescents

	1	2	3	4	5	6	7	8	9	10	11	12	13	14	15	16	17	18	19	20	21	22	23	24	25	26	27	28	29	30	31	32	33	34	35	36
1. Self-esteem	1.00	.38	-.38	-.50	-.40	-.17	.05	.16	.10	.00	-.06	-.01	-.08	.10	.09	.10	.02	.06	.14	.18	-.16	-.12	-.29	-.21	-.29	-.24	-.20	-.13	.17	.02	.19	-.04	.00	.17	-.17	-.09
2. Resiliency	.28	1.00	-.15	-.25	-.24	-.11	.16	.16	-.01	.04	-.06	.06	.05	.24	.18	.27	.07	.18	.21	.17	-.10	.03	-.18	-.14	-.11	.12	-.29	.02	.28	.09	.12	.18	-.14	.35	-.06	-.07
3. Anger	-.32	-.24	1.00	.50	.22	.25	-.11	-.04	.01	-.01	.10	.10	-.10	-.21	-.10	-.13	-.07	-.02	-.17	-.07	.22	.11	.31	.29	.31	.17	.18	.06	-.16	-.06	-.08	.12	-.01	-.03	.27	.19
4. Depressive affect	-.39	-.25	.50	1.00	.37	.25	-.06	-.06	.03	.08	.14	.12	.05	-.17	-.04	.08	.02	.17	-.04	.12	.30	.31	.30	.45	.25	.16	.16	.05	-.18	-.06	-.15	.04	.08	.07	.28	.20
5. Eating disorders	-.25	-.24	.22	.37	1.00	.38	.15	.04	.02	-.11	.16	.10	.06	-.11	.01	-.18	.07	.11	.23	.09	.19	.23	.16	.41	.33	.29	.37	.16	-.04	.01	-.22	.04	.05	.03	.16	.25
6. Negative chances	-.11	-.22	.25	.25	.38	1.00	.05	-.01	.02	-.11	.05	.09	-.04	-.04	.01	-.04	.07	.04	-.09	.00	.31	.31	.33	.14	.19	.31	.23	.18	-.09	.05	-.16	-.09	-.03	-.05	.42	.31
7. R/E importance	.05	.16	-.11	.06	.15	.05	1.00	.38	.07	-.06	.19	.16	.14	.20	.05	.18	-.03	.06	.06	.00	-.04	.00	-.04	.06	.08	-.03	-.03	.09	.21	.22	.22	.37	.18	.14	-.15	-.01
8. R/E behavioral involvement	.10	.16	-.04	-.06	.04	-.01	.38	1.00	.29	.00	.09	.13	.18	.10	.12	.13	.06	.08	.08	.06	-.08	-.11	-.07	-.01	.12	.13	.16	.09	.18	.23	.08	.16	.05	.29	-.09	.25
9. Same R/E friends	.00	-.01	.01	.03	.02	.02	.07	.29	1.00	.05	.05	.02	.10	.05	.05	-.03	-.04	.02	.02	.09	-.12	.01	.06	.04	.06	.01	-.03	.01	.04	.06	.03	.08	.26	.07	-.09	-.04
10. Cross R/E friends	.00	.04	-.01	.08	-.11	-.11	-.06	.00	.05	1.00	-.10	-.13	.06	.04	.04	-.01	-.01	.11	.01	.01	.01	.01	.05	-.05	.10	-.06	-.02	-.03	.06	-.05	-.02	.03	.06	.23	-.09	.03
11. Expected R/E discrimination	-.06	-.06	.10	.14	.16	.05	.19	.09	.05	-.10	1.00	.40	.45	.07	.14	.09	.13	.18	.11	.11	.05	.16	.05	.10	.10	.02	.06	-.01	.02	-.01	.05	.04	-.05	.03	.04	-.08
12. John Henryism	-.01	.06	.10	.12	.10	.09	.16	.13	.02	-.13	.40	1.00	.33	.11	.07	.11	.12	.13	.13	-.02	.11	.05	.11	.05	.10	.05	-.01	-.01	.02	.07	.01	.02	.07	.03	.02	.12
13. Parent worries about discrimination	-.08	.05	-.10	.05	.06	-.04	.14	.18	.10	.06	.45	.33	1.00	.09	.09	.18	.12	.11	.11	.02	.11	.11	.02	.00	-.07	-.07	.04	.00	.05	.11	.03	.02	.04	.10	.01	.02
14. GPA	.10	.24	-.21	-.17	-.11	-.04	.20	.10	.05	.04	.07	.11	.09	1.00	.12	.11	.11	.11	.31	.27	-.10	-.09	-.12	-.02	-.17	-.08	.20	.10	.18	.14	.07	.10	.09	.17	-.01	.08
15. Educational aspirations	.09	.18	-.10	-.04	.01	.01	.05	.12	.05	.04	.14	.07	.09	.12	1.00	.63	.62	.17	.19	.24	-.09	-.15	.01	.01	-.10	.13	.07	.09	.13	.05	.13	.09	.07	.14	-.01	-.05
16. Educational expectations	.10	.27	-.13	.08	-.18	-.04	.18	.13	-.03	-.01	.09	.11	.18	.11	.63	1.00	.37	.16	.24	.14	-.14	-.13	.05	.02	-.05	.13	.09	.05	.16	.11	.05	.11	.09	.28	-.11	-.03
17. Occupational aspirations	.02	.07	-.07	.02	.07	.07	-.03	.06	-.04	-.01	.13	.12	.12	.11	.62	.37	1.00	.16	.07	.16	.03	-.02	-.03	.00	.00	-.16	.03	.03	.03	.05	.03	.07	.07	.24	.01	-.03
18. Academic importance	.06	.18	-.02	.17	.11	.04	.06	.08	.02	.11	.18	.13	.11	.11	.17	.16	.16	1.00	.58	.22	-.22	-.13	-.10	-.01	-.06	-.07	-.12	.03	.24	.11	.18	.24	.00	.12	.00	-.13
19. Academic self-concept	.14	.21	-.17	-.04	.23	-.09	.06	.08	.02	.01	.11	.13	.11	.31	.19	.24	.07	.58	1.00	.35	-.13	-.19	-.10	-.10	-.14	.15	.22	.01	.22	.11	.11	.30	.05	.32	-.20	-.13
20. Positive school identification	.18	.17	-.07	.12	.09	.00	.00	.06	.09	.01	.11	-.02	.02	.27	.24	.14	.16	.22	.35	1.00	-.19	-.10	-.15	.05	-.13	.27	.04	.13	.13	.24	.01	.22	.14	.29	-.28	-.10
21. School problems	-.16	-.10	.22	.30	.19	.31	-.04	-.08	-.12	.01	.05	.11	.02	-.10	-.09	-.14	.03	-.22	-.13	-.19	1.00	.23	.56	.30	.21	.25	.19	.11	-.27	-.24	-.22	-.19	-.10	-.22	.29	.26
22. Cigarette use	-.12	.03	.11	.31	.23	.31	.00	-.11	.01	.01	.16	.05	.11	-.09	-.15	-.13	-.02	-.13	-.19	-.10	.23	1.00	.66	.37	.44	.14	.05	.04	-.14	-.11	-.09	.04	-.02	-.09	.13	.20
23. Delinquent behaviors	-.29	-.18	.31	.30	.16	.33	-.04	-.07	.06	.05	.05	.11	.02	-.12	.01	.05	-.03	-.10	-.10	-.15	.56	.66	1.00	.34	.42	.20	.09	-.09	-.08	-.07	-.15	-.01	-.04	-.23	.28	.24
24. Alcohol use	-.21	-.14	.29	.45	.41	.14	.06	-.01	.04	-.05	.10	.05	.00	-.02	.01	.02	.00	-.10	-.10	.05	.30	.37	.34	1.00	.60	.11	.11	-.21	-.12	.04	-.16	-.02	-.16	-.08	.30	.33
25. Marijuana use	-.29	-.11	.31	.25	.33	.19	.08	.12	.06	.10	.10	.10	-.07	-.17	-.10	-.05	.00	-.06	-.14	-.13	.21	.44	.42	.60	1.00	.09	.01	-.25	-.16	.01	-.12	-.09	.06	-.16	.01	.20
26. Intrusive parenting	-.24	.12	.17	.16	.29	.31	-.03	.13	.01	-.06	.02	.05	-.02	-.08	.13	.13	-.16	-.07	.15	.27	.25	.14	.20	.11	.09	1.00	.51	.26	-.18	-.25	-.36	.04	-.14	-.02	.00	.07
27. Negative interactions with parent	-.20	-.29	.18	.16	.37	.23	-.03	.16	-.03	-.02	.06	-.01	.04	.20	.07	.09	.03	-.12	.22	.04	.19	.05	.09	.11	.01	.51	1.00	.22	-.04	-.10	-.39	.00	-.08	-.08	.00	.13
28. Strict parenting	-.13	.02	.06	.05	.16	.18	.09	.09	.01	-.03	-.01	-.01	.00	.10	.09	.05	.03	.03	.01	.13	.11	.04	-.09	-.21	-.25	.26	.22	1.00	.05	-.10	-.04	.01	.01	-.04	.00	.07
29. Family social support	.17	.28	-.16	-.18	-.04	-.09	.21	.18	.17	.06	.02	.02	.05	.18	.13	.16	.03	.24	.22	.13	-.27	-.14	-.08	-.12	-.16	-.18	-.04	.05	1.00	.27	.43	.30	.39	.17	-.24	.07
30. Parent-adolescent communication	.02	.09	-.06	-.06	.01	.05	.22	.23	.32	-.05	-.01	.07	.11	.14	.05	.11	.05	.11	.11	.24	-.24	-.11	-.07	.04	.01	-.25	-.10	.01	.27	1.00	.17	.30	.31	.23	-.21	-.15
31. Positive identification with parent	.19	.12	-.08	-.15	-.22	-.16	.22	.08	.22	-.02	.05	.01	.03	.07	.13	.05	.03	.18	.11	.01	-.19	-.09	-.15	-.16	-.12	-.30	-.37	-.04	.43	.17	1.00	.25	.29	.20	-.22	-.16
32. Peer communication	-.04	.18	.12	.04	.04	-.09	.37	.16	.08	.03	.04	.02	.02	.10	.09	.11	.07	.24	.30	.22	-.19	.04	-.01	-.02	-.09	.04	.00	.13	.30	.23	.08	1.00	.33	.21	.10	-.05
33. Peer support	.00	-.14	-.01	.08	.05	-.03	.18	.05	.26	.06	-.05	.07	.04	.09	.07	.09	.07	.00	.05	.14	-.10	-.02	-.04	-.17	.06	-.04	-.17	.06	.39	.31	.29	.33	1.00	.19	.10	-.13
34. Positive peers	.17	.35	-.03	.07	.03	-.05	.14	.29	.07	.23	.03	.03	.04	.17	.14	.28	.24	.12	.32	.30	-.22	-.09	-.23	-.08	-.16	-.02	.00	-.24	.17	.23	.20	.17	.23	1.00	-.26	-.30
35. Negative peers	-.17	-.06	.27	.28	.16	.42	-.15	-.09	-.09	-.09	.04	.02	.04	-.18	-.01	-.11	-.01	-.14	-.17	-.28	.29	.13	.28	.30	.05	.18	.00	-.10	-.22	-.17	.06	-.38	.10	-.26	1.00	.42
36. Peer drug norms	-.09	-.07	.19	.20	.25	.31	-.01	.25	-.04	.03	-.08	.09	-.04	-.12	-.06	-.03	-.03	-.13	-.13	-.10	.26	.20	.24	.33	.10	.07	.13	.07	-.08	-.15	-.16	-.05	-.13	-.30	.42	1.00

Note. African American males are at the bottom half of the correlation matric; African American females are at the top half of the correlation matric. When r > .15, p < .05, when r > .20, p < .01.

TABLE 4
Correlations Among Wave 3 Measures for European American Adolescents

	1	2	3	4	5	6	7	8	9	10	11	12	13	14	15	16	17	18	19	20	21	22	23	24	25	26	27	28	29	30	31	32	33	34
1. Self-esteem	1.00	.48	-.43	-.60	-.52	-.30	.03	-.06	-.13	.19	-.14	-.10	.09	.19	.08	.31	.33	.22	-.12	-.35	-.19	-.23	.05	-.27	-.20	-.08	.27	.15	.20	-.01	.02	.22	-.13	-.19
2. Resiliency	.38	1.00	-.44	-.43	-.23	-.35	.05	-.09	-.13	.38	-.23	-.13	.16	.26	.02	.33	.47	.23	-.13	-.26	-.22	-.09	-.12	-.23	.09	.29	.05	.42	.30	.12	.05	.42	-.33	-.23
3. Anger	-.18	-.38	1.00	.54	.31	.32	.17	.14	.13	.15	.26	.15	-.14	-.18	.05	-.23	-.18	-.18	.29	.25	.37	.27	.27	-.09	.27	.16	.09	-.04	-.13	.09	.13	-.36	.31	.26
4. Depressive affect	-.44	-.23	.39	1.00	.40	.30	-.02	-.06	.18	.19	.18	.19	-.19	-.21	.02	-.28	-.18	-.14	.25	.29	.37	.25	.29	-.09	.22	.10	-.01	-.12	-.21	.02	-.01	-.30	.27	.20
5. Eating disorders	-.40	-.13	.24	.35	1.00	.21	-.04	.02	.03	.00	.08	-.10	.08	-.07	-.02	-.19	-.21	-.15	.18	.30	.24	.25	.14	.12	.09	.02	.19	.10	.03	.07	-.21	-.01	-.30	.20
6. Negative chances	-.06	-.20	.32	.39	.35	1.00	-.04	-.18	-.19	.03	.09	.02	-.09	-.14	-.16	.24	.28	.16	-.13	-.20	-.17	-.09	-.08	-.04	-.15	-.01	-.09	.07	-.12	.02	.02	-.04	.32	.20
7. Same R/E friends	.19	.14	.17	-.14	.01	-.04	1.00	-.77	-.18	-.18	-.13	-.07	-.01	-.02	.03	-.16	-.09	.02	-.06	-.10	.04	.08	.06	-.01	-.12	.03	-.08	-.02	-.02	.00	-.15	.07	.07	.14
8. Cross R/E friends	-.11	-.07	.20	-.04	.01	.08	-.84	1.00	.09	.14	.11	-.07	-.01	-.02	.03	-.07	.01	.04	-.07	-.10	.04	-.07	-.04	.00	.11	.06	-.03	-.02	.00	.11	.13	.07	.04	-.08
9. Expected R/E discrimination	-.14	-.15	.17	.18	.03	.04	-.18	.09	1.00	.39	.55	-.14	-.13	-.32	-.09	-.07	-.01	.02	-.05	-.10	.04	-.01	-.07	.12	.21	.23	-.08	-.01	-.08	.06	.10	-.13	.02	.01
10. John Henryism	-.14	-.23	.29	.19	.00	.03	-.18	.14	.25	1.00	.36	-.06	-.06	-.12	.01	.07	.01	.02	-.14	.24	.19	.07	-.06	.17	.24	.14	-.16	.08	-.22	.08	.00	.26	.26	.18
11. Parent worries about discrimination	-.05	-.08	.15	.23	.08	.09	-.13	.11	.37	.12	1.00	-.15	-.10	-.06	-.01	-.05	-.01	.09	.09	.08	.09	.03	-.07	-.02	.11	.14	.02	.07	-.03	.13	.14	-.17	-.03	-.02
12. GPA	.18	.30	-.35	-.22	-.10	.02	-.07	-.02	-.10	.12	-.09	1.00	.26	.33	.00	.22	.37	.17	-.21	-.21	-.21	-.24	-.24	.05	-.16	-.02	.14	.11	.06	-.03	-.01	.33	.01	-.32
13. Educational aspirations	.20	.17	-.20	-.14	.08	.07	-.06	-.19	.15	.00	-.18	.26	1.00	.68	.17	.24	.28	.16	-.13	-.20	-.17	.00	-.11	-.04	-.15	-.01	.10	.19	.09	.02	-.04	.32	.01	-.10
14. Educational expectations	.23	.27	-.23	-.05	-.13	-.13	-.17	-.22	-.09	-.18	-.09	.33	.77	1.00	.20	.35	.35	.14	-.10	-.17	-.22	-.09	-.08	-.05	-.19	.00	.17	.11	.07	-.03	.06	.34	.07	-.23
15. Occupational aspirations	-.04	.02	-.16	-.06	-.16	-.04	-.16	-.13	.37	.13	.05	.00	.01	.22	1.00	.08	.10	.13	.05	-.14	.05	-.21	.05	.00	-.16	-.01	.05	.08	.06	-.06	.15	-.06	.04	.17
16. Academic importance	.26	.23	-.26	-.24	-.07	-.29	-.07	.05	-.08	.07	-.05	.22	.11	.12	.10	1.00	.61	.27	-.18	-.34	-.27	-.32	-.08	-.10	-.16	-.01	.12	.16	.22	.11	.12	.26	-.16	-.26
17. Academic self-concept	.41	.30	-.42	-.39	-.20	-.20	.06	.17	-.03	.01	-.01	.36	.28	.36	.04	.56	1.00	.31	-.23	-.36	-.27	-.17	-.23	.00	.09	.04	.20	.17	.20	.11	.17	.20	-.20	-.21
18. Positive school identification	.25	.27	-.33	-.20	.11	.11	-.07	-.03	-.15	.02	.09	.17	.16	.16	.19	.31	.31	1.00	-.20	-.24	-.24	-.17	.31	.08	-.12	.21	.24	.20	.15	.02	.24	.14	-.23	-.21
19. School problems	-.11	-.07	.27	.20	.05	.02	-.04	-.07	-.11	-.20	.09	-.20	-.13	-.10	-.05	-.18	-.22	-.20	1.00	.45	.57	.31	.31	.12	.07	.03	-.10	-.13	-.15	.17	-.01	-.27	.40	.32
20. Cigarette use	-.10	.01	.20	.08	.14	.35	.08	-.04	.06	.07	.02	-.21	-.21	-.06	.02	-.06	-.28	-.24	.45	1.00	.47	.62	.57	.04	.08	.03	-.15	-.20	.25	.12	.12	-.27	.35	.36
21. Delinquent behaviors	-.18	-.13	.29	.09	.10	.41	.14	.08	.01	.24	.00	-.07	-.20	.03	.07	-.13	-.32	-.18	.51	.68	1.00	.51	.69	.10	.23	.09	-.10	-.13	-.12	.17	.05	-.26	.35	.36
22. Alcohol use	-.02	.00	.08	.05	.04	.44	.14	-.05	.00	.00	.03	-.22	-.09	.00	.00	.13	-.16	.07	.61	.51	.61	1.00	.69	.10	.23	.33	.03	-.13	-.12	.00	.00	-.24	.35	.53
23. Marijuana use	-.07	.03	.20	.10	-.10	.28	.14	-.05	-.21	.05	-.21	-.17	-.01	-.03	.05	-.21	-.14	.31	.51	.69	.47	.13	1.00	.05	.18	.33	-.09	.01	-.09	-.03	.01	-.03	.37	.07
24. Intrusive parenting	-.30	-.32	.36	.20	.16	.20	-.03	-.01	-.14	.17	.10	.05	-.10	-.11	.00	-.19	-.29	-.27	.12	.14	.05	.12	.13	1.00	.48	.33	.24	-.21	-.31	-.09	-.08	-.28	.06	.20
25. Negative interactions with parent	-.18	-.17	.25	.29	.16	.20	.04	.17	.10	.10	.13	-.07	.00	-.04	.13	-.08	-.13	-.17	.14	.07	.13	.15	.05	.48	1.00	.23	-.06	-.18	-.40	.07	-.03	-.21	.07	.20
26. Strict parenting	-.07	-.06	.00	-.01	.21	.21	-.03	.10	.03	.03	.10	.14	.10	.10	.05	.34	.38	.18	.01	.02	.16	.15	.18	.33	.23	1.00	-.05	.09	.03	-.13	.04	-.09	.03	.06
27. Family social support	.48	.42	-.22	-.36	-.15	-.19	.01	.05	-.14	-.07	-.20	.14	.11	.07	.07	.38	.38	.18	-.19	-.15	-.19	-.17	.02	-.21	-.28	-.05	1.00	.39	.55	.13	.16	.35	-.36	-.32
28. Parent–adolescent communication	.20	.15	-.05	-.18	.05	.03	.01	.06	-.12	.08	.05	.11	.29	.28	.08	.16	.30	.15	-.13	-.20	-.13	.11	.23	-.18	-.11	.09	.37	1.00	.55	.36	.36	.16	-.20	-.20
29. Positive identification with parent	.27	.19	-.13	-.25	.03	-.22	-.01	.00	-.08	-.22	.00	.06	.11	.07	.06	.34	.20	.20	-.15	-.13	-.12	-.12	.18	-.42	-.40	.03	.42	.58	1.00	.29	.28	.35	-.09	-.18
30. Peer communication	.11	.07	.05	-.10	.02	-.03	.10	.03	.13	.08	.13	.08	.08	.06	-.06	.05	.01	.18	.17	.12	.12	.00	.03	.03	-.10	.13	.20	.29	.43	1.00	.30	.12	-.11	-.11
31. Peer support	.17	.02	-.12	-.16	-.04	-.09	-.01	.02	.10	.07	.14	-.01	.21	.20	.14	.20	.24	.26	-.01	.00	.00	.00	.47	.06	-.03	.04	.03	.13	.05	.30	1.00	.26	-.43	-.19
32. Positive peers	.12	.28	-.29	-.17	.08	-.35	.00	.02	.11	.20	-.17	.33	.34	.34	.07	.26	.37	.14	-.26	-.26	-.26	-.24	.09	-.28	-.08	.06	.35	.16	.36	.49	.26	1.00	-.44	-.38
33. Negative peers	-.16	-.21	.47	.19	.14	.59	.14	.10	.11	.13	.11	.01	.01	.07	.05	-.06	-.06	-.06	.40	.35	.37	.35	.37	.06	.07	.07	-.36	-.23	-.24	-.09	-.43	-.44	1.00	.60
34. Peer drug norms	-.07	-.06	.28	.12	.03	.51	.11	.01	.08	.18	.13	-.32	-.10	-.23	.17	-.26	-.21	-.21	.32	.36	.36	.53	.07	.20	.20	.06	-.32	-.27	-.27	-.11	-.19	-.38	.50	1.00

Note. European American males are at the bottom half of the correlation matrix; European American females are at the top half of the correlation matrix. When r > .15, p < .05; when r > .20, p < .01.

stronger associations between resiliency and GPA than between self-esteem and GPA, further supporting our decision to examine separately each of these positive indicators of psychological well-being as opposed to combining them into a higher-order factor (see Tables 3 and 4). Within the Wave 3 measures, there were also significant correlations within and across domains that were generally similar in magnitude among all four groups (see Tables 3 and 4). For example, the correlations between negative school chances and school problems were .31 for African American males, .35 African American females, .39 for European American males, and .34 for European American females. Thus, these associations generally support our assumption that the psychological well-being scales have comparable meanings for these four subgroups.

For *R/E identity and discrimination*, the same measures were significantly associated across waves, for the most part, showing convergent validity across time (see Supporting Information Tables S3 and S4). Within Wave 3, the correlations between the two R/E identity measures, between the two friendship measures, and among the three discrimination measures were generally medium to large in magnitude (see Tables 3 and 4), demonstrating convergent validity. However, the correlations among the R/E identity, friendship, and discrimination measures were low, demonstrating discriminant validity. Among the four groups, we could not assess similarities for the R/E identity measures, as these were only assessed for African American adolescents, but they were generally similar in magnitude for African American males and females. The R/E friendship measures were generally associated weakly with measures in other domains for both African American and European American adolescents. For R/E discrimination, there were generally weak associations with measures in other domains, but there were moderate associations with many of the measures in the psychological well-being and academic functioning domains for European American adolescents. These findings suggest that the R/E discrimination measures have different meanings across race/ethnicity.

For our measures of *academic functioning*, there were significant associations within the same construct across waves that were medium to large in magnitude, showing convergent validity across time (see Supporting Information Tables S5 and S6). Within Wave 3, the magnitude of the correlations among measures of academic functioning were generally medium in magnitude, demonstrating convergent validity (see Tables 3 and 4). Across domains, the magnitude of many of the correlations between psychological well-being, problem behaviors, and academic functioning were generally medium, also supporting the assumption of convergent validity; whereas the magnitude of the correlations between measures of academic functioning and family characteristics were generally small, showing discriminant validity. There is also good evidence that these constructs have different meanings and should be kept as first-order rather than second-order variables. For example, educational expectations had stronger correlations with self-esteem and resiliency compared to the correlations between educational aspirations and these two constructs. Among the four groups, the correlations were generally similar in both magnitude and direction, showing that these constructs have similar meanings across gender and race/ethnicity (see Tables 3 and 4). For example, the correlations between resiliency and academic self-concept were .47 for European American females, .30 for European American males, .36 for African American males, and .38 for African American females.

For *problem behaviors*, there were positive correlations for measures across waves that were generally small to medium in magnitude, showing convergent validity across time (see Supporting Information Tables S7 and S8). Within Wave 3, the correlations among the problem behavior measures were often large in magnitude, particularly among similar types of behaviors such as school problems and delinquent behaviors, demonstrating convergent validity (Tables 3 and 4). Across domains, the correlations between problem behaviors and many indicators of mental health as well as positive and negative peers were generally medium in magnitude, providing further evidence of convergent validity. However, the magnitude of the correlations between problem behavior measures and R/E discrimination measures were small in magnitude, showing discriminant validity. There was also good evidence that these measures had distinct associations with other measures, highlighting the importance of keeping them as first- rather than second-order variables. For example, alcohol use generally had stronger correlations with mental health problems than did marijuana use.

Among the four groups, correlations were similarly small to medium in magnitude and were in the same direction thus supporting the assumption that these constructs have similar meanings across both gender and race/ethnicity. For example, engaging in problem behaviors and having negative peers had associations that were medium in magnitude for all four groups, with the correlations being .28 for African American females, .36 for African American males, .35 for European American females, and .44 for European American males. This was not the case, however, for substance use behaviors. The correlations between cigarette, marijuana, and alcohol use and measures in other domains often differed among the four groups. For example, cigarette use had stronger correlations with psychological well-being for European American females compared to the other three groups, whereas marijuana use had lower associations with measures in other domains for females compared to males. However, given that these measures were based on a single items used in population studies such as monitoring the future (cf. O'Malley et al., 1987) regarding behaviors in the past 30 days, these findings likely reflect low frequencies for these groups rather than construct invariance.

For *family characteristics*, correlations of the same construct across waves were generally medium to large in magnitude, demonstrating convergent validity across time (see Supporting Information Tables S9 and S10). Within Wave 3, family characteristics had medium to large associations with each other in the expected direction, showing convergent validity (see Tables 3 and 4). Across domains, the correlations were small to medium in magnitude, showing both convergent and discriminant validity. For example, the correlations between parent–adolescent communication and peer communication were medium in magnitude, but the correlations between intrusive parenting and peer communication were small in magnitude. Furthermore, the strength of these associations often differed, supporting our decision to keep these measures separate. For example, although negative interactions with parents generally had negative, significant associations with positive identification with parents, it generally was not significantly associated with parent–adolescent communication. Among the four groups, there was good evidence that associations were similarly small to medium in magnitude and in the expected direction (see Tables 3 and 4). For example, the associations between strict parenting and negative interactions with parents were .20 for African American males, .22 for African American females, .24 for European American females, and .23 for European American males. Furthermore, the correlations between measures of parental control and psychological functioning were generally small to medium in magnitude for all four groups, supporting our assumption that the measures of family characteristics have similar meanings across both race/ethnicity and gender.

For *peer characteristics*, correlations for the same construct across waves were generally small to medium in magnitude, demonstrating convergent validity across time (see Supporting Information Tables S11 and S12). Within Wave 3, having positive peers was positively correlated with psychological well-being, good relationships with parents, and academic functioning, whereas negative peers was positively correlated with poor mental health and engagement in problem behaviors. For example, the correlations between negative peers and negative chances were large in magnitude, showing convergent validity. On the other hand, the correlations between peer communication and eating disorders were small in magnitude, demonstrating discriminant validity. Within Wave 3, patterns for the associations both within and across domains also varied, supporting our decision to keep these measures separate (see Tables 3 and 4). For example, the associations between negative peers and delinquent behaviors were stronger in the positive direction than the associations between positive peers and delinquent behaviors in the negative direction, confirming that these two measures are not simply opposite ends of the same dimension. Among the four groups, there is good evidence that the correlations among the peer measures and the correlations between the peer measures and measures in other domains are similar in magnitude and direction, supporting the assumption that these constructs have similar meanings across gender and race/ethnicity. For example, the correlations between positive peers and peer support were .23 for African American females, .19 for African American males, .26 for European American males, and .19 for European American females. Furthermore, the correlations between positive peers and delinquent behaviors were −.23 for African American females, −.18 for African American males, −.20 for European American males, and −.26 for European American females.

Summary

The correlational analyses showed evidence of both convergent and discriminant validity of our measures across both time and domains. They also provided support for our decision to treat the various measures within each domain as separate constructs rather than aggregating them up to a more general level. The patterns of correlations further provided support for our assumption that most of the scales operate similarly both within and across time for the four groups, with the exception of the R/E discrimination measures. Given that the patterns of correlations showed that the R/E discrimination measures varied across race/ethnicity, we next explored the source of these differences by testing whether their measurement properties (e.g., factor-loading patterns) were invariant across race/ethnicity and gender, focusing on Wave 3 measures.

Invariance Tests of R/E Discrimination Measures

We tested successive degrees of measurement invariance using M*plus* 5.21 (Muthén & Muthén, 1998–2010) for our R/E discrimination measures. To do this, we constructed a series of models examining race/ethnicity and gender separately to determine whether and where the differences might lie. In the first (i.e., configural) model (Meredith, 1993), which assesses whether items load only on the intended factor, we estimated factor loadings between each construct and its theoretically specified indicators (with one factor loading per construct set to 1 for identification purposes). In the second (i.e., weak) model, the factor loadings were constrained to be equal across race/ethnicity or gender. In the final (i.e., strong) model, the item intercepts were also constrained to be equal across race/ethnicity or gender. Weak and strong invariance were tested for each construct separately by constraining appropriate parameters of each construct, in turn.

We examined the change in both the χ^2 and the comparative fit index (CFI) between successive models. The χ^2 statistic and the change in χ^2 test are influenced by sample size. When sample size is large, as in this study, the change in χ^2 test can be statistically significant even when the change in the model is relatively small. Therefore, we used ΔCFI $\geq$ .01 to determine the form of measurement invariance for each construct (Cheung & Rensvold, 2002).

Table 5 presents the findings of the race/ethnicity invariance tests. Overall, the R/E discrimination measures showed weak invariance across both race/ethnicity and gender, where ΔCFI $\geq$ .01. The R/E discrimination measures showed strong invariance for gender, where ΔCFI $\geq$ .01, but not for race/ethnicity. Table 6 presents the Wave 3 item-level means of the R/E discrimination measures for the R/E and gender groups. Here we can see that there were greater differences in some of the items between the R/E groups, which explains why tests of strong invariance failed. This is most evident in expected R/E discrimination, where there was a greater differential regarding

TABLE 5

INVARIANCE TESTS FOR R/E DISCRIMINATION MEASURES

	df	χ^2	CFI	Δdf	$\Delta\chi^2$	ΔCFI
Configural						
R/E measures—gender	12	21.67***	.996			
R/E measures—ethnicity	12	25.15***	.993			
Weak						
Expected R/E discrimination—gender	13	26.61***	.994	1	4.94	−.002
Expected R/E discrimination—ethnicity	13	29.72***	.991	1	4.57	−.002
R/E John Henryism—gender	13	22.00***	.996	1	.33	.000
R/E John Henryism—ethnicity	13	25.32***	.993	1	.17	.000
Parents' worries about discrimination—gender	13	21.71***	.996	1	.04	.000
Parents' worries about discrimination—ethnicity	13	41.00***	.984	1	15.85***	−.009
Strong						
Expected R/E discrimination—gender	15	29.98***	.994	2	8.31	−.002
Expected R/E discrimination—ethnicity	15	247.31***	.870	2	222.16***	−.123
R/E John Henryism—gender	15	33.68***	.992	2	12.01***	−.004
R/E John Henryism—ethnicity	15	288.88***	.847	2	263.73***	−.146
Parents' worries about discrimination—gender	15	22.55***	.997	2	.88	.001
Parents' worries about discrimination—ethnicity	15	225.47***	.882	2	200.32***	−.111

Note. Because our R/E discrimination measures each have two or three indicators, we grouped these measures together in separate race/ethnicity and gender configural models, for identification purposes.
***$p < .001$.

TABLE 6
ITEM-LEVEL MEANS FOR THE R/E DISCRIMINATION MEASURES

	R/E			Gender		
	African American	European American	F-Test	Male	Female	F-Test
Race/ethnicity						
Expected R/E discrimination						
Discrimination—job	1.87	1.23	$(1, 936) = 80.45^{***}$	1.78	1.87	$(1, 936) = .77$
Discrimination—education	2.10	1.30	$(1, 936) = 61.60^{***}$	1.65	1.65	$(1, 936) = 2.32$
R/E John Henryism						
Work harder	2.50	1.58	$(1, 926) = 103.37^{***}$	2.17	2.18	$(1, 926) = .34$
Do better	2.52	1.61	$(1, 926) = 103.96^{***}$	2.28	2.13	$(1, 926) = 2.85$
Parents' worries about discrimination						
At school	2.02	1.70	$(1, 933) = 8.70^{***}$	1.94	1.87	$(1, 933) = .91$
At work	2.35	1.46	$(1, 933) = 63.04^{***}$	2.05	2.02	$(1, 933) = .22$

$^{***}p < .001.$

discrimination on a job versus in education for African American versus European American adolescents. This is also shown in parents' worries about education, where African American parents were more worried about discrimination at work and European American parents were more worried about discrimination at school. As expected, there were no significant differences according to gender for these measures.

Summary

Using correlational analyses and measurement invariance tests, we examined the construct and measurement invariance of our constructs. Our findings showed that R/E discrimination measures did not show construct invariance or strong measurement invariance across race/ethnicity. Therefore, although we included gender, race/ethnicity, and the gender by race/ethnicity interaction in our models, we did not directly compare R/E differences in mean levels of the intercepts and slopes for the R/E discrimination measures where describing the findings. The significance of these differences across the respective groups, which are presented in the tables, should thus be interpreted with caution.

Overall, however, the correlational analyses indicated that the majority of the constructs were related similarly to each other across groups. Therefore, we believe that most of the measures used in this study can be assessed meaningfully using items that may mean something slightly different for different people or for the same person at different points in time. For the purposes of the descriptive analyses reported here, and consistent with the idea that abstract concepts can have the same meaning across groups and time, despite the possibility of differences in the meaning of specific item content (Nesselroade et al., 2007), we assume that the meaning of the scores on the majority of scales in this study are sufficiently similar across groups and time to warrant meaningful comparisons of growth parameters across our four race/ethnicity and gender groups.

ANALYTIC PLAN

Overview of Data Analyses

In order to describe the developmental trajectories, we used a two-level hierarchical linear model (Raudenbush, Bryk, Cheon, & Congdon, 2000). As there are multiple observations, waves of data are nested within adolescents. Two types of models define a two-level HLM. The Level-1 model provides the average trajectory across time, and the Level-2 model accounts for the variation across individuals. For the Level-1 model, we used adolescents' age rather than wave to account for time. Using age, rather than wave, provides a more sensitive time metric where analyzing MADICS data because the date of survey responses for any given individual, and thus their age at each wave, varied substantially both within and between individuals (e.g., a given person could be the first to respond at one wave and the last to respond in another wave). Using age as the time metric also allowed us to graph our results by reference to changes from early to late adolescence, ranging from 12 to 20 years. The Level-2 model included SES, adolescent's gender and race/ethnicity, the interaction between gender and race/ethnicity, and parents' marital status.

Level-1 Model

We assume that Y_{ti}, the observed status at time t for individual i, is a function of a systematic growth curve trajectory or growth curve plus random error (Bryk & Raudenbush, 1992):

$$Y_{ti} = \pi_{0i} + \pi_{1i}(\text{Age}_{ti} - 14.23) + \pi_{2i}(\text{Age}_{ti} - 14.23)^2 + e_{ti}$$

In this equation, the mean age of target adolescents at Wave 3 (i.e., 14.23 years) was subtracted from the individual's age so that π_{0i} represents the score on the outcome at age 14.23, π_{1i} represents the rate of change in the outcome at age 14.23, and π_{2i} estimates changes in the rate of change in the outcome over time, characterizing growth patterns that are not linear. By "centering" the equation in this manner, parameters that would be otherwise meaningless can be interpreted in relation to the age in the middle of the developmental period being studied (Bryk & Raudenbush, 1992, pp. 25–29). The coefficient, e_{ti}, represents the proportion of Y_{ti} that is not modeled; that is, the conditional error or residual variance.

Level-2 Model

π_{0i}, π_{1i}, and π_{2i} are the outcome measures for the Level-2 equations:

$$\pi_{0i} = \beta_{00} + \beta_{01}(\text{SES})_i + \beta_{02}(\text{Gender})_i + \beta_{03}(\text{Race/Ethnicity})_i$$
$$+\beta_{04}(\text{Gender}*\text{Race/Ethnicity})_i + \beta_{05}(\text{Single})_i + \beta_{06}(\text{Married})_i$$
$$+ \beta_{07}(\text{Mean Age})_i + \beta_{08}(\text{Mean Age})_i^2 + r_{0i}$$

$$\pi_{1i} = \beta_{10} + \beta_{11}(\text{SES})_i + \beta_{12}(\text{Gender})_i + \beta_{13}(\text{Race/Ethnicity})_i$$
$$+\beta_{14}(\text{Gender}*\text{Race/Ethnicity})_i + \beta_{15}(\text{Single})_i + \beta_{16}(\text{Married})_i$$
$$+ r_{1i}$$

$$\pi_{2i} = \beta_{20} + \beta_{21}(\text{SES})_i + \beta_{22}(\text{Gender})_i + \beta_{23}(\text{Race/Ethnicity})_i$$
$$+ \beta_{24}(\text{Gender} * \text{Race/Ethnicity})_i + \beta_{25}(\text{Single})_i + \beta_{26}(\text{Married})_i$$
$$+ r_{2i}$$

The set of constant terms for the Level-2 equations defines the growth curve when all of the covariates in the model are set to zero. Given the coding of the Level-2 covariates (described below), β_{00} is the sample mean at age 14.23, β_{10} is the average rate of change in the outcome variable at age 14.23, and β_{20} is the degree of curvature averaged across the sample (Bryk & Raudenbush, 1992, pp. 25–29). The coefficients, r_{0i}, r_{1i}, and r_{2i} represent the residual variances of the intercept, linear slope, and quadratic slope, respectively. The residual variance for the quadratic slope, r_{2i}, was not estimated in models with only three waves of data due to insufficient degrees of freedom (Morgan, Farkas, & Wu, 2009).

SES was standardized (i.e., mean centered and divided by its sample standard deviation) so that the coefficients, β_{01}, β_{11}, and β_{21} reflect differences in the outcome per one standard deviation change in the predictor variable. The coefficients for gender, β_{01}, β_{12}, and β_{22}, represent the difference in the growth curves for male and female adolescents, where all other covariates are held constant. The coefficients for race/ethnicity, β_{03}, β_{13}, and β_{23} represent the difference in the growth curves for African American and European American adolescents where all other covariates are held constant. Gender and race/ethnicity were coded with $-.5$ assigned to males and African Americans and $+.5$ assigned to females and European Americans. Using contrast codes rather than dummy codes allows one to interpret more easily the equations with interaction terms (Cohen, Cohen, West, & Aiken, 2003). Positive values indicate higher means, slopes, and more convex curvature for European Americans and females, whereas negative values indicate higher means, slopes, and more concave curvature for African Americans and males.

The coefficients, β_{04}, β_{14}, and β_{24} represent the interactions between gender and race/ethnicity. Because we found very little evidence of SES by race/ethnicity or gender interactions in our preliminary analyses, we limited our assessments of interactions to those involving gender by race/ethnicity. Thus, two- and three-way interactions among other demographics variables were not included in the final models due to their overall lack of significance. The coefficients, β_{05}, β_{15}, and β_{25} represent the growth curves for adolescents of single, never married parents. The coefficients, β_{06}, β_{16}, and β_{26} represent the growth curves for adolescents of married, intact parents.

Individuals' means for age and age-squared were included at the intercept, π_{0i}. These terms ensure that the equations for linear and quadratic change reflect only within-individual change and not stable individual differences that are confounded due to the timing of data collection or attrition that may be associated with differences between individuals in each wave. Otherwise, growth curve estimates could be influenced not only by within-individual change over time but, also, by any stable individual differences between those who stayed in the study and those who dropped out (Bryk & Raudenbush, 1992, pp. 121–123).

Reporting Findings and Presentation of Tables and Figures

In the next several chapters, we present the results of the HLM analyses according to domain (i.e., psychological well-being, R/E identity and discrimination, academic functioning, problem behaviors, family character-istics, and peer characteristics). For each domain, three sets of HLM analyses were performed. First, we examined the unconditional means model, which is a model with no predictors at either level. The unconditional means model partitions the total outcome variation into between- and within-person variation. Using the unconditional means model, we calculated the intraclass correlation (ICC), which estimates the total proportion of variation that lies between individuals, regardless of time. Second, we examined an uncondi-tional growth model, which is a model with age as the only Level-1 predictor and no Level-2 predictors added. The unconditional growth model estimates the baseline amount of change. Using the first two models, we calculated the proportional reduction in the Level-1 variance components explained by time (R^2). Third, we examined the conditional growth curve model, with the Level-2 predictors added. We then calculated how much of the within-person variation was explained by the Level-2 predictors.

For each construct, key results are reported in two tables. The first table provides the coefficients in the full conditional growth curve model, with the Level-2 predictors. The second table provides the residual variance in the unconditional means model, unconditional growth model, and conditional growth model (i.e., listed in the tables as "With Level-2 Predictors"), as well as the ICC, R^2 of the within-person variation associated with time, and the percent of variance that was explained in the intercept and slope parameters by adding the Level-2 predictors. Figures for each measure are presented showing mean-level trajectories adjusted for model covariates according to race/ethnicity and gender, regardless of their significance, for the purpose of comparison across and within domains. For SES and parents' marital status, figures are presented only where either variable moderates quadratic trends, where $p < .01$. Given that the growth curve trajectories were calculated using adolescents' age rather than wave, the x-axis was labeled with adolescents' age from 12 to 20 years. For clarity and consistency across measures, the figures were constructed using the full range of responses for each measure on the y-axis, with the exception of educational aspirations, educational expectations, and occupational aspirations. Note that the full range of responses vary across figures so that it is not warranted to directly compare the figures without taking into account the range being shown.

In each section, we begin with a brief overview of the measures and then discuss the findings for each construct. In light of the large sample and number of statistical analyses performed, we limit our discussion to cases where $p < .01$, although tables report significance levels where $p < .05$. Findings related to gender and race/ethnicity are highlighted, although significant results relating to SES and parents' marital status are also mentioned briefly. Lastly, we provide a summary of our findings within each domain. This overview focuses on the significant findings within each domain for the average adolescent as well as significant trends in the differences according to adolescents' gender, race/ethnicity, and their interaction, as well as parents' marital status and SES.

Supporting Information

Additional supporting information may be found in the online version of this article at the publisher's website.

IV: PSYCHOLOGICAL WELL-BEING

Leslie Morrison Gutman, Stephen C. Peck, Oksana Malanchuk,
Arnold J. Sameroff, and Jacquelynne S. Eccles

This article is part of the issue "Moving Through Adolescence: Developmental Trajectories of African American and European American Youth" Gutman, Peck, Malanchuk, Sameroff, and Eccles (Issue Authors). For a full listing of articles in this issue, see: http://onlinelibrary.wiley.com/doi/10.1111/mono.v82.4/issuetoc.

Our measures of psychological well-being reflect positive indicators, including self-esteem and resiliency, as well as negative aspects of functioning, including depressive affect, anger, eating disorders, and negative life chances. Results are shown in Tables 7 and 8 and Figure 1.

SELF-ESTEEM

Although we expected self-esteem to increase from early to late adolescence based on previous studies (Erol & Orth, 2011; Galambos et al., 2006; Orth & Robins, 2014), we found both a significant linear increase and negative quadratic trend in our sample (see Table 7). On average, these adolescents' self-esteem increased from 12 to 15 years, then decreased from 16 to 20 years (see Figure 1). Why was there an average decrease in self-esteem from ages 16 to 20? Perhaps the reason is because the late-adolescent transition for this group at this historical point is linked to a reassessment of

Corresponding author: Leslie Morrison Gutman, Department of Clinical Educational and Health Psychology, University College London, 1-19 Torrington Place, London WC1E 7HB, email: l.gutman@ucl.ac.uk

DOI: 10.1111/mono.12330

TABLE 7

GROWTH MODELS FOR PSYCHOLOGICAL WELL-BEING

	Self-Esteem	Resiliency	Anger	Depressive Affect	Eating Disorders	Expected Negative Life Chances
For intercept						
Intercept	3.81***	3.77***	2.29***	1.32***	1.99***	1.44***
SES	-.00	.09***	-.12***	-.02	-.04	-.04
Gender	-.28***	-.05	-.11*	.11***	.55***	-.11**
Ethnicity	-.07	.07	-.18**	-.00	.10	-.00
GXE	-.27**	-.02	-.09	.06	.57***	.06
Single	.04	.08	.09	-.05	-.23	-.37
Intact	.05	.03	.00	-.02	-.09	-.06
Age	-.03	-.07	.00	-.03	.02	.02
Age²	-.00	.01	-.01	.01	-.00	-.01
For linear slope						
Intercept	.08***	.10***	.01	.18***	-.08	.05***
SES	-.01	.02	-.01	.03*	.03	-.02
Gender	.00	.01	-.02	-.05*	.02	.03*
Ethnicity	-.02	-.03	.00	.03	.05	-.01
GXE	.01	.05	.01	-.03	-.06	.00
Single	.06	.04	.03	.01	.20	-.03
Intact	.00	-.01	.02	-.01	.06	-.01
For quadratic slope						
Intercept	-.02***	-.02***	-.01*	-.04***	.00	.01*
SES	.00	-.01**	.00	-.01**	-.01	.00
Gender	.00	-.00	.00	.01	-.00	-.02*
Ethnicity	-.00	-.00	.00	-.01	-.00	.02*
GXE	.00	-.01	.00	.01	.01	-.00
Single	-.02*	-.01	-.00	.01	-.03	.04*
Intact	.00	.00	-.01	-.00	-.01	.00

*** $p < .001$, ** $p < .01$, * $p < .05$.

TABLE 8

RESIDUAL VARIANCE FOR PSYCHOLOGICAL WELL-BEING

Level 1 Variable	Unconditional Means Model	ICC	Unconditional Growth Model	Level 1 R^2	With Level 2 Predictors	% Explained
Self-esteem		.41		.24		
Level 1	.532		.406			
Intercept	.364***		.409***		.388***	5%
Linear slope			.017***		.017***	<1%
Quad slope			.000		.000	<1%
Resiliency		.27		.30		
Level 1	.381		.268			
Intercept	.142***		.189***		.181***	4%
Linear slope			.017***		.016***	6%
Quad slope			.000		.000	<1%
Anger		.35		.12		
Level 1	.647		.571			
Intercept	.343***		.452***		.427***	6%
Linear slope			.008		.008	<1%
Quad slope			.000		.000	<1%
Depressive affect		.22		.40		
Level 1	.107		.064			
Intercept	.031***		.073***		.071***	3%
Linear slope			.004***		.004***	<1%
Eating disorders		.52		.09		
Level 1	.468		.424			
Intercept	.503***		.595***		.514***	14%
Linear slope			.006***		.005***	17%
Expected negative life chances		.32		.36		
Level 1	.270		.174			
Intercept	.127***		.136***		.127***	7%
Linear slope			.015***		.015***	<1%

***$p < .001$.

one's general state of being. The slight decline indicates a slight increase in how often youth wished they were somewhat different than they currently are. The transitions that 16–20-year-olds in this culture, at this historical time point, are experiencing should increase the average levels of competence of the people with whom they interact and thus to whom they can compare themselves. For example, if they move to college after graduation from high school, they will find themselves in a more academically select group of peers. Those who move into the work force may also find this period particularly stressful: they will either have a hard time getting a job with a living wage, or they will find themselves in a job with many more competent peers. As Ruble

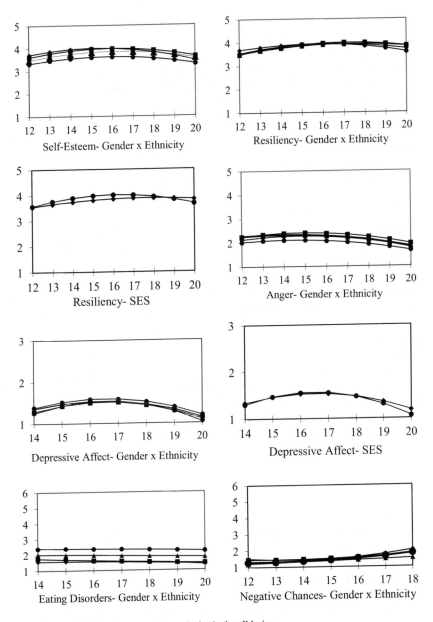

FIGURE 1.—Growth curves for psychological well-being.
Note. The *x*-axis represents age in years, whereas the *y*-axis represents the mean of the scale, controlling for the covariates. For the gender and race/ethnicity growth curves, European American females are represented by the circle, European American males are represented by the diamond, African American females are represented by the triangle, and African American males are represented by the square. For the SES growth curves, high-SES adolescents are represented by the circle, whereas low-SES adolescents are represented by the diamond.

and Seidman (1996) argued, these are the kinds of transitions that should lead to reevaluating the self and perhaps wishing one were somewhat different than one is currently. It is important to note, however, that the declines after age 16 are quite small, and the average levels remain quite high.

In contrast to previous findings (Baldwin & Hoffmann, 2002; Block & Robins, 1993; Zimmerman et al., 1992), but in support of Erol and Orth (2011), we found no gender differences in trajectories of self-esteem in this sample. However, unlike Erol and Orth (2011), we also found no evidence of R/E differences in the trajectories. The slopes were also not modified by parents' marital status or family SES, indicating that the pattern of decline in self-esteem in later adolescence is equally characteristic of youth moving into residential colleges, the labor market, or more local tertiary educational settings.

At age 14 (the intercept), there was a significant gender by race/ethnicity interaction, indicating that the mean-level gender difference in self-esteem was higher for European American than for African American adolescents, with European American females having the lowest self-esteem of the three gender by R/E groups (see Table 7). This finding is consistent with previous studies showing that gender differences are more evident in European American than in African American youth, with European American but not African American females having lower self-esteem compared to their male peers (Kling, Hyde, Showers, & Buswell, 1999; Major, Barr, Zubek, & Babey, 1999).

Adjusted for the covariates, the mean levels were above the midpoint on this scale and hovered between 3.5 ("sometimes") and 4 ("often"), suggesting that these adolescents in general were satisfied with themselves. All of these youth had just made the transition into junior high school at Wave 1, suggesting an increase in their self-esteem following this transition.

RESILIENCY

In contrast to our expectations based on previous studies indicating stability in resiliency (Vecchione et al., 2010), both the linear and quadratic trends were significant (see Table 7). As shown in Figure 1, on average these adolescents showed a slight increase in resiliency from the ages of 12 to 16 years and then a slight decrease from 17 to 20 years. It is a welcome sign that these adolescents' resiliency improved over their high school years. However, consistent with the findings for self-esteem, their sense of resiliency decreased on average as they made the transition from high school into either some form of tertiary education or the work force. This decline was evident for all of the gender by R/E groups.

The rate of change in resiliency also varied across SES groups. As shown in Figure 1, higher-SES adolescents experienced a greater increase in resiliency from 12 to 16 years than did lower-SES adolescents. Higher-SES adolescents also experienced a decrease from age 17 to 20, whereas lower-SES adolescents showed no such decrease during this same period. As a result, higher-SES adolescents reported higher levels of resiliency than did lower-SES adolescents from 12 to 18 years, but this advantage disappeared by age 18.

At age 14, higher-SES youth reported more resiliency than did lower-SES youth, and there were no significant differences associated with race/ethnicity, gender, the race/ethnicity interaction, or parents' marital status (see Table 7). As was true for adolescents' self-esteem, the mean levels were well above the midpoint of this scale (3), taking into account the demographic covariates. Specifically, the average youth reported feeling ego-resilient between "sometimes" (3.5) and "often" (4).

It is interesting that family SES was linked to adolescents' resiliency, particularly during the high school years. Family wealth likely influences the neighborhood in which one lives as well as the resources one has had access to throughout one's development. Both of these contextual characteristics are likely to result in having had to confront fewer major challenges to one's agency. If so, adolescents growing up in higher-SES families may have had fewer opportunities to have their resiliency challenged, leading to greater confidence in their ability to cope with life's challenges. They may also have been exposed to parents who had more effective coping skills and strategies and thus acquired greater confidence through role modeling.

ANGER

Contrary to previous research (Galambos & Krahn, 2008; Galambos et al., 2006), there were no significant changes in anger from early to late adolescence (see Figure 1). Neither the linear nor quadratic slopes were significant, where $p < .01$ (see Table 7). There also were no significant modifications in the slopes by SES, gender, race/ethnicity, the gender by race/ethnicity interaction, or parents' marital status. These findings suggest that adolescents, regardless of their demographic characteristics, experience an overall stable trajectory of their angry feelings from early to late adolescence.

At age 14, adolescents who were lower SES and African American reported having angrier feelings than did adolescents who were higher SES and European American. The SES difference could well reflect differences in what the youth experienced as a result of where they lived and the extra stresses with which they had to deal as a result of their lower-SES status. The R/E group difference, given that family SES is taken into account, may reflect differences in the frequency with which African American and European American youth were confronted with day-to-day R/E-related stigma and discrimination as well as their increasing awareness of institutional and structural racism (Cross, 1991; Wong et al., 2003). Thus, both of these slight differences could reflect the greater likelihood of these youth having been confronted with situations to which anger is an appropriate response. There was no significant gender difference in anger at age 14 where $p < .01$. This finding is consistent with Archer's (2004) meta-analysis of anger and aggression in adolescence, in which he concluded that males display more physical aggression compared to females but report similar levels of angry feelings.

It is important to note that the mean levels of anger being expressed were quite low. As expected, given the relatively high levels of adolescents' self-esteem and resiliency, the mean levels were below the midpoint of the scale. Adjusted for the covariates, mean levels ranged between 1.5 and 2.5 (with 2 equal to "once in awhile" and 3 equal to "sometimes"). Clearly, these frequencies are not consistent with the general stereotype of adolescence being a time of anger. Although the fact that they were experiencing any anger at all might reflect hormonal changes associated with puberty, it seems just as likely that they reflect reasonable responses to the world in which these adolescents lived (Eccles et al., 1993). One could argue that these levels of anger accurately reveal the number of times they would be expected to be confronted by a situation that justifiably elicited angry feelings. The fact that the levels were highest for African American and low-SES students is consistent with this interpretation.

DEPRESSIVE AFFECT

Both the linear and the quadratic trends were significant (see Table 7). Consistent with our expectations from previous research (Cole et al., 2002; Galambos et al., 2006; Garber, Keiley, & Martin, 2002), the average adolescent experienced an increase in the frequency of depressive affect from ages 14 to 16 and then reported a decrease from 17 to 20 years (see Figure 1). Thus, unlike self-esteem and resiliency, which increased over the high school years, suggesting increasingly positive development during the high school years followed by a decrease, reports of depressive affect increased until age 16–17 and then decreased. Both positive feelings about the self and feelings of depression are consistent with the notion of early to middle adolescence as a period of increased moodiness (Steinberg & Morris, 2001), but it is important to note that feelings of depression were much less frequent compared to feelings of satisfaction with oneself (depressive affect occurring on average "once in a while" versus feeling satisfied with oneself "sometimes" to "often").

There was also a significant but slight difference in the quadratic trend of depressive affect according to SES. As shown in Figure 1, higher-SES adolescents experienced a slightly greater rate of decrease from 18 to 20 years than did lower-SES adolescents. As a result of these very small changes, on average and controlling for all other demographic characteristics, lower-SES youth reported more frequent rates of depressive affect at age 20 than did higher-SES youth. This difference is inconsistent with the SES differences in resiliency at age 20 where, if anything, high-SES youth reported lower feelings of resiliency than did low-SES youth.

At age 14, there was a significant gender difference but no other significant demographic effects. As one would expect (Angold, Erkanli, Silberg, Eaves, & Costello, 2002; Ge, Conger, & Elder, 2001; Ge, Lorenz, Conger, Elder, & Simons, 1994; Twenge & Nolen-Hoeksema, 2002), females reported slightly more frequent feelings of depression than did males.

Consistent with the findings for self-esteem, resiliency, and anger, the frequencies with which these young people reported feeling depressed were quite low, particularly given the cultural stereotype of adolescents being moody and depressed. Taking into account the covariates, adolescents reported such feelings slightly more than "once in a while"—scores ranged from 1 to 1.5 on a 3-point scale, with 2 as the midpoint. Furthermore, although statistically significant, the group differences were quite small.

EATING DISORDERS

Although other studies have shown increases in eating disorders during adolescence (Hudson et al., 2007; Measelle et al., 2006), in this sample the linear and quadratic slopes of eating disorders were nonsignificant, indicating that the incidence of eating disorders remained stable from 14 to 20 years (see Figure 1 and Table 7). Furthermore, neither of the slopes were moderated by SES, gender, race/ethnicity, the interaction of gender by race/ethnicity, or parents' marital status.

There were clear differences in the levels of eating disorders at the intercept, however. At 14 years, there was a significant gender by race/ethnicity interaction showing that the gender difference in eating behavior was much more marked among European American than African American youth and that the R/E difference was much more marked among the females. As other researchers have found (Hoek, 2006), there was a much higher incidence of eating disorders for European American than African American female adolescents. These findings are consistent with evidence that (a) European American females are more aware of a thinness standard compared to African American females (Abrams & Stormer, 2002), (b) African American females have more positive body images compared to European American females (Molloy & Herzberger, 1998), and (c) a broader range of female body types are considered attractive in the African American community (Parker et al., 1995).

The mean levels, however, indicate that eating disorders were quite rare for all groups when taking into account the covariates, whose reported rates vary between "less than rarely" (1.5) to "rarely" (2) on a 6-point scale (with 3.5 as the midpoint), with the exception of European American females. Although their mean level was still quite low (averaging near 2.5, between "rarely" and "sometimes"), the rates for European American females are troubling and consistent with public health data suggesting that we should be concerned about the implications of such behaviors for young women's long-term health trajectories. Some of these eating-disorder behaviors are sufficiently risky to jeopardize future health, even if done only occasionally.

EXPECTED NEGATIVE LIFE CHANCES

There has been increasing discussion about the role that expectations about one's future options and risks can play in shaping individuals' developmental trajectories (e.g., McDade et al., 2011; Schulenberg & Maggs, 2002; Stoddard, Zimmerman, & Bauermeister, 2011). Research has demonstrated that holding high educational expectations predicts an increased likelihood of completing high school and attending tertiary education (e.g., Beal & Crockett, 2010; Eccles, Vida, & Barber, 2004; Mello, 2008). But what about such expectations as becoming unemployed or involved in risky or delinquent behaviors? Do such expectations also become self-fulfilling prophecies? Little research has addressed this question, but the work on negative neighborhood effects suggests that the presence of large numbers of adult role models who engage in risky or illegal behaviors can lead adolescents living in these neighborhoods to develop high expectations that they will become involved in these behaviors as well (Elliot et al., 1996); these expectations, in turn, may increase the likelihood that they actually follow these risky pathways. Few studies have looked at the developmental trajectories or consequences of such negative life expectations, but one could argue that such beliefs might influence optimism and investment in one's future.

In this sample, we found a significant increasing linear slope (see Table 7) in the youths' reports of the likelihood that they will become engaged in risky and delinquent behaviors, even death, from early to late adolescence. Thus, on average, expectations of negative life chances increased for these adolescents as they grew older (see Figure 1). There were no significant differences in the slopes according to SES, gender, race/ethnicity, the gender by race/ethnicity interaction, or parents' marital status (where $p < .01$).

At the intercept (age 14), as expected, males reported higher expectations for negative life chances than females. However, there were no other significant differences at the intercept after accounting for our other demographic variables. In terms of the mean level, adolescents' expectations of negative outcomes started quite low, varying between a score of 1 and 1.5, which corresponds to adolescents saying that the average likelihood of these negative life experiences occurring was "very low" to "low" (controlling for the covariates). By age 18, the average mean level increased to above 1.5. Part of the increase in these negative expectations could reflect the fact that a score of 6 was given if the events had already happened. Because several of these events increase in frequency with age, the odds that one of them has already happened increases with age as well. In fact, some of these acts become almost normative by age 16 and 17, like skipping school or having sex. Thus, although it is worrisome that some of these youth believed that such negative life experiences were likely in their future, this was not true for most of the youth in this sample. The contrast of these findings with expectations for positive educational outcomes presented in the next section reinforces this point. Most of the youth in this sample, in the late 1990s, were quite optimistic about their future lives, and this optimism did not depend on their SES or race/ethnicity.

SUMMARY OF PSYCHOLOGICAL WELL-BEING

Developmental trajectories showed a convex curvature with a slight increase in early adolescence followed by a slight decrease in late adolescence for many of our measures of psychological well-being, including feelings of self-esteem, resiliency, anger, and depression, although the trends for anger were not statistically significant (where $p < .01$). The prevalence of eating disorders remained stable while expectations of negative life chances increased from early to late adolescence. This was somewhat in line with our predictions, although we expected that resiliency would remain stable and eating disorders would increase throughout adolescence.

This convex pattern was consistent across both positive and negative indicators of psychological well-being, suggesting that mental health-related changes are tied to the normative events of this age period in interesting but possibly contradictory ways. The highest levels of both positive and negative indicators of emotional functioning occurred in middle adolescence, around ages 16 and 17, a time of relative stability in these adolescents' lives. They were in the final years of high school but were not yet involved in the transition out of high school. Many would have either gained confidence in their abilities to thrive in the high school context or reconciled themselves to a nonacademic life track and thus reduced the importance they attached to doing well academically. Many would also have found their social niche in this setting, as well as in settings outside of school, leading to increases in self-esteem and confidence in one's resiliency.

So why, although absolutely low, were the levels of anger and depressive affect highest at these ages? The most likely explanation is that different parts of the population were contributing to these means, with those who were doing the best at the tasks and settings of middle adolescence accounting for the higher levels of the positive emotional characteristics and those who were not doing as well in these settings accounting for the higher levels of the negative emotional characteristics. The relatively small changes across time in all of these indicators could well result from small shifts in which parts of the larger population were selecting the more extreme scores. It could also be that this is a period of great moodiness so that many adolescents showed more extreme forms of both positive and negative self-appraisals and emotions and, thus, gave equally extreme responses to both positive and negative indicators of mental health (Buchanan, Eccles, & Becker, 1992; Graber, 2004). Both explanations may be equally true with small segments of adolescents reacting more strongly to their moods due to biological and experiential dispositions (Davidson, Jackson, & Kalin, 2000) and features of their environment (Eccles et al., 1993; Powers, 2011). What is most interesting is that none of our other demographic categories showed consistent associations with these patterns during the middle adolescent years, providing support for the idea that major challenges faced by adolescents in the United States are fairly consistent across demographic groups (Buchanan et al., 1992).

As expected, the lowest levels of these self-appraisal and emotional reactions occurred both (a) during the early adolescent transitional period, right after these children moved into junior high school and while they were in the midst of pubertal development, particularly for males (Baumrind, 1991; Eccles et al., 1993; Simmons & Byth, 1987), and (b) during the transition out of high school when these youth faced a variety of major new challenges (Ruble & Seidman, 1996) likely to make them question themselves and their relative competencies. These findings are in keeping with the idea that school transitions may be times of increased risk for adolescents due to stage-environment misfit, eliciting self-reappraisal leading to lower satisfaction with the self and the self's coping abilities (Eccles et al., 1993). But why the lower levels of depressive affect in early than middle adolescence? One might expect that depressive affect would also be highest at these times, particularly if adolescents doubted their coping abilities more and were feeling less satisfied with themselves. Instead, consistent with other studies (Cole et al., 2002; Garber et al, 2002), we found the opposite pattern for both average levels of reported depressive affect and within each of our subpopulations, suggesting that this pattern of change is normative in American samples during this period.

Although we expected that females would show lower and worsening trajectories for self-esteem, depressive affect, and eating disorders, we found significant gender differences in the mean levels only, rather than in the shape of the adolescents' trajectories. In support of previous research (Hankin et al., 1998; Kling et al., 1999; Zahn-Waxler, Shirtcliff, & Marceau, 2008), females at age 14 were more at risk of experiencing internalizing mental health problems compared to males. Female adolescents reported a higher prevalence of eating disorders, greater feelings of depression and lower levels of self-esteem than did the males. As we expected, males reported higher expectations of becoming involved in risky and illegal behaviors than did females at age 14.

We also predicted that African American adolescents would have more positive trajectories of self-esteem compared to European American adolescents, but there were no R/E differences in any of the slopes. There was only one significant R/E difference, which occurred at the intercept: African American adolescents reported more anger than did European American adolescents at age 14, understandably, as they are just learning of the injustices perpetrated on their race/ethnicity. There were, however, several gender by R/E interactions, again at the mean level only with European Americans showing greater gender differences compared to African Americans. As a result, and consistent with previous findings (Hoek, 2006), these European American females reported a greater incidence of eating disorders and lower self-esteem than did both African American females and European American males (Richman, Clark, & Brown, 1985), highlighting their uniquely heightened vulnerability to mental health difficulties during the adolescent years. These gender by race/ethnicity interactions emphasize the importance of an intersectionality perspective where considering the potential impact of these two very powerful demographic characteristics.

SES was a significant factor in both the mean levels and trajectories of our mental health–related characteristics. Lower-SES adolescents reported more frequent feelings of anger and less frequent feelings of resiliency than did higher-SES adolescents. However, there were also differences in the trajectories of psychological well-being, such that differences associated with SES decreased in late adolescence. For example, higher-SES adolescents experienced a greater increase in resiliency from 12 to 16 years than did lower-SES adolescents, but their trajectories converged in later adolescence. Similarly, lower-SES adolescents experienced more frequent feelings of depression in early adolescence than did higher-SES adolescents, but again their trajectories converged as they approached the transition to adulthood. Apparently, in this sample, SES differences in our indicators of psychological well-being narrowed as the adolescents matured into young adults. In the case of adolescents' depressive affect, this shift reflects the movement of both groups toward better mental health. In contrast, this shift also reflects the downward movement of both groups toward a more moderate level of confidence in their resiliency, perhaps due to the challenging nature of the transition out of high school for all youth.

Contrary to studies finding more internalizing problems for adolescents from single families versus those from intact families (e.g., Lansford et al., 2006), we found no significant differences (where $p < .01$) in psychological well-being on our six measures according to parents' marital status, suggesting that living in an always-single home does not have significant or necessarily negative consequences for adolescent psychological well-being. However, it must be kept in mind that we only included parents' marital status when the adolescent was 12 years old. As a result, we do not know how changes in parents' marital status reflect changes in mental health across the adolescent years.

Overall, most of the variation in psychological well-being was attributable to differences within adolescents, with the exception of eating disorders. Between 9% (eating disorders) and 40% (depressive affect) of the within-person variation was associated with age. Demographic characteristics accounted for between 3% and 14% of the variance in the intercept (see Table 8), with the greatest amount of variance being accounted for in eating disorders and the least amount of reliable variance accounted for in depressive affect. The amount of reliable variance accounted for in slopes also varied across our six indicators, with the most being explained for eating disorders (17%), followed by resiliency (6%). Finally, covariates explained little of the variation in the other slopes, including self-esteem, anger, depressive affect, and expected negative life chances. Clearly, there is a great deal of intra-individual variance left to be explained. Both age and classic demographic characteristics explained relatively little of the inter-individual and intra-individual differences in psychological well-being. On the whole, the psychological well-being of these young people looked very good, and what changes there were do not suggest a great deal of risk despite the major social and biological changes that these youth experience as they pass through this developmental period. One is not left with the impression that our young people were at high risk of negative life events or negative life outcomes. Rather, they showed positive psychological functioning, more generally.

V: R/E IDENTITY AND DISCRIMINATION

Leslie Morrison Gutman, Stephen C. Peck, Oksana Malanchuk,
Arnold J. Sameroff, and Jacquelynne S. Eccles

This article is part of the issue "Moving Through Adolescence: Developmental Trajectories of African American and European American Youth" Gutman, Peck, Malanchuk, Sameroff, and Eccles (Issue Authors). For a full listing of articles in this issue, see: http://onlinelibrary.wiley.com/doi/10.1111/mono.v82.4/issuetoc.

When MADICS began, there were very few measures of either R/E identity or perceived discrimination. The Multidimensional Inventory of Black Identity (MIBI) was in the process of being developed (Sellers, Smith, Shelton, Rowley, & Chavous, 1998), and the Multigroup Ethnic Identity Measure (MEIM) (Phinney, 1992) had just become available (by Wave 3). As a result, we began our study with open-ended questions in order to explore the meaning of race/ethnicity to the young people in our study. We then used content analysis of their responses to develop closed-ended scales, and we incorporated the newly emerging MEIM and MIBI scales as they became available. Therefore, many of our R/E-related measures have very few items in common across all of the waves. Nevertheless, in order to use HLM most appropriately, we needed to focus on those items that were assessed in a consistent manner across time. By and large, we succeeded in meeting this goal through the examination of R/E identity, R/E segregation of friendship networks, and R/E discrimination. Results are shown in Tables 9 and 10 and Figure 2.

Corresponding author: Leslie Morrison Gutman, email: l.gutman@ucl.ac.uk
DOI: 10.1111/mono.12331
© 2017 The Society for Research in Child Development, Inc.

TABLE 9

GROWTH MODELS FOR R/E IDENTITY AND DISCRIMINATION

	R/E Importance	R/E Behavioral Involvement	Same R/E Friends	Cross R/E Friends	Expected R/E Discrimination	R/E John Henryism	Parents' Worries About Discrimination
For intercept							
Intercept	3.55***	2.93***	3.89***	2.10***	1.59***	2.09***	1.94***
SES	.07*	.08	.07*	−.07*	.03	.06	−.03
Gender	.03	.03	.16***	−.12**	.12**	−.04	.02
Ethnicity			−.63***	.53***	−.77***	−.91***	−.64***
GXE			.03	−.05	.24**	−.10	.23*
Single	.00	−.11	.19*	−.02	−.20	.04	−.33*
Intact	.00	.07	−.01	−.02	.04	.06	.09
Age	.02	−.06	.04	−.00	−.02	−.11	−.12
Age²	.01	.05	−.04	−.02	.01	.02	.02
For linear slope							
Intercept	−.06*	−.03*	.11***	−.11***	.01	−.09*	−.09*
SES	−.04	.03	.02	−.02*	.04	−.04	.10**
Gender	−.06	−.01	.00	−.02	−.06	−.01	.00
Ethnicity			.00	.04	.02	.08*	.09*
GXE			−.07	.01	.07	.09	.12
Single	−.06	−.01	−.06	.05	.15	−.03	.27*
Intact	.02	.00	−.03	.05*	.03	.06	−.02

(Continued)

TABLE 9. (*Continued*)

	R/E Importance	R/E Behavioral Involvement	Same R/E Friends	Cross R/E Friends	Expected R/E Discrimination	R/E John Henryism	Parents' Worries About Discrimination
For quadratic slope							
Intercept	.00	-.02*	-.02***	.01*	.00	.03***	.00
SES	.01	-.01	.00	.00	-.01	.01	-.02**
Gender	.01	-.01	.00	.00	.00	.00	-.01
Ethnicity			.01	-.02***	-.01	-.04***	-.03**
GXE			.01	.00	-.02	-.02	-.02
Single	.01	.01	.01	-.01	-.03	.00	-.05*
Intact	.01	.00	.01	-.01	-.01	-.02	.01

Note. ***$p < .001$, **$p < .01$, *$p < .05$. R/E importance and R/E behavioral involvement were estimated for African American adolescents only. Given that our R/E discrimination measures lacked both construct and measurement invariance across R/E groups, significant differences between African Americans and European Americans should be interpreted with caution.

TABLE 10

RESIDUAL VARIANCE FOR R/E IDENTITY AND DISCRIMINATION

	Unconditional Means Model	ICC	Unconditional Growth Model	Level 1 R^2	With Level 2 Predictors	% Explained
R/E importance		.28		.19		
Level 1	.253		.205			
Intercept	.097***		.090***		.090***	<1%
Linear slope			.005***		.005***	<1%
R/E behavioral involvement		.36		.08		
Level 1	.513		.472			
Intercept	.294***		.278***		.270***	3%
Linear slope			.004		.003	25%
Same R/E friends		.31		.41		
Level 1	.563		.462			
Intercept	.251***		.302***		.209***	31%
Linear slope			.021***		.021**	0%
Quad slope			.0008		.0008	0%
Cross R/E friends		.30		.41		
Level 1	.498		.419			
Intercept	.210***		.303***		.240***	21%
Linear slope			.008*		.006**	25%
Quad slope			.000		.000	<1%
Expected R/E discrimination						
Level 1	.500	.35	.440	.12		
Intercept	.274***		.307***		.176***	43%
Linear slope			.009***		.009***	<1%
R/E John Henryism		.47		.14		
Level 1	.468		.404			
Intercept	.411***		.433***		.275***	36%
Linear slope			.005**		.004**	20%
Parents' worries discrimination		.38		.21		
Level 1	.635		.504			
Intercept	.388***		.624***		.543***	13%
Linear slope			.020***		.019***	5%

***$p < .001$, **$p < .01$, *$p < .05$.

R/E IDENTITY

R/E identity is a multidimensional construct that incorporates the significance and meaning that individuals place on race/ethnicity in defining

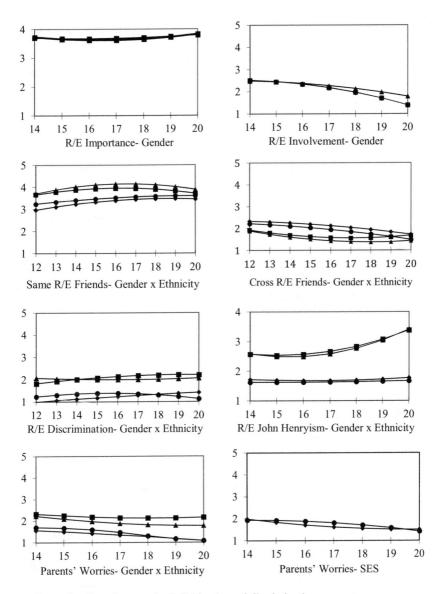

FIGURE 2.—Growth curves for R/E identity and discrimination.

Note. The *x*-axis represents age in years, whereas the *y*-axis represents the mean of the scale, controlling for the covariates. For the gender and race/ethnicity growth curves, European American females are represented by the circle, European American males are represented by the diamond, African American females are represented by the triangle, and African American males are represented by the square. For the SES growth curves, high-SES adolescents are represented by the circle, whereas low-SES adolescents are represented by the diamond.

themselves (Sellers et al., 1998). Our measures of R/E identity include adolescents' feelings of importance and pride in their R/E identity and their behavioral involvement in R/E-related activities. Because we did not include these measures at age 12, and European American adolescents were not asked these questions at age 14, the results are limited to African American adolescents from ages 14 to 20.

R/E Importance

This scale measures the importance of, and pride in, R/E identity in the lives of African American adolescents. The linear and quadratic trends were not statistically significant at the $p < .01$ level (see Table 9). Therefore, these beliefs remained quite stable during adolescence for these African American youth (see Figure 2).

There were also no significant differences in mean levels of R/E importance at age 14 (the intercept) associated with gender, SES, or parents' marital status, where $p < .01$. Taking into account the other covariates, their mean responses across time hovered above 3.5 on a 4-point scale, with (3) meaning "somewhat important" and (4) meaning "very important." Clearly, the importance of one's race/ethnicity was quite high for the African American youth throughout their adolescence. These results are consistent with the reports of other researchers (Phinney & Ong, 2007) who have found that this aspect of African Americans' R/E identity tends to be well-developed by age 14.

R/E Behavioral Involvement

Another indicator of R/E identity is the frequency of engaging in R/E related activities. As with R/E importance, the linear and quadratic slopes of R/E Behavioral Involvement were not significant, where $p < .01$ (see Figure 2), and did not vary significantly by gender, SES, or parents' marital status (see Table 9).

At age 14, there were also no significant differences associated with gender, SES, or parents' marital status. Adjusting for the other covariates, the mean levels across time for the African American youth ranged between 1.5 and 2.5 (with 1 equal to "almost never" and 3 equal to "occasionally"). Therefore, the African American youth engaged in these behaviors between "almost never" to "occasionally."

R/E FRIENDSHIPS

The proportion of one's friends who are members of one's own R/E group (Same R/E Friends) relative to those in other R/E groups (cross R/E friends) are also indicators of the centrality of one's own R/E group membership in one's life. There have been a few studies that pointed out the very strong tendency for R/E peer groups in the United States to segregate themselves from one another (e.g., Kao & Joyner, 2004; Quillian & Campbell, 2003), but there has been much less longitudinal research examining how such segregation in one's friendship networks changes over the adolescent years for African American and European American youth.

Same R/E Friends

For the average adolescent, there were significant linear and quadratic slopes (see Table 9). Same R/E friends increased from early adolescence and then decreased slightly in late adolescence. There were similar trajectories for both African American and European American adolescents.

At age 14, there were significant differences according to gender and race/ethnicity. African American adolescents reported that, of their friends, between "most of them" (4) and "all of them" (5) are African American, taking into account the other covariates. In contrast, European American adolescents reported that, of their friends, a little more than "about half of them" were European American. For both African American and European American adolescents, females reported having slightly more same R/E friends than did males.

Cross R/E Friends

There was a significant linear decrease indicating that the proportion of cross R/E friends decreased, on average, from early to late adolescence (see Table 9). The quadratic slope was also moderated by race/ethnicity. African American adolescents had a slight increase in the proportion of other R/E friends in late adolescence, whereas European American adolescents reported a slight decrease (see Figure 2).

At age 14, there were significant differences in cross R/E friends associated with gender and race/ethnicity. African American adolescents reported that, of their friends, "few of them" (2) were European American, taking into account the other covariates. In contrast, European American adolescents reported that less than half of their friends were African American, with mean levels ranging from "a few of them" (2) to "half of them" (3). Again, males reported having slightly more cross R/E friends than did females.

EXPECTATIONS OF FUTURE R/E DISCRIMINATION

Here we focus on expectations of discrimination in the future, making a distinction between expectations of R/E discrimination and the

89

anticipation of having to work harder than others to get ahead in the future because of one's race/ethnicity. Following the work of Sherman James (1994), we call the latter R/E John Henryism. There has also been growing interest in the role that the family plays in socializing children's understanding of racism and discrimination. In this section, we present the results for these indicators of anticipated discrimination and adolescents' perceptions of their parents' concerns about the likelihood that they (the adolescents) will be confronted with R/E discrimination in the future. As a reminder, although we described the mean levels of the intercepts and slope of the trajectories of these measures for African American and European American adolescents, we did not directly compare them. Significant R/E differences are presented in Table 9 but should be interpreted with caution given the lack of construct and measurement invariance across these R/E groups.

Expected R/E Discrimination

The linear and quadratic slopes were not significant (see Table 9). As shown in Figure 2, both African American and European American adolescents had relatively stable expectations of experiencing R/E discrimination in the future. There were no significant differences in the slopes associated with any of our covariates.

Taking into account the other covariates, at the intercept (age 14), European American male adolescents reported the lowest possible choice of 1 or "not at all" and European American females reported slightly less than between "not at all" (1) and "just a little" (2). African American male and female adolescents reported levels around 2.

R/E John Henryism

There was a significant positive quadratic slope for the extent to which our participants reported that they would have to work harder than others to get ahead due to their race/ethnicity (see Table 9). As shown in Figure 2, on average, African American adolescents reported a stable level of R/E John Henryism from 14 to 16 years and then a sharp rise from 17 to 20 years. European American adolescents, on average, reported a stable, but very low level of R/E John Henryism from 14 to 20 years.

Together, looking at the actual values of the youth's responses (adjusting for the other covariates), the African American youth began neither agreeing nor disagreeing with the idea that they would have to work harder than others to get ahead due to their race/ethnicity (a mean score of 2.5 at age 14 that lies midway between "agree" and "disagree"). However, by age 20, their mean-level response lay between "agree" and "strongly agree." European American adolescents consistently disagreed with this belief from 14 to 20 years, with a score hovering around 1.5.

Parents' Worries About R/E Discrimination

On average, there were neither significant linear nor quadratic slopes, where $p < .01$ (see Table 9). As shown in Figure 2, African American adolescents experienced a slight decrease from ages 14 to 17 that leveled off at ages 17–20. European American adolescents experienced a steady decrease from ages 14 to 20.

Both the linear and quadratic slopes were moderated by SES. Lower-SES adolescents had a more negative linear slope but a more positive quadratic slope than did higher-SES adolescents. As shown in Figure 2, compared to higher-SES adolescents, lower-SES adolescents experienced a greater decrease in their perceptions of their parents' worries from ages 14 to 18, which stabilized between 18 and 20 years. Higher-SES adolescents, on the other hand, experienced little change from ages 14 to 16 and then a steady decline from ages 16 to 20. As a result, levels of perceived parents' worries were similar at ages 14 and 20, with some variation during the middle adolescent years across the two SES groups.

At age 14, African American youth reported that their parents worried about such discrimination more than "a little" (2). Thus, although the African American youth did not think their parents were extremely concerned about current and future R/E discrimination, they did think that possible R/E discrimination was one of their parents' concerns. European American youth, at age 14, reported that their parents worried about such discrimination between "not at all" (1) and "a little" (2).

SUMMARY OF R/E IDENTITY AND DISCRIMINATION

Our longitudinal study is unique in that it includes both self-identified European Americans and African Americans from all SES groups within the same geographic location. Contrary to our expectations for African American adolescents, their R/E identity, expectations of R/E discrimination, and parents' worries about discrimination did not significantly change from early to late adolescence, where $p < .01$. However, the anticipation that one will have to work harder to get ahead because of one's race/ethnicity increased dramatically over the years for the African American youth. European American adolescents reported stable expectations of R/E discrimination and John Henryism but declining perceptions of their parents' worries about

R/E discrimination as they approached late adolescence. These changes in late adolescence for both African American and European American adolescents may reflect their departure from relatively racially/ethnically homogeneous high schools and their transition to higher education or employment. However, given that our measure of R/E John Henryism lacked both construct and measurement invariance across race/ethnicity groups, the meaning of the late-adolescence differences between African Americans and European Americans should be interpreted with caution.

Regarding the mean levels, these African American adolescents did anticipate that future discrimination was likely to play some role in their lives and that they may have to work harder than others to succeed due to their race/ethnicity. Nevertheless, they did not anticipate that R/E discrimination would be a major obstacle to their educational and occupational goals. Furthermore, our correlational analyses showed only weak associations between the R/E discrimination measures and the measures of psychological well-being and academic functioning for the African American adolescents. We have shown elsewhere that believing one will face future discrimination in work and education predicts increased investment in one's academic achievement for these African American youth (Wong et al., 2003), suggesting that on average the African American youth in this county actively cope with anticipated future discrimination by working to increase their personal human capital.

European American adolescents in this sample reported, on average, having little to no expectations of discrimination and disagreed that they would have to work harder to succeed in the future because of their race/ethnicity. Our correlational analyses showed that having higher expectations of R/E discrimination and John Henryism were moderately and significantly correlated with lower levels of psychological well-being and academic functioning for the European American adolescents. These findings underscore that the meaning of R/E discrimination appears to be very different for African American compared to European American adolescents. Other factors in these adolescents' lives associated with their race/ethnicity may have also played a role in buffering the effects of R/E discrimination. Other research has shown, for example, that R/E identity and socialization practices protect African American adolescents from experiencing negative outcomes associated with R/E discrimination (Miller & MacIntosh, 1999; Sellers et al., 2006; Tynes et al., 2012).

For R/E friendships, there were significant changes during adolescence. As expected for both African American and European American adolescents, segregation accelerated during the secondary school years and then was asymptote at a fairly high level. Overall, these findings are consistent with studies on the R/E composition of friendship networks in the high school

92

years (see Fuligni et al., 2009, for a review). Contrary to previous research (Aboud & Janani, 2007; Epstein, 1989), however, there was also a very slight shift toward less segregation after high school, especially for African American youth. However, the levels of segregation at all ages were quite high. The slight increase in mixed R/E group friendships in late adolescence could reflect the fact that some youth had moved into racially/ethnically heterogeneous social contexts with their transition into college or employment. Although some of the African American youth who went to college went to historically Black colleges (21%), the majority went to racially/ethnically heterogeneous colleges. This may explain the increase in the proportion of other R/E friends, particularly for African American adolescents.

As noted in previous literature (see Fuligni et al., 2009, for a review), African American adolescents reported having more African American than European American friends. European American adolescents, on the other hand, reported that about half of their friends were European American. What is most interesting here is that the possible peer networks in these high schools are predominantly African American, so the apparent segregation among the African American youth could be driven, in part, by the R/E composition of the schools. In contrast, in these schools, the segregation of the European American students runs counter to the R/E composition of the school and, thus, probably reflects an active sorting process. Interestingly, however, the European American youth reported that a smaller proportion of their friends are of their same R/E group than did African American youth. This finding counters research showing that European American teens, in particular, are less likely to have cross R/E friendships (Hamm, Brown, & Heck, 2005), but likely reflects the greater proportion of African American youth in the student bodies in all of the schools in this sample.

In terms of gender differences, as predicted and consistent with Way and Chen (2000), the females reported that a higher percentage of their friends are of similar race/ethnicity than did the males. Analyses using qualitative interview data have also revealed that males tend to be more flexible compared to females regarding friendship selection, and this flexibility may result from being involved in formal or informal sporting activities that encourage more contact among adolescents from different R/E groups. As we expected from previous research (Smith-Bynum et al., 2014; Wang & Huguley, 2012), African Americans males reported higher expectations of future R/E discrimination than did African American females. Given previous research highlighting the negative impact of perceived discrimination (e.g., Caldwell et al., 2004; Seaton et al., 2011; Smith-Bynum et al., 2014; Wang & Huguley, 2012; Williams et al., 2003; Wong et al., 2003), these findings are particularly salient for the future expected outcomes of African American males.

93

On the whole, the other family demographic characteristics had few significant associations with this set of adolescents' beliefs, with the exception of parents' worries about R/E discrimination. During the high school years, lower-SES youth evidenced a greater decline in their parents' worries about future R/E discrimination than did higher-SES youth. However, higher-SES adolescents evidenced a greater decline in later adolescence, perhaps associated with their entry into college or employment. Parents' marital status was not associated with variations in either the intercept or slopes for any of the measures, where $p < .01$.

Overall, most of the variation in R/E identity and discrimination was attributable to differences within adolescents, with about one-third of the variation found between adolescents (see Table 10). On average, less than 20% of the within-group variation was associated with age, with the exception of R/E friendships which were at 41%. The final models accounted for up to 43% of the variance in the intercept (see Table 10), with the greatest variance accounted for in expected R/E discrimination and up to 25% of the variance accounted for in the slopes, with the greatest variance accounted for in cross R/E friends and R/E behavioral involvement. Nevertheless, substantial amounts of variance in both the intercepts and developmental trajectories remain to be studied.

VI: ACADEMIC FUNCTIONING

Leslie Morrison Gutman, Stephen C. Peck, Oksana Malanchuk,
Arnold J. Sameroff, and Jacquelynne S. Eccles

This article is part of the issue "Moving Through Adolescence: Developmental Trajectories of African American and European American Youth" Gutman, Peck, Malanchuk, Sameroff, and Eccles (Issue Authors). For a full listing of articles in this issue, see: http://onlinelibrary.wiley.com/doi/10.1111/mono.v82.4/issuetoc.

In this chapter, we first report changes in academic achievement, followed by the results for educational and occupational expectations and aspirations. We then present the results for several different indicators of academic motivational beliefs and perceptions of the school environment, ending with a summary of the findings. Results are shown in Tables 11 and 12 and Figure 3.

GRADE POINT AVERAGE (GPA)

There was a significant negative linear slope moderated by SES and gender (see Table 11). Consistent with our predictions, GPA declined steadily across the school years for the average adolescent (see Figure 3). Higher-SES and female adolescents experienced a smaller decline in GPA than did lower-SES and male adolescents. There were no differences in the slopes according to race/ethnicity, the gender by race/ethnicity interaction, or parents' marital status.

Corresponding author: Leslie Morrison Gutman, email: l.gutman@ucl.ac.uk
DOI: 10.1111/mono.12332

TABLE 11

GROWTH MODELS FOR ACADEMIC FUNCTIONING

	GPA	Educational Aspirations	Educational Expectations	Occupational Aspirations	Academic Importance	Academic Self-Concept	Positive School Identification
For intercept							
Intercept	3.04***	7.77***	6.87***	8.34***	5.38***	5.18***	3.36***
SES	.16**	.37***	.51***	1.85**	.07	.15***	-.02
Gender	.26***	.42***	.40***	2.11*	-.03	-.00	.08
Ethnicity	.19***	-.23*	-.04	-2.84***	-.29***	.02	-.07
GXE	-.04	-.07	.11	1.19	-.01	.00	.21*
Single	-.05	-.01	.23	.35	.15	.17	-.06
Intact	.15***	-.08	.15	.57	-.11	-.04	.02
Age	-.02	-.08	-.15	1.56	.21**	.02	.06
Age²	.00	.01	.03	-.02	-.07*	.01	-.02
For linear slope							
Intercept	-.07***	.04	.04	-.22	-.15***	-.07***	-.05**
SES	.03**	.04	.03	.09	.09***	.00	.00
Gender	.05***	.08**	.05	.33	.03	.02	.03
Ethnicity	.00	-.05	-.01	-.16	-.04	-.01	-.02
GXE	.00	-.04	-.07	-.91	-.02	.03	.06
Single	.02	.02	.01	-.41	.04	-.02	.02
Intact	.00	-.06	-.01	-.38	-.01	-.02	-.02
For quadratic slope							
Intercept	-.00	-.03*	-.03*	.00	-.01	-.01	.02**
SES	-.01	.01	.02	.00	-.02	-.00	.00
Gender	-.01	-.01	.03	.00	.03	-.01	.00
Ethnicity	-.01	-.01	-.03	.00	-.03	-.00	.01
GXE	.00	.02	.00	.01	.05**	-.01	-.03
Single	.02	.02	-.03	.00	-.01	-.00	-.02
Intact	-.01	.02	-.01	.00	.03	.01	.01

*** $p < .001$, ** $p < .01$, * $p < .05$.

TABLE 12

RESIDUAL VARIANCE FOR ACADEMIC FUNCTIONING

	Unconditional Means Model	ICC	Unconditional Growth Model	Level 1 R^2	With Level 2 Predictors	% Explained
GPA		.39		.30		
Level 1	.257		.180			
Intercept	.166***		.178***		.123***	31%
Linear slope			.020***		.012***	40%
Educational aspirations		.44		.14		
Level 1	1.226		1.056			
Intercept	.945***		1.008***		.885***	12%
Linear slope			.034***		.031***	9%
Educational expectations		.46		.09		
Level 1	1.419		1.285			
Intercept	1.200***		1.237***		.971***	22%
Linear slope			.025***		.020**	20%
Occupational aspirations		.28		.17		
Level 1	260.221		215.591			
Intercept	101.845***		113.566***		107.960***	5%
Linear slope			5.344***		5.167***	3%
Quad slope			.001***		.001***	<1%
Academic importance		.23		.15		
Level 1	1.376		1.168			
Intercept	.406***		.458***		.418***	9%
Linear slope			.029***		.024***	17%
Academic self-concept		.41		.20		
Level 1	.745		.595			
Intercept	.518***		.543***		.534***	2%
Linear slope			.018***		.018***	<1%
Quad slope			.000*		.000*	<1%
Positive school identification		.25		.04		
Level 1	.442		.425			
Intercept	.144***		.149***		.145***	3%
Linear slope			.002		.002	<1%

***$p < .001$, **$p < .01$, *$p < .05$.

At age 14, adolescents who were higher SES, female, European American, and lived with intact, always-married parents had higher GPAs than did those who were lower-SES, male, African American, and lived in other family types. Taking into account the other covariates, the average

97

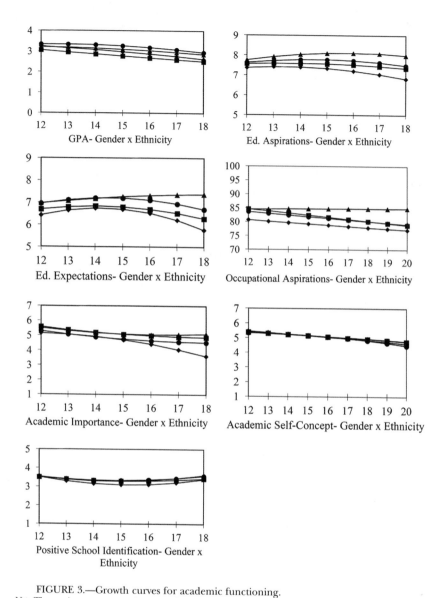

FIGURE 3.—Growth curves for academic functioning.

Note. The *x*-axis represents age in years, whereas the *y*-axis represents the mean of the scale, controlling for the covariates. For the gender and race/ethnicity growth curves, European American females are represented by the circle, European American males are represented by the diamond, African American females are represented by the triangle, and African American males are represented by the square.

GPA of these students ranged from a C to a B. Males began with a B average and dropped to a C by the end of high school; females began with a slightly higher than B average and ended with nearer to a C+.

One of the benefits of this population is to be able to separate out R/E differences from socioeconomic differences. For GPA, both social class and race/ethnicity predicted GPA in the manner typical of most studies in the United States, with European American and high-SES youth having a higher GPA compared to African American and lower-SES youth (see Kao & Thompson, 2003, for a review). It is likely that different processes explain these two effects on school achievement, with SES effects being carried mostly by lack of resources and differences in experiences at home (Davis-Kean, 2005; Gutman et al., 2003; McLoyd, 1998) and the unique effect of race/ethnicity likely reflecting the impact of R/E discrimination in school (see Wong et al., 2003). In this sample, the African American youth reported higher levels of R/E discrimination than did the European American youth, and both Wong et al. (2003) and Chavous et al. (2003) demonstrated that experiences of R/E discrimination in this population predicted declines in GPA over the secondary school years.

EDUCATIONAL ASPIRATIONS AND EXPECTATIONS AND OCCUPATIONAL ASPIRATIONS

Evidence has documented the importance of high occupational aspirations and educational aspirations and expectations for later academic and career success (Clausen, 1993; Schoon, Martin, & Ross, 2007; Mello, 2008; Wigfield et al., 2006). According to Eccles's Expectancy-Value Theory, these beliefs help to guide adolescents' high school course choices and provide an impetus for increased engagement in learning the academic content in these courses (Eccles, 1994). In this way, these beliefs reflect the influence of young people's conceptualization of their own talents, goals, and interests and serve as vehicles through which young people may actualize their emerging identities (Eccles, 1994; Lent, Brown, & Hackett, 1994; Meece, Eccles-Parsons, Kaczala, Goff, & Futterman, 1982; Savickas, 2005). Here, we examine educational and occupational aspirations, which reflect adolescents' hopes regarding their educational attainment and the social status of their ideal occupation, as well as their expectations regarding the educational level they expect to actually achieve.

Educational Aspirations

Neither the linear nor quadratic slopes were significant at the $p < .01$ level, but the linear slope was moderated by gender (see Table 11). On average, these adolescents' educational aspirations were stable from 12 to 18 years, but there was a slight decline over time for males (see Figure 3). There were no significant differences in the slopes according to adolescents' race/ethnicity, the gender by ethnicity interaction, or parents' SES or marital status.

At 14 years, higher-SES and female adolescents had higher educational aspirations than did lower-SES and male adolescents. There were no significant differences at the intercept according to adolescents' race/ethnicity, the gender by race/ethnicity interaction, or parents' marital status.

On average and controlling for all covariates, these students' educational aspirations were very high, ranging between graduating from a 4-year university and obtaining a master's degree. This level increased over time for some of the participants, such that on average females were close to aspiring to a master's degree by age 18. In contrast, the average aspirations of males dropped closer to graduating from a 4-year college.

Educational Expectations

A quite similar pattern emerged for adolescents' educational expectations (see Table 11). As shown in Figure 3, on average, educational expectations were stable from 12 to 18 years. There were no significant differences in the linear and quadratic slopes at the $p < .01$ level, and the slopes were not moderated by SES, gender, race/ethnicity, the gender by race/ethnicity interaction, or parents' marital status.

There were significant differences for SES and gender at the intercept but no differences according to race/ethnicity, the gender by race/ethnicity interaction, or parents' marital status. At age 14, higher-SES and female adolescents had higher educational expectations than did lower-SES and male adolescents.

As expected, the mean levels were lower for educational expectations than for educational aspirations. Taking into account the other covariates, the average adolescent expected to obtain slightly less than a bachelor's degree. Both higher-SES and female adolecents expected to obtain more than a bachelor's degree, whereas lower-SES and male adolescents expected to obtain between an associate's degree and a bachelor's degree.

Occupational Aspirations

As with educational aspirations, there were no significant changes in the linear and quadratic slopes for the average adolescent (see Table 11). As shown in Figure 3, on average these adolescents' occupational aspirations had the same status level from early to late adolescence. There also were no significant differences in the slopes according to the demographic variables.

There were, however, significant mean-level group differences at the intercept. At age 14, higher-SES and African American adolescents aspired to higher status occupations than did lower-SES and European American adolescents. There were no significant differences according to gender, the gender by race/ethnicity interaction, or parents' marital status.

In terms of the actual ratings, taking into account the other covariates, the average adolescent aspired to a career in a mid-level managerial or professional position. At age 14, African American youth aspired to higher status occupations (at the level of accountants, auditors, or supervisors of police and detectives, mean = 85) than did European American youth (police officers, health care practitioners, editors, or public relations specialists, mean = 80).

ACADEMIC MOTIVATIONAL BELIEFS

Motivational psychologists have stressed the importance of task- and self-related beliefs as influences on academic engagement and educational aspirations and expectations. Eccles, Wigfield, and their colleagues (Eccles et al., 1993; Wigfield & Eccles, 2002); Marsh and his colleagues (Marsh, 1992; Marsh & Craven, 2006; Marsh & Shavelson, 1985); and Bandura (1977, 1997) have stressed the importance of beliefs related to task importance and domain-specific self-efficacy. There is now considerable evidence (Wigfield et al., 2006) that these sets of beliefs predict levels of school engagement during the secondary school years, secondary school course choice, and longer-term educational and occupational aspirations. In this monograph, we included one measure of task-related beliefs and one reflecting self-related beliefs.

Academic Importance

In keeping with the idea that it is the relative importance of various tasks that influence behavioral choice, we measured perceived academic importance in relative terms: how important school subjects are to the person in comparison to other things. Consistent with existing literature, we found a significant negative linear slope (see Table 11). On average, the relative importance these adolescents attached to academic subjects declined across their secondary school years (see Figure 3). This linear slope was moderated by SES. Lower-SES youth experienced a sharper decline in academic importance across the school years compared to higher-SES youth. Although we believe this may be the first study to document a more rapid decrease in the importance attached to school subjects for lower- than higher-SES students, this finding is consistent with both (a) studies showing higher drop-out rates and declining academic achievement among lower-SES youth (Eccles, 2012; Rumberger, 1987) and (b) the other SES differences we report in this section. The quadratic slope was also moderated by a gender by race/ethnicity interaction: European American male adolescents experienced a sharper decline in perceived academic importance compared to the other groups as they approached the end of high school.

In terms of the intercept, there was a significant race/ethnicity effect. At age 14, African American adolescents, on average, rated academics as more important than did European American adolescents. There were no significant differences according to SES, gender, the gender by race/ethnicity interaction, or parents' marital status. With regard to the means of their responses, controlling for the covariates, the youth in this sample, like the youth in other studies (Jacobs, Lanza, Osgood, Eccles, & Wigfield, 2002), attached quite high relative importance to school subjects at age 12, averaging close to 5.5 on a 7-point scale, with 7 being "much more important to me than other things." These initially high levels then showed a steady decline across adolescence to 4.5, meaning academics were seen as only slightly more important than other things.

Academic Self-Concept

Our measure captures both an absolute confidence in one's academic abilities and a social-comparative assessment of one's academic abilities relative to other students. Consistent with other studies (De Fraine et al., 2007; Eccles et al., 1993; Gniewosz et al., 2012), we found a significant negative linear slope for this construct (see Table 11). For the average adolescent, self-perceptions of their academic skills significantly declined from early to late adolescence (see Figure 3). Importantly, this slope was not moderated by any of the other demographic characteristics.

Consistent with the SES difference in GPA, higher-SES adolescents had a higher self-concept of their academic skills than did lower-SES adolescents at the intercept (age 14). In contrast to previous studies (De Fraine et al., 2007; Dotterer et al., 2014), there were no significant effects for race/ethnicity or gender, perhaps because this construct assessed ability self-concepts across math and other school subjects rather than focusing on specific academic domains. Taking this broad approach would average across the typical gender differences for math and English academic self-concepts. Consistent with widely reported SES differences in school achievement, higher-SES youth reported higher academic self-concepts than did lower-SES youth (Eccles, 2012). As noted earlier, one of the advantages of this sample is our ability to unconfound race/ethnicity with SES. Clearly, in this case, SES is a more powerful predictor of individual differences than race/ethnicity. Like academic importance, mean levels of academic self-concept started quite high—at 5.5 on a 7-point scale (controlling for the covariates)—and decreased over time to slightly above 4.5.

POSITIVE SCHOOL IDENTIFICATION

We end this section with our results on the adolescents' perceptions of positive school identification. Motivational psychologists have argued that having a positive general identification with one's school should increase the likelihood of attending and being positively engaged with the school's agenda (Eccles & Roeser, 2011; Finn, 1989; Fredricks, Blumenfeld, & Paris, 2004; Voelkl, 1997). Scholars concerned with school drop-out and school disengagement have stressed the importance of a lack of identification with one's school as an institution (Fine, 1986; Finn, 1989; Rumbauer, 2001). Finally, scholars have also argued that the drops in achievement across the middle school and high school transition result, in part at least, from declines in one's general sense of fit with the social context (Eccles et al., 1993; Eccles & Midgley, 1989; Gutman & Midgley, 2000). However, there have been very few studies looking at longitudinal changes in school identification among different demographic groups of adolescents.

We found a significant negative linear slope and a significant positive quadratic slope (see Table 11). On average, these adolescents' positive identification with their school environment resembled a concave-shaped trajectory (see Figure 3). Adolescents experienced a decrease in their identification with their school from age 12 to 15 followed by an increase from ages 16 to 18. This pattern did not vary according to SES, gender, race/ethnicity, the gender by race/ethnicity interaction, or parents' marital status.

There were no significant differences in demographic variables at the intercept at the $p < .01$ level. Taking into account the covariates, on average these adolescents' scores ranged from 3 to 3.5, with 3 equal to "neither agree nor disagree," to 4, with 4 equal to "agree." Thus, despite the slight dip during the transition to high school, most of our adolescents agreed somewhat but not strongly that their school was good, they liked their school, and they would recommend their school to other students.

SUMMARY OF ACADEMIC FUNCTIONING

With the exception of adolescents' aspirations and expectations, the developmental trajectories of academic functioning supported our hypotheses, showing a significant but slight decline across junior and senior high schools. Our findings are comparable to the general literature, which has shown that declines in academic functioning tend to occur during the early adolescence years as these youth move through junior high school and then, again, during the transition into senior high school (Anderman, Maehr, & Midgley, 1999; Barber & Olsen, 2004; Benner & Graham, 2009; Eccles et al., 1993; Eccles & Roeser, 2010; Gutman & Midgely, 2000; Juvonen, Le, Kaganoff, Augustine, & Constant, 2004; Roeser, Eccles, & Freedman-Doan, 1999; Rumberger, 2001; Wigfield, Eccles, & Pintrich, 1996). Our young people experienced declines in their feelings of both academic importance and scholastic competence from early to late adolescence. They also experienced a decrease in their generally positive feelings about school during junior high school and in the first few years of senior high school. More worrisome is that their GPAs dropped as they moved through high school—a full grade point in some cases. Despite these changes, our youth remained on the positive side of the midpoints of our scales. Academic beliefs related to the future, including educational expectations and aspirations and occupational aspirations, remained quite high from early to late adolescence.

As we predicted, there were significant gender differences in academic functioning. Consistent with other studies (Gutman & Schoon, 2012; Mello, 2008; Schoon et al., 2007; Voyer & Voyer, 2014), females had higher educational aspirations and expectations and achieved higher GPAs than did males. There were several gender differences in the shape of trajectories. First, males experienced a greater decline in their school grades than did females from early to late adolescence. Second, females experienced an increase while males experienced a slight decrease in educational aspirations. Contrary to our expectations based on other research (De Fraine et al., 2007; Dotterer, Lowe, & McHale, 2014), however, there were no gender differences in the trajectories of academic motivational beliefs.

In line with our expectations, African American adolescents, particularly females, reported being more academically motivated than did European American adolescents, especially compared to European American males who reported a sharp decline in the importance they attached to academics as they neared the end of high school. African American adolescents also reported having higher occupational aspirations than did European American adolescents. Nevertheless, African American adolescents had lower GPAs than did European American adolescents, highlighting the persistence of the Black–White achievement gap, even among middle- and upper-class populations (Kao & Thompson, 2003; Magnuson & Waldfogel, 2008). Together, these findings suggest there is an attitude-achievement paradox in our sample, as the African American adolescents reported more positive attitudes toward education yet had lower academic achievement, despite having similar SES backgrounds to the European American adolescents (Mickelson, 1990).

As is true in many studies, SES also predicted developmental changes in academic functioning. Lower-SES adolescents were at risk of having lower mean intercept levels and more negative trajectories compared to higher-SES adolescents. In line with previous research (Kao & Tienda, 1998; Schoon et al., 2007), lower-SES adolescents reported lower educational and occupational aspirations, educational expectations, and self-concepts of academic skills. Lower-SES adolescents had a lower average GPA than did higher-SES adolescents at age 14, and they also experienced a greater linear decrease in their GPA across the school years. Furthermore, their perceptions of academic importance had a greater decline across the school years compared to higher-SES adolescents. These findings present a consistent picture of greater disengagement from education among lower-SES than higher-SES adolescents.

For parents' marital status, there was only one statistically significant difference. Adolescents of intact, never-divorced parents had a higher GPA than did adolescents of other family types. In comparison to SES, there were also fewer significant effects of parents' marital status highlighting the fact that family configuration has little impact on educational outcomes once its association with SES is taken into account.

Overall, the majority of the variation in academic functioning was attributable to differences between individuals rather than between groups or ages. Of the systematic group differences, between 4% (positive school identification) and 30% (GPA) was due to age. The demographic variables explained between 2% and 31% of the variance in the intercepts (see Table 12), with the greatest variance explained in educational expectations (22%) and GPA (31%) and up to 40% of the variance in the linear slope, with the greatest variance explained for GPA (40%).

VII: PROBLEM BEHAVIORS

Leslie Morrison Gutman, Stephen C. Peck, Oksana Malanchuk,
Arnold J. Sameroff, and Jacquelynne S. Eccles

This article is part of the issue "Moving Through Adolescence: Developmental Trajectories of African American and European American Youth" Gutman, Peck, Malanchuk, Sameroff, and Eccles (Issue Authors). For a full listing of articles in this issue, see: http://onlinelibrary.wiley.com/doi/10.1111/mono.v82.4/issuetoc.

Here we report our findings for school problems, delinquent behaviors, cigarette use, alcohol use, and marijuana use. Results are shown in Tables 13 and 14 and Figure 4.

SCHOOL PROBLEMS

Our measure focuses on breaking school rules and getting punished for these infractions. There was a significant positive linear slope coupled with a negative quadratic slope that did not vary by SES, gender, race/ethnicity, the gender by race/ethnicity interaction, or parents' marital status (see Table 13). On average, these adolescents reported slightly increasing levels of school problems from 12 to 16 years, which then stabilized from 16 to 17 years and decreased somewhat from 17 to 18 years (see Figure 4).

At age 14, males reported more school problems than did females. There were no significant differences in school problems according to SES, race/ethnicity, the race/ethnicity interaction, or parents' marital status. For all youth, the average reports of school problems such as cheating, skipping

Corresponding author: Leslie Morrison Gutman, Department of Clinical, Educational and Health Psychology, University College London, 1-19 Torrington Place, London WC1E 7HB, email: l.gutman@ucl.ac.uk

TABLE 13

GROWTH MODELS FOR PROBLEM BEHAVIORS

	School Problems	Cigarette Use	Delinquent Behaviors	Alcohol Use	Marijuana Use
For intercept					
Intercept	.40***	1.34***	1.65***	.46***	.26***
SES	-.01	-.04	-.02	-.03	-.03
Gender	-.12***	-.04	-.25***	-.10	-.20***
Ethnicity	-.02	.29***	-.00	.24***	.14**
GXE	-.09*	.14	-.13*	-.09	.01
Single	-.03	-.02	-.07	-.06	-.04
Intact	-.03	-.04	-.06	-.01	.00
Age	-.03	-.03	-.06	.02	-.04
Age²	.01	-.00	.01	.03	.00
For linear slope					
Intercept	.05***	.13***	-.02*	.08***	.15***
SES	-.00	-.01	.00	.01	-.01
Gender	-.01	.00	-.00	-.02	-.08***
Ethnicity	.02	.10***	.02*	.06*	.09***
GXE	-.02	.08*	.00	.03	.01
Single	-.01	-.02	-.00	.00	.02
Intact	.01	-.01	.01	.01	-.02
For quadratic slope					
Intercept	-.01***	.00	-.01***	.03***	.00
SES	.00	.00	-.00	.01	.00
Gender	.00	-.01*	.00	.00	.00
Ethnicity	-.00	.00	-.01*	.02	-.01*
GXE	.01	-.00	.00	-.01	-.00
Single	.01	.00	.01	.00	.00
Intact	.00	-.00	.00	-.01	.00

*** $p < .001$, ** $p < .01$, * $p < .05$.

TABLE 14

Residual Variance for Problem Behaviors

	Unconditional Means Model	ICC	Unconditional Growth Model	R^2 Level 1	With Level 2 Predictors	% Explained
School problems						
Level 1	1.842	.24	1.400	.24		
Intercept	.569***		.682***		.624***	9%
Linear slope			.030***		.030***	<1%
Cigarette use						
Level 1	.739	.28	.363	.55		
Intercept	.284***		.309***		.294***	5%
Linear slope			.042***		.037***	12%
Quad Slope			.002***		.002***	<1%
Delinquent behaviors						
Level 1	1.493	.34	1.233	.17		
Intercept	.762***		1.068***		.966***	10%
Linear slope			.030*		.030*	<1%
Quad slope			.001		.001	<1%
Alcohol use						
Level 1	.981	.19	.503	.49		
Intercept	.223***		.312***		.296***	5%
Linear slope			.025*		.024*	4%
Quad slope			.002***		.002***	<1%
Marijuana use						
Level 1	.843	.23	.328	.61		
Intercept	.248***		.262***		.246***	6%
Linear slope			.055***		.051***	7%
Quad slope			.003***		.003***	<1%

***$p < .001$, *$p < .05$.

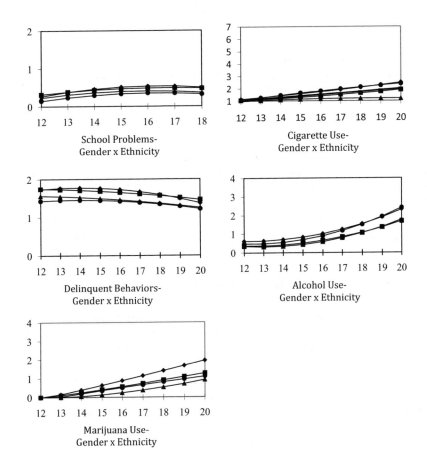

FIGURE 4.—Growth curves for problem behaviors.
Note. The *x*-axis represents age in years, whereas the *y*-axis represents the mean of the scale, controlling for the covariates. For the gender and race/ethnicity growth curves, European American females are represented by the circle, European American males are represented by the diamond, African American females are represented by the triangle, and African American males are represented by the square.

classes, or being sent to the principal's office were very low. Taking into account the covariates, on average, these adolescents reported frequencies no greater than .5, with "never" (0) to "1–9 times" (1). Essentially, this scale was dichotomous, with 50–70% of the students saying "never" and the remaining students saying "a few times."

CIGARETTE USE

There was a significant positive linear slope for cigarette use that was moderated by race/ethnicity (see Table 13). On average, these adolescents' reports of smoking cigarettes increased linearly from early to late adolescence (see Figure 4); this increase was greater for European American adolescents than for African American adolescents. The overall linear increase in smoking likely reflects the fact that cigarette use is legal for individuals over 18 and, thus, a subset of the adolescents is increasingly adopting an acceptable adult behavior as they get closer to 18. This finding supports research that has found smoking typically begins during adolescence, if it begins at all (Johnston et al., 2011).

There was one significant difference at the intercept. In line with other findings (Johnston et al., 2011), European American adolescents reported higher levels of smoking cigarettes than did African American adolescents. Interestingly, unlike some other recent reports, which showed slightly more males likely to smoke cigarettes compared to females (Johnston et al., 2011), we found no gender difference in these patterns.

In terms of mean levels, cigarette smoking increased from slightly more than "one a day" to close to "1–5 a day" from ages 12 to 20 (controlling for the covariates). For European American youth, smoking increased from about "one a day" to about "1–5 a day" by age 20. For African American youth, it remained slightly more than "one a day" throughout adolescence. So although smoking increased, it still remained at a relatively low level, especially among our African American youth. In fact, the majority of adolescents (i.e., 94% at Wave 1, 89% at Wave 3, 74% at Wave 4, and 70% at Wave 5) reported never smoking cigarettes.

DELINQUENT BEHAVIORS

There was a significant negative quadratic slope (see Table 13). On average and consistent with other studies (Hirschi & Gottfredson, 1983; Moffitt, 1993), these adolescents reported the highest frequency of engagement in delinquent behaviors at ages 12–14; these reports then declined from ages 15 to 20 years (see Figure 4). There were no significant differences in the slopes according to SES, gender, race/ethnicity, the gender by race/ethnicity interaction, or parent's marital status, where $p < .01$.

At age 14, males reported more frequent engagement in delinquent behaviors than did females. But in terms of absolute levels, the rates of delinquent behaviors were quite low. Given that the measure is a count of the extent to which adolescents participated in a range of delinquent behaviors that included stealing a motor vehicle, being in a gang fight, hitting someone, damaging property for fun, stealing, and lying to parents, the low absolute counts indicate that, on average, adolescents had only engaged in between 1 and 2 of these behaviors in the past 6 months to a year (controlling for the covariates). Such low frequencies are to be expected given the severity of many of these behaviors, with the exception of lying to one's parents.

ALCOHOL USE

Like smoking cigarettes, there was a significant linear increase for drinking alcohol and a significant positive quadratic slope resulting from accelerated alcohol use in late adolescence (see Table 13). On average, these adolescents' reports of alcohol use remained stable from 12 to 14 years and then increased from 14 to 20 years, with the sharpest increase from 17 to 20 years (see Figure 4), supporting findings that alcohol use peaks during early adulthood (Johnston et al., 2011) and that these increases reflect taking up of behaviors that are legal in adulthood.

At 14 years, European American adolescents reported drinking more alcohol than did African American adolescents. By and large, these findings are consistent with other studies and suggest very limited use of alcohol by African American youth, in particular (Johnston et al., 2011). Controlling for the covariates, on average, adolescents' reports of drinking alcohol ranged from .5 to 2, with 0 equal to "never" and 2 equal to "2–3 times per month."

MARIJUANA USE

There was a significant linear increase in smoking marijuana that was moderated by gender and race/ethnicity (see Table 13). For the average adolescent, smoking marijuana increased steadily from early to late adolescence. The increase was particularly marked for male and European American adolescents (see Figure 4).

There were also several significant mean-level differences at the intercept. At 14 years, male and European American adolescents reported more use of marijuana than did female and African American adolescents, in support of previous findings (Chen & Jacobson, 2012; Johnston et al., 2011). Consequently, European American males reported the highest levels, whereas African American females reported the lowest levels.

In terms of the mean levels, these adolescents' marijuana use increased from virtually "never" to slightly more than "rarely" (taking into account the covariates). Thus, although there were increases over adolescence, the rates remained quite low, with the exception of European males who reported, on average, using marijuana two to three times per month by age 20. It is important to note that the high percentage of missing data on this variable at Waves 1 and 3 may have resulted in underestimates of the usage of marijuana, particularly in early adolescence.

SUMMARY OF PROBLEM BEHAVIORS

In line with our expectations, developmental trajectories of problem behaviors increased during adolescence, with the exception of delinquent behaviors. Consistent with recent research on national rates of adolescent drug use (Johnston et al., 2011), adolescents' use of cigarettes, alcohol, and marijuana increased from early to late adolescence. Similar to the other measures of academic functioning, they also reported increasing school problems from early to middle adolescence that stabilized somewhat as they approached high school graduation. In contrast, they engaged in fewer delinquent behaviors of other kinds as they matured into late adolescence. Most importantly, these adolescents reported very low levels of engagement in any of the problem behaviors, and the developmental changes were quite small, suggesting that the emergence of problem behaviors during adolescence is neither inevitable nor typical and, if it occurs, it tends to happen at quite low frequencies.

There were significant mean-level differences in these negative behaviors according to gender. As predicted, 14-year-old males, on average, engaged in more problematic behaviors, both in and out of school, and were more likely to use marijuana and increase their use of marijuana throughout adolescence compared to females. These findings are supported by previous research showing that gender differences in the usage of drugs emerge in middle to late adolescence (Johnston et al., 2011), and males are more likely to engage in delinquent and problem behaviors compared to females (see Farrington, 2009, for a review). Contrary to other studies (Bray et al., 2001; Wallace et al., 2002; Webb et al., 2002), we found no gender differences in the slope of the trajectories of alcohol and cigarette use, only marijuana use.

There were also consistent R/E differences. In line with our predictions and other studies (Chen & Jacobson, 2012; Gutman et al., 2011), European Americans reported higher mean levels of cigarette, alcohol, and marijuana use, as well as a greater rate of increase in cigarette and marijuana use, than did African Americans from early to late adolescence. These findings further highlight the higher risk of European American adolescents for a range of negative health behaviors compared to African American adolescents.

112

Similar to contemporary findings (Johnston et al., 2011) documenting parallel trends in the use of cigarette, alcohol, and most other drugs; we found no significant differences according to SES and family composition. Although previous studies have shown that adolescents who are lower SES or reside in a single-parent household engage in more problematic behaviors than those residing in higher-SES households with two biological parents (e.g., Barrett & Turner, 2006; Fergusson, Horwood, & Lynskey, 1994), we found no evidence of these associations. Further, given previous findings on the high levels of drinking among college students, we also expected to find that SES would moderate the quadratic increase in drinking in late adolescence (Johnston et al., 2011). We found no evidence that SES and parents' marital status were associated with increases in drinking alcohol in our sample, however.

Overall, one-fifth to one-third of the variance in these indicators was attributed to differences between adolescents. Of the variation by group, approximately one-fifth to more than one-half of the variance was explained by age. Demographic variables accounted for between 5% and 10% of the intercept variance (see Table 14), with the greatest amount of variance accounted for in delinquent behaviors (10%) and up to 12% of the linear slope variance accounted for in cigarette use.

VIII: FAMILY CHARACTERISTICS

Leslie Morrison Gutman, Stephen C. Peck, Oksana Malanchuk,
Arnold J. Sameroff, and Jacquelynne S. Eccles

This article is part of the issue "Moving Through Adolescence: Developmental Trajectories of African American and European American Youth" Gutman, Peck, Malanchuk, Sameroff, and Eccles (Issue Authors). For a full listing of articles in this issue, see: http://onlinelibrary.wiley.com/doi/10.1111/mono.v82.4/issuetoc.

In this chapter, we report our findings for two aspects of the parent–dolescent relationship: (a) parental control, which includes attitudes and practices concerning adolescents' compliance with, and maintenance of, parental rules and regulations and (b) parental support and closeness, which includes positive aspects of the parent–adolescent relationship. Results are shown in Tables 15 and 16 and Figure 5.

PARENTAL CONTROL

Rather than merely conceptualizing parental control as high or low, consistent with other developmental psychologists (e.g., Barber, Stolz, Olsen, Collins, & Burchinal, 2005), we distinguish between two dimensions of parental control: psychological and behavioral control. On the one hand, parents' use of psychological control involves attempting to control adolescents' thoughts and feelings by psychological manipulation; Psychological control includes manipulating the love relationship between the

Corresponding author: Leslie Morrison Gutman, University College London 1-19 Torrington Place London WC1E 7HB. email: l.gutman@ucl.ac.uk
DOI: 10.1111/mono.12334

TABLE 15

GROWTH MODELS FOR FAMILY CHARACTERISTICS

	Intrusive Parenting	Negative Interactions	Strict Parenting	Family Social Support	Parent–Adolescent Communication	Positive Identification With Parents
For intercept						
Intercept	2.88***	1.83***	2.86***	4.26***	3.71***	3.18***
SES	-.01	.00	.01	.06	-.07	-.02
Gender	-.06	-.05	-.09	.15**	.49***	.02
Ethnicity	-.18**	-.02	-.15**	-.06	-.01	-.14***
GXE	-.21	-.05	-.08	.15	.30*	.20**
Single	-.05	.11*	-.22	.03	-.40*	-.02
Intact	-.08	-.03	-.11	.10	-.13	.03
Age	-.19	-.02	-.09	-.07	.03	.05
Age^2	.04	-.00	.04	.01	-.01	-.01
For linear slope						
Intercept	.03	-.04**	-.09***	-.05	-.01	-.08***
SES	.02	.01	-.01	.01	-.00	.01
Gender	.02	.01	-.01	-.00	.07*	.02*
Ethnicity	.07	.04***	.04	-.01	.07*	-.03*
GXE	.12	-.01	-.07	.00	.01	.06**
Single	.04	-.04*	-.08	-.01	-.07	.00
Intact	.07	.03*	.02	-.03	-.06*	-.00
For quadratic slope						
Intercept	-.02*	.01**	-.02	.02	-.01	.01**
SES	-.00	-.00	.01	-.00	.00	-.00
Gender	-.01	-.01	.00	.00	-.01	-.00
Ethnicity	-.02*	-.01**	.00	.00	-.01	.01
GXE	-.01	.00	.03	-.01	-.01	-.01
Single	.00	.01*	.02	-.00	.03	-.00
Intact	-.01	-.00	.01	.01	.02**	.00

*** $p < .001$, ** $p < .01$, * $p < .05$.

TABLE 16

RESIDUAL VARIANCE FOR FAMILY CHARACTERISTICS

	Unconditional Means Model	ICC	Unconditional Growth Model	R^2 Level 1	With Level 2	% Explained
Intrusive parenting		.33		.13		
Level 1	.596		.517			
Intercept	.293***		.216***		.212***	2%
Linear slope			.009***		.008***	11%
Negative interactions		.30		.23		
Level 1	.289		.223			
Intercept	.126***		.176***		.176***	<1%
Linear slope			.006***		.005***	17%
Quad slope			.000		.000	<1%
Strict parenting		.33		.16		
Level 1	.912		.768			
Intercept	.448***		.490***		.485***	1%
Linear slope			.018***		.018***	<1%
Family social support		.32		.06		
Level 1	.389		.364			
Intercept	.184***		.174***		.162***	7%
Linear slope			.003**		.003**	<1%
Parent–adolescent communication		.37		.14		
Level 1	1.208		1.034			
Intercept	.724***		.882***		.821***	7%
Linear slope			.017*		.015	12%
Quad slope			.000		.000	<1%
Positive identification		.39		.29		
Level 1	.214		.151			
Intercept	.137***		.174***		.162***	7%
Linear slope			.003**		.003**	<1%

***$p < .001$, **$p < .01$, *$p < .05$.

parent and adolescent and gaining compliance through the use of love withdrawal, guilt, and shame through criticism (Barber, 1996; Schaefer, 1965). The use of psychological control has been shown to undermine adolescents' psychological development at all ages (Barber, 1996, 2002; Gray & Steinberg, 1999).

On the other hand, parents' use of behavioral control, such as monitoring, rules, management, and supervision, involves the degree to which parents attempt to control their adolescent's behavior or the manner in which such control is exercised (e.g., rule setting, consequences)

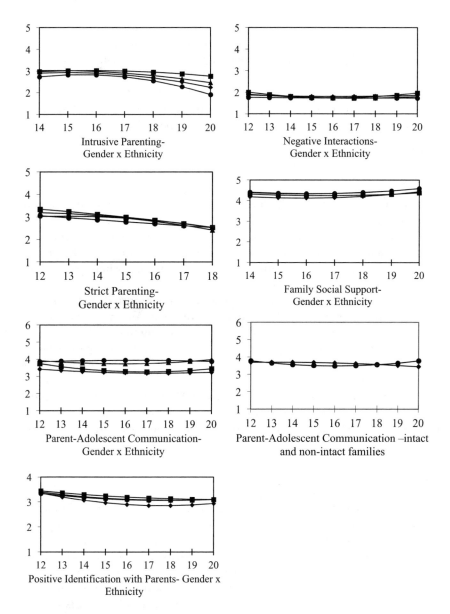

FIGURE 5.—Growth curves for family characteristics.

Note. The *x*-axis represents age in years, whereas the *y*-axis represents the mean of the scale, controlling for the covariates. For the gender and race/ethnicity growth curves, European American females are represented by the circle, European American males are represented by the diamond, African American females are represented by the triangle, and African American males are represented by the square. For the marital status growth curves, adolescents from intact families are represented by the circle, whereas adolescents from non-intact families are represented by the diamond.

(McElhaney, Allen, Stephenson, & Hare, 2009). Behavioral control allows parents to keep track of their adolescents' activities while granting them greater autonomy (Smetana et al., 2006). In general, use of behavioral control has positive associations with adolescent development during early adolescence (Eccles et al., 1993; Steinberg & Morris, 2001). We examined two measures of psychological control (i.e., intrusive parenting and negative interactions with parents) and one measure of behavioral control; namely, strict parenting.

Intrusive Parenting

Our measure of intrusive parenting focuses on adolescents' perceptions that their parent exerts high levels of control concerning how the adolescent should feel and act. On average, these adolescents reported a relatively stable and low trajectory of intrusive parenting (see Figure 5). Neither the linear nor quadratic slopes were significant, where $p < .01$ (see Table 15).

At age 14, these African American adolescents reported slightly higher levels of intrusive parenting than did these European American adolescents. This finding is consistent with previous studies showing that adolescents from African American families report higher levels of authoritarian parenting—a parenting style that focuses on control, obedience, and conformity among children—compared to adolescents from European American families (Dornbusch et al., 1987; Steinberg et al., 1991). In terms of the mean levels, however, the average adolescent reports of intrusive parenting were low, between (2) "rarely" and (3) "occasionally" on a 5-point scale, with 5 = "almost always."

Negative Interactions With Parents

This construct measures adolescents' perception that their parent engages in harsh, critical parenting. There was a significant negative linear slope and a significant positive quadratic slope (see Table 15). On average, these adolescents' reports of negative interactions with their parents declined from 12 to 15 years and then increased from 17 to 20 years. The linear and quadratic slopes were both moderated by race/ethnicity. As shown in Figure 5, African American adolescents experienced a decrease in negative interactions with their parents from 12 to 15 years followed by a slight but significant increase from 17 to 20 years. European American adolescents, however, experienced a fairly stable and very low trajectory.

At age 14, there were no significant differences in negative interactions with parents according to the demographic variables. In terms of mean levels, the rates were quite low across the entire age period. On average, the adolescents reported negative relations with their parents about 1–2 times in the previous month (controlling for the covariates). These rates were highest at ages 12 and 20 and were lowest for all groups around age 16. Contrary to the stereotype of adolescence as a time of increasing negative relationships in the family, these data suggest that adolescents themselves think that negative interactions with parents occur relatively infrequently and change very little in frequency over the adolescent years.

Strict Parenting

This measures parents' use of restricting privileges as a punishment for breaking rules. As we might expect during adolescence, there was a significant linear decrease in strict parenting from early to late adolescence (see Figure 5). Adjusting for the covariates, this decrease represented a drop from a frequency of a little more than "about half of the time" to a frequency of slightly more than "not too often."

At age 14, African American adolescents reported higher levels of strict parenting than did European American adolescents. There were no other significant demographic differences at the intercept. These findings thus suggest that, on average, most parents decrease their use of strict parenting strategies as their children move through adolescence.

CLOSENESS AND SUPPORT

We included several measures that are commonly used as indicators of family closeness and support; including family social support, parent–adolescent communication, and positive identification with parents (Laursen & Collins, 2009).

Family Social Support

On average, these adolescents reported stable perceptions of their family social support from early to late adolescence (see Figure 5). The linear and quadratic slopes were not significant (see Table 15) and did not differ by any of the demographic groups.

At age 14, females reported more family social support than did males. On average, taking into account the covariates, adolescents rated their parental social support halfway between 4 ("often") and 5 ("almost always"). This demonstrates that these adolescents, on the whole, had a stable perception of their parents as very positive and supportive throughout their adolescent years. These findings are consistent with the work of Smetana and others who have repeatedly demonstrated that adolescents maintain quite positive relationships with their family during their teen years (Smetana, 1988; Steinberg, 2001).

Parent–Adolescent Communication

There were no significant differences in the linear or quadratic slopes for adolescents' perceptions of their communication with their parents, with the exception of intact families (see Table 15). As shown in Figure 5, the average adolescent experienced a relatively stable and high trajectory of parent–adolescent communication from early to late adolescence. However, adolescents from intact, married families experienced a convex-shaped pattern, with a decrease in family communication from 12 to 15 years and then an increase from 17 to 20 years. In contrast, adolescents from nonintact–parent families experienced a slight decrease in family communication over the adolescent years.

At age 14, there was a significant difference according to gender: females reported more frequent communication with their parents than did males. This gender difference is consistent with other studies that have found greater communication between female adolescents and their parents than between male adolescents and their parents (Noller & Callan, 1990).

In terms of the mean levels, on average, these adolescents reported talking with their parents about their future plans and what was going on with their friends almost "once a week" (taking into account the covariates). Overall, these levels suggest that a substantial amount of parent–adolescent communication about these important issues goes on throughout this period. As shown later, these levels are about the same as the frequency of such communications with peers. Thus, consistent with the findings of Smetana and her colleagues (Smetana et al., 1996), communication with parents remains very important, as important as communication with peers, during adolescence.

Positive Identification With Parents

This construct measures how much adolescents respect and feel close to their parents. There was a significant negative linear slope, moderated by the interaction of gender by race/ethnicity, and a significant positive quadratic slope (see Table 15). On average, these adolescents reported a decline in positive identification with their parents from 12 to 16 years that stabilized from 16 to 20 years (see Figure 5). These results are consistent with other studies indicating that middle to older adolescents are much less likely to idealize their parents compared to younger adolescents and preteens (Beyers & Goossens, 1999; Levpušček, 2006). The significant moderating effect of

120

gender by race/ethnicity reflects the fact that European American males showed the steepest decline that leveled off between ages 17 and 20. African American males also showed a steady decline from ages 12 to 20. In contrast, the African American and European American females showed the shallowest decline over time. In line with our hypothesis, these findings support research that females have closer relationships with their parents than do males from middle to late adolescence (De Goede et al., 2009; Kim et al., 2015), although our results show that this gender difference may exist for European American adolescents only.

At 14 years, there was a significant gender by race/ethnicity interaction with African American males reporting the highest levels of positive identification with their parents and European American males reporting the lowest levels. African American and European American females reported similar levels of identifying with their parents.

In terms of mean levels, controlling for the covariates, on average these adolescents reported identifying with their parents between (3) "some of the time" and (4) "often." Although there was a significant decline across time, it was quite small (less than .5 on a 5-point scale). Adolescents' positive identification with their parents remained on the positive side of the midpoint of the scale for all four groups throughout adolescence.

SUMMARY OF FAMILY RELATIONSHIPS

Contrary to our predictions based on previous research (Conger & Ge, 1999; Larson et al. 1996; Steinberg, 1988; Wang et al., 2011), adolescents' perceptions of their relationship with their parents changed relatively little and remained quite positive over their adolescent years. This was true for the extent to which they talked with their parents about important issues and their perceptions of their parents' support. The extent to which adolescents positively identified with their parents showed a somewhat different pattern: adolescents reported decreases in identification with their parents from early to middle adolescence that then stabilized in later adolescence. This is in line with our expectations based on previous studies suggesting that positive relationships with parents decline from early to middle adolescence and then increase or stabilize from middle to late adolescence (Shanahan et al., 2007). For positive identification with parents, this may reflect the process of separation when adolescents begin to redefine themselves and their parents as autonomous individuals in a relationship (Meeus et al., 2005). Together, our findings suggest that, for most adolescents, positive emotional aspects of family relationships do not undergo severe transformations during adolescence. These results are consistent with studies showing positive, well-

121

functioning relationships, with most parents and adolescents reporting frequent supportive interactions and a low incidence of communication difficulties across the adolescent years (see Laursen & Collins, 2009; Steinberg, 2001, for reviews).

In contrast, and as predicted from previous research (De Goede et al., 2009; Rubin et al., 2011), aspects of parental control *did* change across adolescence. Parents gave their adolescents more autonomy, in the form of less strict parenting, as their child approached middle and late adolescence. Adolescents also reported a decrease in their perceptions of negative interactions with their parents from early to middle adolescence, with a slight increase during late adolescence. This latter finding contradicts our own predictions, but makes sense developmentally, as adolescents are in the process of forming their own identities and may spend more time away from home and assert themselves more with their parents, particularly in late adolescence. As adolescents mature, they become more self-assertive and less willing to accept parental authority (Fuligni, 1998). As a result, they may begin to view discipline techniques such as power assertion more negatively (Paikoff, Collins, & Laursen, 1988) and become less accepting of parental directives than younger teens (Perkins & Turiel, 2007). However, these shifts were quite small, and the overwhelming pattern was reflective of continually strong and very positive relationships between these teens and their parents.

The race/ethnicity and gender differences in these patterns were generally consistent with our expectations. In line with other findings (e.g., McAdoo, 1993; Smetana et al., 2004), African American adolescents reported having less autonomy from, but a closer relationship with, their parents than did European American adolescents. The African American youth reported that their parents engaged in more intrusive parenting than did the European American youth. At the same time, African American adolescents reported higher levels of positive identification with their parents and a greater linear decline in negative interactions with their parents than did European American adolescents. These two sets of findings suggest that R/E differences are not so much about authoritarianism, per se, as they are about greater parental involvement in their adolescents' lives—what one might call cultural differences in the developmental timing associated with the shift from parental control to adolescent autonomy. Given the racial context in the United States at this time, it is understandable that African American parents might maintain stricter control of their teens.

As hypothesized, females reported higher mean levels in their relationships with parents, including more support and communication, than did males. Other research has also found gender differences in the slopes of parental closeness and support (De Goede et al., 2009; Kim et al. 2015). Our findings also show a gender by race/ethnicity interaction in the intercept and slope of positive identification with parents. European American males had both the lowest mean level and the steepest decline in their reported closeness with their parents of all four groups, suggesting that they may be at risk of having especially poor relationships with their parents.

Contrary to the emphasis that has been placed on SES and parents' marital status in many studies on human development, we found no evidence of such differences in our set of indicators. For parents' marital status, adolescents from intact, married families experienced an increase in communication with their parents from 17 to 20 years, whereas adolescents from nonintact families experienced a decrease throughout adolescence. But, again, this difference was quite small.

Overall, around one-third of the variance in these measures existed between adolescents. Between 6% (family social supports) and 29% (positive identification with parents) of the group variance was explained by age. The demographic variables accounted for only a small percentage of the variance in the intercept, up to 7% for family social support, parent–adolescent communication, and positive identification with parents (see Table 16) and up to 17% of the variance in the slopes, with the greatest variance explained for negative interactions with parents (17%) and parent–adolescent communication (12%). There were several measures where little or no group-level variation was explained in either the intercept or slopes, such as strict parenting, suggesting that factors other than age or social demographics are important here.

IX: PEER CHARACTERISTICS

Leslie Morrison Gutman, Stephen C. Peck, Oksana Malanchuk,
Arnold J. Sameroff, and Jacquelynne S. Eccles

This article is part of the issue "Moving Through Adolescence: Developmental Trajectories of African American and European American Youth" Gutman, Peck, Malanchuk, Sameroff, and Eccles (Issue Authors). For a full listing of articles in this issue, see: http://onlinelibrary.wiley.com/doi/10.1111/mono.v82.4/issuetoc.

In this chapter, we summarize our findings for both positive aspects of peer relationships (peer communication, peer support, and positive friends) and negative aspects of peer relationships (negative friends and peer drug norms). These different measures were chosen, in part, to parallel our parent measures. For example, we have parent and peer measures of support and communication as well as assessments of positive and negative aspects of both types of relationships. This allowed us to assess the nature of changes in our adolescents' relationships with their parents versus their peers. Although there is great deal of interest in the changes in these two social contexts, very few studies have looked at changes over time in both contexts. This is quite odd given the amount of rhetoric linking these two systems and suggesting that adolescence is largely about the conjoint declines in connections with one's parents and increases in one's connections with one's peers. One of our main goals was to help to fill this void. Our results are shown in Tables 17 and 18 and Figure 6.

Corresponding author: Leslie Morrison Gutman, Department of Clinical, Educational and Health Psychology, University College London, 1-19 Torrington Place, London WC1E 7HB, email: l.gutman@ucl.ac.uk

TABLE 17

GROWTH MODELS FOR PEER CHARACTERISTICS

	Peer Communication	Peer Support	Positive Peers	Negative Peers	Peer Drug Norms
For intercept					
Intercept	3.71***	2.78***	3.36***	1.48***	1.98***
SES	.13*	.00	.08***	-.00	.04
Gender	.97***	.33***	.31***	-.13**	-.10
Ethnicity	-.08	.03	-.07**	-.04	.12
GXE	.43*	.22*	-.04	-.09	-.20
Single	.22	-.19*	.00	-.04	-.06
Intact	-.06	.04	.05	-.01	-.12
Age	.02	-.04	-.03	-.16	-.16
Age²	-.01	.02	.00	.03*	.03
For linear slope					
Intercept	.27***	-.04*	-.03*	.15***	.31***
SES	-.02	.00	.05***	-.01	.01
Gender	-.00	-.06**	.02	-.06***	-.02
Ethnicity	.10	-.03	.00	-.01	.07**
GXE	-.12	-.08	-.04	.01	-.09**
Single	-.32*	-.06	.05	.02	.03
Intact	-.04	.01	.00	.02	-.01
For quadratic slope					
Intercept	-.04***	.04***	-.01**	-.04***	-.03***
SES	.00	.00	-.01*	-.00	-.00
Gender	-.00	.03*	-.01	-.00	-.02
Ethnicity	-.03*	.03*	-.00	.00	-.02
GXE	.03	-.01	.01	.01	.05**
Single	.04	.01	-.02	.01	.01
Intact	.01	.00	.01	-.00	.01

*** $p < .001$, ** $p < .01$, * $p < .05$.

125

TABLE 18

RESIDUAL VARIANCE FOR PEER CHARACTERISTICS

	Unconditional Means Model	ICC	Unconditional Growth Model	R^2 Level 1	With Level 2 Predictors	% Explained
Peer communication						
Level 1	1.060	.38	.855	.19		
Intercept	.652***		.969***		.763***	21%
Linear Slope			.029***		.029***	<1%
Peer support						
Level 1	.585	.25	.540	.08		
Intercept	.199***		.220***		.181	18%
Linear slope			.008**		.008**	<1%
Positive peers						
Level 1	.452	.29	.346	.23		
Intercept	.187***		.225***		.194***	14%
Linear slope			.005*		.004*	20%
Quad slope			.000		.000	<1%
Negative peers						
Level 1	.271	.13	.173	.36		
Intercept	.039***		.073***		.069***	5%
Linear slope			.006***		.006***	<1%
Peer drug norms						
Level 1	1.044	.08	.658	.37		
Intercept	.091***		.213***		.207***	3%
Linear slope			.010***		.010***	<1%

*** $p<.001$, ** $p<.01$, * $p<.05$.

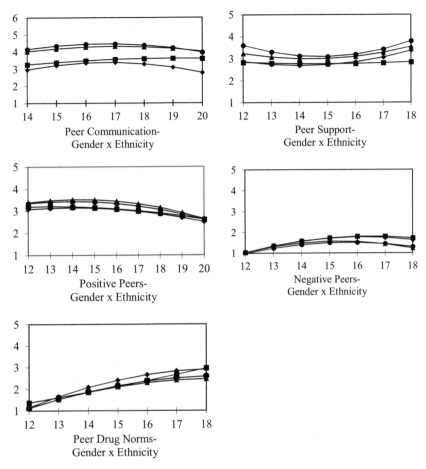

Figure 6.—Growth curves for peer characteristics.
Note. The *x*-axis represents age in years, whereas the *y*-axis represents the mean of the scale, controlling for the covariates. For the gender and race/ethnicity growth curves, European American females are represented by the circle, European American males are represented by the diamond, African American females are represented by the triangle, and African American males are represented by the square.

PEER COMMUNICATION

As with their communication with their parents, we asked the adolescents how often they talked with their friends about important matters using exactly the same questions. Unlike their communication with their parents, which remained stable during adolescence, there was a significant positive linear slope and a significant negative quadratic slope for peer communication

127

(see Table 17). On average, these adolescents' communication with their peers increased from 14 to 16 years, remained stable from 16 to 18 years, and then decreased from 18 to 20 years (see Figure 6). There were no significant differences in either of the slopes according to gender, race/ethnicity, the gender by race/ethnicity interaction, SES, or parents' marital status.

At age 14 (the intercept), females reported more frequent conversations with their peers than did males. These gender differences are consistent with other studies of peer communication (Belle, 1989; Keijsers & Poulin, 2013; McNelles & Connolly, 1999). In terms of actual frequencies, the average adolescent talked with friends about important issues between a few times per week to once per week (controlling for the covariates). This is the same number of times they talked with their parents about these issues. Thus, although we found an increase in the frequency of these types of communication with one's friends over adolescence, this did not result from a concomitant decline in the frequency of such communications with one's parents. Instead, peers became an additional source of communication.

PEER SUPPORT

Again, we tried to assess social support in a similar manner across parents and friends to make comparisons more meaningful, focusing on emotional support. There was a significant positive quadratic trend for adolescents' perceptions of peer support (see Table 17). Furthermore, the linear trend was significantly moderated by gender. On average, these adolescents' ratings of support from their peers declined from 12 to 14 years and then increased from 15 to 18 years (see Figure 6). This pattern was shown for females who reported higher levels of perceived peer support at age 18 than at age 12. In contrast, on average, males' perceptions of peer support were fairly stable from 12 to 15 years, with an increase from 16 to 18 years.

At 14 years, female adolescents reported having more peer support than did male adolescents. None of the other demographic variables were significant, where $p < .01$, at the intercept. In terms of the mean levels, adolescents at age 14 felt that they received good support "about half the time" (controlling for the covariates) from their peers. This support increased to levels between "about half the time" to "fairly often" by age 18. Interestingly, their perceptions of peer support were lower at all ages than these same adolescents reported for receiving support from their parents. So again, increasing peer connections were not being made at the expense of parental connections.

PREVALENCE OF POSITIVE AND NEGATIVE PEERS

Increasingly, discussions about peer influences during adolescence include mentions of the need to describe the exact nature of the adolescents' group of friends (Rose & Rudolph, 2006). What adolescents do with and learn from their friends and peers will depend on what these friends and peers are doing as well as what they value. Thus, the costs and benefits of peer influence depend on the nature of one's friends and peers. Accordingly, we asked our participants to rate the proportion of their friends who exhibited a wide set of both positive and negative behaviors, goals, and values. We then factored these items and developed two comprehensive scales—one for positive behaviors, goals, and values and one for negative behaviors, goals, and values. We did not collect data on the negative peer characteristics at age 20 because the specific items were no longer age appropriate.

Positive Peers

There were significant negative linear and quadratic trends for reports of the prevalence of positive peers among one's friends (see Table 17). On average, these adolescents' reports of the proportion of their friends who exhibited positive behaviors and values remained stable from 12 to 14 years and then decreased from age 14 onward, with a steep decline in late adolescence (see Figure 6). The linear slope was moderated by family SES. Lower-SES adolescents experienced a steady decrease in prevalence of positive peers from 12 to 20 years, whereas higher-SES adolescents experienced a slight increase over time. Thus, the decline in proportion of positive peers among one's friends is only true for adolescents living in low-SES households. This likely reflects the decrease in the proportion of their friends expecting to go to college and being academically engaged.

At age 14, higher-SES, African American, and female adolescents reported having a higher proportion of positive friends than did lower-SES, European American, and male adolescents. In terms of the mean levels, taking into account the covariates, these adolescents began with a little more than half of their friends being engaged with academics and/or other positive social activities (3 = "half of my friends"). By age 20, adolescents reported that between "a few" to "half" of their friends were academically engaged and prosocial. These results are consistent with the declines we noted earlier in the extent to which the youth themselves are academically engaged. However, although these proportions declined over the adolescent years, the majority of youth maintained a relatively high percentage (close to 50% on average) of prosocial, academically oriented friends.

Negative Peers

The prevalence of negative peers was assessed by asking about the proportion of one's friends who engaged in various risky or problem behaviors, including smoking cigarettes and drinking alcohol. There was a significant positive linear slope and a significant negative quadratic slope across time, with the linear trend significantly more marked for males than for females (see Table 17). The negative quadratic slope reflected a decrease in the proportion of one's friends who engage in these negative behaviors in late adolescence. On average, adolescents' proportion of risky friends increased from 12 to 15 years then decreased from 16 to 18 years (see Figure 6). These results are consistent with our findings showing an increase followed by a decrease in problem behaviors in the middle adolescent years.

At the intercept (age 14), males reported a higher percentage of negative peers than did females. In terms of the means, on average, these 14 year olds reported having a very small percentage of friends who engaged in risky behavior (i.e., less than 1%), controlling for the covariates. By age 18, the proportion of risky friends had increased to somewhat less than 25%.

PEER DRUG NORMS

We asked our participants to rate how "cool" or "uncool" their friends would think they were if they used either alcohol or illegal drugs such as marijuana. We found both a significant positive linear slope and a significant negative quadratic slope for perceived peer norms regarding alcohol and drug use (see Table 17). On average, these adolescents reported that peer norms for alcohol and drug use increased dramatically over time, but this increase slowed down in late adolescence (see Figure 6). The significant gender by race/ethnicity interactions for both the linear and quadratic trends were due to the fact that, unlike the other three groups, these trends did not level off for the African American males.

At the intercept, there were no significant differences according to gender, race/ethnicity, the gender by race/ethnicity interaction, SES, or parents' marital status. In terms of actual ratings, taking into account the covariates, on average, these adolescents began believing that their peers would think they were very uncool if they used drugs. By age 18, they were more likely to believe that their friends had a neutral, although still somewhat negative, attitude toward drug use. This pattern coincides with the average increase in drug use from early to late adolescence seen in our sample.

SUMMARY OF PEER CHARACTERISTICS

As predicted, most of the peer characteristics, with the exception of peer support, peaked during early to middle adolescence and then lessened in later adolescence. These findings support assertions that peers play an especially important role during this period of adolescence (Eccles & Roeser, 2011; Furman & Buhrmester, 1992; Hartup, 1996; Steinberg & Morris, 2001). Although perceived peer support increased in late adolescence, trajectories of the other peer characteristics either declined or stabilized as adolescents matured. This suggests that the influence of peers became less important, and their relationships were more stable yet supportive, as they approached late adolescence.

There were significant differences associated with gender, reflecting variation in the meaning and importance of peer relationships. As expected based on previous research (see Rose & Rudolph, 2006, for a review), young females generally experienced more positive, supportive friendships than did their male peers. For example, females reported more peer communication, prosocial and academically engaged friends, and supportive friendships than did males. Male adolescents, on the other hand, reported more friends who were engaged in risky or problematic behaviors than did their female counterparts. These findings highlight that females' friendships are more oriented toward relationship intimacy, whereas males' friendships are more focused on agency, power, and excitement (Rose, 2002). Although we did not expect gender differences in the trajectories of peer characteristics, we found that males reported a greater increase in having negative peers than did females, suggesting that males are at a heightened risk for deviant peer affiliation, particularly during middle to late adolescence. Females, on the other hand, reported a greater decrease in peer support over their teenage years compared to males. This latter finding may reflect females' lessening reliance on their friends for support as they grow older, perhaps reflecting a shift to romantic partners or greater independence as they mature.

We did not make any predictions regarding R/E differences, due to lack of evidence, but found some differences according to race/ethnicity. At age 14, African American adolescents reported having more positive peers than did European American adolescents. European American males, furthermore, experienced a greater linear increase in having friends who endorsed the use of drugs compared to the other three groups, following a similar pattern to their actual reported marijuana use. At age 17, however, the extent to which European American males reported their friends thought drugs were "cool" decreased; whereas, at the same time, friends' endorsement of drugs increased sharply for African American males. This finding highlights that the timing of risk regarding the negative influence of friends using drugs may differ for European American versus African American males.

There were few significant differences according to SES, with the exception of having positive peers. Our higher-SES adolescents generally reported having more positive peer relationships than did our lower-SES adolescents. Lower-SES adolescents reported lower levels of, and a greater decline in, the proportion of prosocial and academically engaged friends than did higher-SES adolescents. There were no significant differences, where $p < .01$, associated with parents' marital status.

Overall, most of the variance in these measures was attributed to within-person differences, with between 8% (peer drug norms) and 38% (peer communication) of the variance explained by between-person differences (see Table 18). Of the within-person variation, between 8% and 37% was accounted for by age, with the most variance explained in peer drug norms (37%) and negative peers (36%). Demographic differences accounted for up to 21% of the variance in the intercept, with the greatest percentage of variance being explained for peer communication (21%) and peer support (18%). For the linear slope, the demographic differences accounted for 20% of the variance for positive peers.

X: INTEGRATIVE SUMMARY

Leslie Morrison Gutman, Stephen C. Peck, Oksana Malanchuk,
Arnold J. Sameroff, and Jacquelynne S. Eccles

This article is part of the issue "Moving Through Adolescence: Developmental Trajectories of African American and European American Youth" Gutman, Peck, Malanchuk, Sameroff, and Eccles (Issue Authors). For a full listing of articles in this issue, see: http://onlinelibrary.wiley.com/doi/10.1111/mono.v82.4/issuetoc.

In this monograph, we have examined the development of a large number of adolescents from diverse socioeconomic and racial/ethnic backgrounds. Overall, these young Americans showed much stronger evidence of positive than problematic development, even at their most vulnerable times. Absolute levels of their engagement in healthy behaviors, supportive relationships with parents and friends, and positive self-perceptions and psychological well-being were much higher than their angry and depressive feelings, engagement in risky behaviors, and negative relationships with parents and peers.

We did not find much evidence that adolescence is a time of heightened risk. Rather, most of these adolescents experienced relatively stable and developmentally healthy trajectories across a wide range of beliefs, behaviors, emotional functioning, and relationships, with slight increases or decreases at different points in development that varied across domains. That said, however, some developmental periods were riskier than others, depending on the outcome assessed as well as the gender and race/ethnicity of the adolescent. An examination of the entirety of adolescence (ages 12–20) allows us to pinpoint when, on average, such changes occurred.

Corresponding author: Leslie Morrison Gutman, Department of Clinical, Educational and Health Psychology University College London 1-19 Torrington Place London WC1E 7HB. email: l.gutman@ucl.ac.uk

DOI: 10.1111/mono.12336

DEVELOPMENTAL CHANGES DURING ADOLESCENCE

Within risk-protection and positive youth development frameworks, our findings highlight the optimal timing to reduce risk and promote positive youth development among different groups of adolescents in multiple spheres of development. During early adolescence, youth often experience multiple, simultaneous changes associated with puberty, the transition from elementary to middle school, and their relationships with parents and friends. As other researchers have noted (cf. Roeser, Eccles, & Sameroff, 2000), early adolescence is a critical time for changes in both positive and negative functioning. This was highlighted in our findings where changes were evident in psychological well-being, peer relationships, and positive identification with parents—suggesting that this is an optimal period for reducing risk and boosting protection in these areas.

For many adolescents, the teenage years are a vulnerable period for engaging in problem behaviors, experimenting with various substances, and associating with negative friends. Engaging in problem behaviors and having negative friends both peaked in middle to late adolescence, suggesting that this is an important time to prevent delinquency. Later adolescence, however, was a time of risk for substance use and abuse. Both using various substances and having friends who endorsed drug use increased steadily across adolescence and peaked in late adolescence, highlighting the importance of continued preventive efforts related to substance use through secondary school and into the later adolescent years.

As we expected from previous studies (De Fraine et al. 2007; Eccles et al., 1993; Gniewosz et al., 2012; Roeser & Eccles, 1998; Wang & Dishion, 2012; Wang & Eccles, 2012), academic self-beliefs and school motivation declined somewhat across the school years. However, these adolescents maintained high aspirations and expectations for their future educational and occupational prospects throughout adolescence. This suggests that supporting school-related achievement, motivation, and identification is more critical than a focus on increasing students' aspirations during the junior and high school years. Lastly, R/E identity and perceptions of discrimination remained relatively stable throughout adolescence, indicating that prevention in this area should most likely target specific groups of adolescents who show vulnerability in these domains.

GENDER AND R/E DIFFERENCES IN ADOLESCENT TRAJECTORIES

Developmental trajectories showed some differences according to gender and race/ethnicity, but these variations depended on the domain being examined. For psychological well-being and academic outcomes, the main gender and R/E differences were found for the mean levels at the intercept rather than in the slopes of the developmental trajectories. However, there were two exceptions: males experienced a sharper decline in their grades during high school compared to their female peers and females experienced an increase while males experienced a slight decrease in educational aspirations. As other studies have found (Gutman & Schoon, 2012; Huang, 2012; Mello, 2008; Schoon et al., 2007; Voyer & Voyer, 2014), females reported higher levels of educational aspirations and expectations and better grades than did males. In line with previous research (Graber & Sontag, 2004), however, females also reported higher levels of the psychological characteristics linked to internalizing problems than did males, whereas males reported higher expectations of negative outcomes than did females.

As other research has noted (Johnson et al., 2001), the African American adolescents reported higher levels of occupational aspirations and attached more importance to school subjects than did the European American adolescents. However, the African American adolescents also reported lower GPAs than did the European American adolescents, despite the fact that they were as likely as their European American peers to come from middle to high-SES families, highlighting the Black–White achievement gap (Kao & Thompson, 2003; Magnuson & Waldfogel, 2008). African American adolescents also reported higher levels of anger than European American adolescents. For the most part, however, both the gender and R/E differences were quite small, suggesting that adolescents experience quite similar developmental patterns in these two domains regardless of their gender or race/ethnicity.

For R/E identity, the most obvious feature of these results was the extent to which the R/E groups adhered to their own social identities and friendship networks. R/E discrimination also appeared to play a salient role in the lives of African American adolescents. Overall, we found very few changes in these constructs during adolescence, supporting some research on R/E identity (Seaton et al., 2009) but contrasting with other research on experiences of R/E discrimination (Greene et al., 2006; Seaton et al., 2009). There were, however, some changes in late adolescence for both African American and European American adolescents that were somewhat contradictory to each other. African American adolescents had increasing concerns about R/E discrimination yet reported a slight increase in having more cross R/E friendships. European Americans reported that their parents had fewer worries about discrimination yet were less likely to have cross R/E friendships. These findings may reflect their transition into college or employment in late adolescence when both groups may confront more heterogeneous R/E environments in contrast to their high schools where most students were African American. Such apparent differences, however, need to be viewed

135

cautiously given that the meaning of these measures may have been different for African American versus European American adolescents.

Patterns of change in their engagement in problem behaviors and association with negative peers also showed variation according to gender and race/ethnicity. In support of previous research (Bray et al., 2001; Chen & Jacobson, 2012; Gutman et al., 2011; Wallace et al., 2002; Webb et al., 2002), these European American and male adolescents were at higher risk of engaging in problem behaviors compared to these African American and female adolescents. European American adolescents not only reported higher rates of cigarette, alcohol, and marijuana use, they also reported faster rates of increase in cigarette and marijuana use compared to African American adolescents. Males further reported higher mean levels regarding their marijuana use, engagement in problems behaviors both in and out of school, and association with negative peers as well as faster rates of increase in using marijuana and having negative peers compared to females. These findings highlight the heightened risk of European American adolescents, particularly males, for engagement in problematic behaviors.

Gender and R/E differences were also evident in the mean levels and/or slopes of interpersonal relationships. Consistent with the existing literature (e.g., Rose & Rudolph, 2006; Way & Green, 2006), female adolescents reported higher levels of positive relationships with their parents and peers than did male adolescents. In terms of R/E differences, African American adolescents reported lower levels of autonomy from, as well as more positive relationships with, their parents than did European American adolescents. As others have suggested, stronger parental control is normative in African American families and thus may be viewed as protective rather than confining (Smetana et al., 2004). These African American adolescents also reported having more prosocial and academically engaged peers during early adolescence than did these European American adolescents. Given that these African American adolescents were more academically motivated than were their European American counterparts, it is not surprising that their friends were more academically engaged as well.

In terms of the intersection between gender and race/ethnicity, we found few significant interactions at the $p < .01$ level. Nevertheless, the significant interactions suggest that certain risks are specific to the intersectionality of the gender and race/ethnicity of the adolescent. European American females, for example, had the highest incidence of eating disorders and the lowest self-esteem of the four groups. Of the four groups, European American males reported the least positive relationship with their parents with the steepest decline and the greatest decrease in academic importance as they neared high school graduation. European American males also had the greatest linear increase in having friends who thought using drugs was "cool" from early to middle adolescence, an increase that tapered off in late adolescence. In contrast, African American males had the sharpest increase in the extent to which their friends felt drug use was "cool" in late adolescence. These results suggest that the timing of risk for the negative influence of peer drug norms varies for European American versus African American males.

PARENTS' MARITAL STATUS AND SES DIFFERENCES IN ADOLESCENT TRAJECTORIES

There were few significant differences in adolescent growth trajectories associated with parents' marital status or SES. There was only two significant findings associated with parents' marital status: adolescents with always married parents had higher GPAs and reported a slight increase in parent–adolescent communication as they approached young adulthood compared to adolescents with single or divorced parents. Although the lack of associations may be due to our examination of family structure at only a single point time, only a very small percentage of our sample experienced a change in marital status over the years of the study.

In contrast, the effects of SES were more pervasive in some domains. Lower-SES adolescents were at greater risk of worse mental health, lower academic outcomes, and less positive peer relationships than were higher-SES adolescents. Furthermore, lower-SES youth experienced a greater decline in positive peers, GPA, and academic motivation than did higher-SES youth. However, the mean levels and growth trajectories of problem behaviors and family characteristics were similar regardless of SES. There was also evidence that some of the significant SES differences, such as those associated with psychological well-being, lessen in early adulthood. However, it is important to note that SES differences may be larger in more recent samples of racially/ethnically diverse adolescents, given that wealth inequality has widened along R/E lines since the end of the Great Recession (Kochhar & Fry, 2014).

LIMITATIONS

A number of limitations need to be noted in the context of our findings. First, we based our investigation on adolescents' reports; therefore, we do not capture perceptions of adolescent development from other viewpoints, such as that of parents. However, the purpose of the study was to examine trajectories of adolescents' perceptions of their intra-individual and interpersonal worlds. Nevertheless, it is important to note that agreement between parents' and adolescents' views of their relationship may be low to moderate and may increasingly diverge with age (Smetana, 1988, 1989).

Second, our measures were somewhat limited due to the constraint on the growth curve trajectories that requires exactly the same measures across waves. The relatively small number of items in each scale likely contributed to lower reliabilities for a few of our measures at different waves. We did add items for some of the scales as newer instruments became available. However, HLM analyses work best when the same scales are used at each wave in order to increase the comparability of measurement across waves.

Third, there is a possibility that some of the words in the questions and the numbers on the response scales may mean something different to African American versus European American, male versus female, and younger versus older adolescents. As described in Chapter III, we examined the pattern of correlations among measures reported in this study, revealing substantial support for the assumption that our measures have similar meanings across groups and time, with the exception of the R/E discrimination measures. Thus, consistent with the idea that abstract concepts can have the same meaning even if the meaning of some items varies across groups and time (Nesselroade et al., 2007), we assumed that the meaning of the scores on the majority of scales in this study were sufficiently similar to warrant meaningful comparisons of growth parameters across our four race/ethnicity and gender groups. Apparent violations of this assumption are a limitation of the current study, and future research will be needed to better understand the implications of such variations across groups and time during adolescence.

Fourth, we examined development as a function of chronological age. As other researchers have noted (Collins, 2006; Lerner, Schwartz, & Phelps, 2009), there are other time metrics that might prove potentially useful (e.g., development as a function of pubertal status or specific life changes). This may be particularly relevant where examining within-level differences among R/E groups because there are variations in the timing of pubertal development between European American and African American adolescents. However, the examination of age trajectories represents a first step in understanding adolescent development in this sample, and other approaches should follow in future reports.

Fifth, SES and parents' marital status were only measured at a single time point; therefore, there may have been changes in SES and family structure whose consequences were not captured by our analyses. In fact, however, very few of the adolescents in our sample experienced such changes over the course of this study. For example, the correlation between Wave 1 and Wave 4 SES is 0.85, and 87% of the parents who were married at Wave 1 were still married at Wave 4, with European American males' families showing the most stability at 94%. Furthermore, although we included SES and marital st0atus in all of our analyses, it also important to keep in mind that our status is relatively more affluent than the typical United States population. Therefore, it is possible that this sociodemographic characteristic may account, at least in part, for the relative lack of risky trajectories evidenced by MADICS participants during adolescence. Therefore, it is important to assess whether more tumultuous adolescent trajectories are present for adolescents living in less privileged circumstances.

Sixth, our analysis was restricted to African American and European American youth, neglecting Latinos, Asian Americans, or biracial adolescents. We acknowledge the importance of describing the normative adolescent development of these groups, yet the geographic reality of our sample did not include a large enough percentage of these groups to assess their trajectories reliably. Our goal was to look at the trajectories in these two R/E populations in a context in which their relative SES and educational circumstances were as similar as possible. This goal, and its constraint on selecting the community in which to conduct this study, made obtaining equivalently representative samples of other R/E groups within the United States impossible. We hope that other researchers will replicate our project with other R/E populations living in a variety of different social and national contexts.

Lastly, the developmental trajectories reflect adolescents in the late 20th century. Since that time, significant societal events have taken place such as the election of our first African American president, along with the Great Recession and widening income gap (Kochhar & Fry, 2014). Although these changes are likely to impact contemporary youth development, it is not entirely clear how. For example, recent research has found that the percentage of adolescents in the United States reporting psychological health complaints decreased from 2006 to 2010, despite the economic recession of 2007 (Pfoertner et al., 2014). Other research has also indicated improving trends for adolescents in the United States, with externalizing symptoms decreasing in the 1990s then remaining stable in the last decade (Centers for Disease Control and Prevention, 2012) and with an overall decline in underage drinking from 1991 to 2005 (Newes-Adeyi, Chen, Williams, & Faden, 2007).

Although today's adolescents may show higher or lower mean levels in some of our measures compared to our sample of African American and European American youth, there is little indication that patterns of developmental change from early to late adolescence would differ between our sample and a more contemporary one. Moreover, there is no evidence to suggest that the nature of the scales and items included would have any different meaning currently than in the past few decades. For example, the concept of self-esteem is the same now as it was in the past several decades, and the items we used to assess that construct appear to have the same meaning at present compared to the past several decades. Furthermore, most, if not all, of our measures are relevant for contemporary youth. Our results are thus useful in that they provide information about the trajectories of African American and European American youth in the

United States who grew up in comparable socioeconomic and educational contexts at the end of the 20th century. Whether these patterns definitely hold for different groups and in different sociohistorical periods remain to be determined.

FUTURE STUDIES

Next steps might include examining (a) bidirectional relations between trajectories across time; (b) demographic intersectionality; (c) developmental pathways defined by linking multivariate profiles across time; and (d) the potential heterogeneity across individuals in the functional forms of change. Previous studies using MADICS data have examined how changes in parenting and family dynamics are associated with changes in adolescents' psychological and behavioral outcomes (Gutman & Eccles, 2007; Gutman et al., 2011). Other research has examined the linkages between adolescents' relationship with parents and peers across time (e.g., De Goede, Branje, Delsing, & Meeus, 2009) as well as the influence of parents, peers, and school climate on adolescents' engagement in problem behaviors (e.g., Martino, Ellickson, & McCaffrey, 2009; Wang et al., 2011; Wang & Dishion, 2012). Future studies could expand these findings by investigating the interrelations among changes in multiple domains of risk, promotive, and protective factors during adolescence. Particularly important would be to distinguish between recursive and nonrecursive effects in adolescents' trajectories and to examine whether the nature of these relations varies according to the developmental period in question (e.g., early adolescence versus late adolescence, middle school versus high school).

A further contribution would be to examine more closely the intersectionality between gender and race/ethnicity, as well as SES, and to consider their combined influence on development. Our findings revealed few significant gender-by-race/ethnicity interactions, where p was set at $<.01$. Furthermore, we found few indications of significant race/ethnicity-by-SES interactions in our preliminary analyses. Nevertheless, this may be a function of our unique sample, where the different R/E groups have more similar SES backgrounds than the United States overall. There may be significant differences among gender, race/ethnicity, and SES in samples where some of the adolescents grow up in more disadvantaged circumstances and surroundings. Although previous studies have investigated the moderating role of these factors, linking predictors and outcomes in different domains at one point in time, more research with adolescents living in different locales examining the intersectionality of these factors in moderating the association between contextual influences and longitudinal trajectories of adolescent development is needed.

A further step in examining adolescent development would be to consider a constellation of risk, promotive, and protective factors that exist within individuals at specific point(s) in time (Bergman, Magnusson, & El-Khouri, 2003; Bergman & Vargha, 2013; Magnusson, 1985, 2003; Peck & Roeser, 2003). Given the complex and varying interdependencies that likely exist among many of the variables we examined, a pattern-centered, multivariate profile approach may further reveal additional forms of heterogeneity in adolescents' developmental trajectories. However useful it may be for capturing a normative picture of adolescent development, focusing exclusively on univariate growth trajectories and their interrelations is an inherently limited approach to understanding human development in context because both individuals and social contexts are multidimensional, multilevel phenomena. How such dimensions and levels cohere within individuals and contexts to form integrated patterns, and the implications of these integrated patterns of personal and contextual characteristics for both typical and atypical developmental pathways, are pressing questions that deserve increased attention.

CONCLUSIONS

This monograph represents one of the few comprehensive documents examining risky and positive youth development in multiple domains from early to late adolescence. Our findings suggest that the average youth in the United States experiences relatively stable and positive trajectories in their interpersonal and intrapersonal worlds throughout their adolescence. Developmental fluctuations were evident, but these occurred at different points depending on the domain in question. Furthermore, these shifts were not mutually exclusive; often times, these adolescents experienced changes in risk, promotive, and protective factors at a similar point in development, even within the same domain. Developmental trajectories differed in some expected ways by gender and race/ethnicity, but even these differences were not very marked. Overall, most of the young people, African American and European American alike, navigated through their adolescence into their twenties with little evidence of heightened risk and arrived at young adulthood with good mental and physical health, quite positive relationships with their parents and peers, and high aspirations and expectations for what their future lives might hold. Exploring possible exceptions to these average trends will be hastened by using methods designed explicitly for examining sample heterogeneity and atypical development (Peck, Feinstein, & Eccles, 2008).

In conclusion, we hope that this monograph provides a springboard for future studies that further explore multivariate heterogeneity in adolescents' profiles and developmental trajectories. Although examining such integrated patterns depends critically on variable-centered measurement development, and benefits from the kind of univariate descriptive analyses reported here, more work is sorely needed. Future studies that accomplish such nuanced examinations would add greatly to our understanding of the complexities involved in the both the nature and timing of changes characterizing adolescent development and its multiple interacting influences and contexts. Our data set is archived at the Henry A. Murray Research Archive at Harvard University (http://murray.harvard.edu/), and we encourage others to complement our work by pursuing such analyses.

REFERENCES

Aboud, F. E., & Janani, S. (2007). Friendship and identity in a language-integrated school. *International Journal of Behavioral Development*, **31**, 445–453.

Aboud, F. E., Mendelson, M. J., & Purdy, K. T. (2003). Cross-race peer relations and friendship quality. *International Journal of Behavioral Development*, **27**, 165–173.

Abrams, L. S., & Stormer, C. C. (2002). Sociocultural variations in the body image perceptions of urban adolescent females. *Journal of Youth and Adolescence*, **31**(6), 443–450.

Adkins, D. E., Wang, V., Dupre, M. E., Van den Oord, E. J., & Elder, G. H. (2009). Structure and stress: Trajectories of depressive symptoms across adolescence and young adulthood. *Social Forces*, **88**(1), 31–60.

Anderman, E. M., Maehr, M. L., & Midgley, C. (1999). Declining motivation after the transition to middle school: Schools can make a difference. *Journal of Research & Development in Education*, **32**(3), 131–147.

Anderson, E. (1990). *Streetwise: Race, class, and change in an urban community*. Chicago: University of Chicago Press.

Angold, A., Erkanli, A., Silberg, J., Eaves, L., & Costello, E. J. (2002). Depression scale scores in 8–17-year-olds: Effects of age, gender. *Journal of Child Psychology, Psychiatry*, **438**, 1052–1063.

Archambault, I., Eccles, J. S., & Vida, M. N. (2010). Ability self-concepts and subjective value in literacy: Joint trajectories from grades 1 through 12. *Journal of Educational Psychology*, **102**(4), 804–816.

Archer, J. (2004). Sex differences in aggression in real-world settings: A meta-analytic review. *Review of General Psychology*, **8**, 291–322.

Attar-Schwartz, S. (2015). Emotional closeness to parents and grandparents: A moderated mediation model predicting adolescent adjustment. *American Journal of Orthopsychiatry*, **85**(5), 495–503.

Bachman, J. G., O'Malley, P. M., Freedman-Doan, P., Trzesniewski, K. H., & Donnellan, M. B. (2011). Adolescent self-esteem: Differences by race/ethnicity, gender, and age. *Self and Identity*, **10**(4), 445–473.

Baldwin, S. A., & Hoffmann, J. P. (2002). The dynamics of self-esteem: A growth-curve analysis. *Journal of Youth and Adolescence*, **31**(2), 101–113.

Baltes, P. B., Reese, H. W., & Nesselroade, J. R. (1977). *Life-span developmental psychology: Introduction to research methods*. Monterey, CA: Brooks/Cole.

Bandura, A. (1977). Self-efficacy: Toward a unifying theory of behavioral change. *Psychological Review*, **84**, 191–215.

Bandura, A. (1997). *Self-efficacy: The exercise of control*. New York, NY: Freeman.

Barber, B. K. (1996). Parental psychological control: Revisiting a neglected construct. *Child Development,* **67**(6), 3296–3319.

Barber, B. K. (2002). *Intrusive parenting: How psychological control affects children and adolescents.* Washington, DC: American Psychological Association.

Barber, B. K., & Olsen, J. A. (2004). Assessing the transitions to middle and high school. *Journal of Adolescent Research,* **19**(1), 3–30.

Barber, B. K., Stolz, H. E., Olsen, J. A., Collins, W. A., & Burchinal, M. (2005). Parental support, psychological control, and behavioral control: Assessing relevance across time, culture, and method. *Monographs of the Society for Research in Child Development,* **70**, 1–147.

Barrett A. E., & Turner R. J. (2006). Family structure and substance use problems in adolescence and early adulthood: Examining explanations for the relationship. *Addiction,* **101**, 109–120.

Baumrind, D. (1991). Parenting styles and adolescent development. *The Encyclopedia of Adolescence,* **1**, 169–208.

Beal, S. J., & Crockett, L. J. (2010). Adolescents' occupational and educational aspirations and expectations: Links to high school activities and adult educational attainment. *Developmental Psychology,* **46**(1), 258.

Belle, D. (1989). *Gender differences in children's social networks and supports.* Hoboken, NJ: John Wiley & Sons.

Bender, H. L., Allen, J. P., McElhaney, K. B., Antonishak, J., Moore, C. M., Kelly, H. O. B., et al. (2007). Use of harsh physical discipline and developmental outcomes in adolescence. *Development and Psychopathology,* **19**(01), 227–242.

Benner, A. D., & Graham, S. (2009). The transition to high school as a developmental process among multiethnic urban youth. *Child Development,* **80**(2), 356–376.

Benson, P. L., Scales, P. C., Hamilton, S. F., & Sesma, A. (2006). Positive youth development: Theory, research, and applications. In R. M. Lerner (Ed.), *Theoretical models of human development. Vol. 1 of Handbook of child psychology* (6th ed.). Editors-in-chief: W. Damon & R. M. Lerner. Hoboken, NJ: Wiley.

Bergman, L. R., Magnusson, D., & El-Khouri, B. M. (2003). *Studying individual development in an interindividual context: A person-oriented approach.* Mahwah, NJ: Erlbaum.

Bergman, L. R., & Vargha, A. (2013). Matching method to problem: A developmental science perspective. *European Journal of Developmental Psychology,* **10**, 9–28.

Beyers, W., & Goossens, L. (1999). Emotional autonomy, psychosocial adjustment and parenting: Interactions, moderating and mediating effects. *Journal of Adolescence,* **22**(6), 753–769.

Birkeland, M. S., Melkevik, O., Holsen, I., & Wold, B. (2012). Trajectories of global self-esteem development during adolescence. *Journal of Adolescence,* **35**(1), 43–54.

Block, J., & Robins, R. W. (1993). A longitudinal study of consistency and change in self-esteem from early adolescence to early adulthood. *Child Development,* **64**(3), 909–923.

Bongers, I. L., Koot, H. M., Van Der Ende, J., & Verhulst, F. C. (2004). Developmental trajectories of externalizing behaviors in childhood and adolescence. *Child Development,* **75**(5), 1523–1537.

Bouchey, H. A., Shoulberg, E. K., Jodl, K. M., & Eccles, J. S. (2010). Longitudinal links between older sibling features and younger siblings' academic adjustment during early adolescence. *Journal of Educational Psychology,* **102**(1), 197–211.

Bradley, B. J., & Greene, A. C. (2013). Do health and education agencies in the United States share responsibility for academic achievement and health? A review of 25 years of evidence about the relationship of adolescents' academic achievement and health behaviors. *Journal of Adolescent Health*, **52**(5), 523–532.

Bray, J. H., Adams, G. J., Getz, J. G., & Baer, P. E. (2001). Developmental, family, and ethnic influences on adolescent alcohol usage: A growth curve approach. *Journal of Family Psychology*, **15**, 301–314.

Breslau, N., Kilbey, M. M., & Andreski, P. (1993). Nicotine dependence and major depression: New evidence from a prospective investigation. *Archives of General Psychiatry*, **50**(1), 31–35.

Brody, G. H., Chen, Y., Murry, V. M., Ge, X., Simons, R. L., Gibbons, F. X., et al. (2006). Perceived discrimination and the adjustment of African American youths: A five-year longitudinal analysis with contextual moderation effects. *Child Development*, **77**(5), 1170–1189.

Brody, G. H., Lei, M. K., Chae, D. H., Yu, T., Kogan, S. M., & Beach, S. R. (2014). Perceived discrimination among African American adolescents and allostatic load: A longitudinal analysis with buffering effects. *Child Development*, **85**(3), 989–1002.

Bronfenbrenner, U. (2009). *The ecology of human development*. Boston, MA: Harvard University Press.

Bronfenbrenner, U., & Morris, P. A. (1998). The ecology of developmental processes. In W. Damon & R. M. Lerner (Eds.), *Handbook of child psychology: Theoretical models of human development*. (pp. 993–1028). Hoboken, NJ: John Wiley.

Brown, J. S., Meadows, S. O., & Elder, G. H., Jr. (2007). Race-ethnic inequality and psychological distress: Depressive symptoms from adolescence to young adulthood. *Developmental Psychology*, **43**(6), 1295–1311.

Bryk, A. S., & Raudenbush, S. W. (1992). *Hierarchical linear modeling applications and data analysis methods*. Newbury Park, CA: Sage Publications.

Buchanan, C. M., Eccles, J. S., & Becker, J. B. (1992). Are adolescents the victims of raging hormones? Evidence for activational effects of hormones on moods and behavior at adolescence. *Psychological Bulletin*, **111**(1), 62–107.

Caldwell, C., Kohn-Wood, L., Schmeelk-Cone, K. H., Chavous, T., & Zimmerman, M. (2004). Racial discrimination and racial identity as risk or protective factors for violent behaviors in African American young adults. *American Journal of Community Psychology*, **33**, 91–105.

Card, N. A., Stucky, B. D., Sawalani, G. M., & Little, T. D. (2008). Direct and indirect aggression during childhood and adolescence: A meta-analytic review of gender differences, intercorrelations, and relations to maladjustment. *Child Development*, **79**(5), 1185–1229.

Casillas, A., Robbins, S., Allen, J., Kuo, Y. L., Hanson, M. A., & Schmeiser, C. (2012). Predicting early academic failure in high school from prior academic achievement, psychosocial characteristics, and behavior. *Journal of Educational Psychology*, **104**(2), 407.

Catalano, R. F., Fagan, A. A., Gavin, L. E., Greenberg, M. T., Irwin, C. E., Ross, D. A., et al. (2012). Worldwide application of prevention science in adolescent health. *The Lancet*, **379**(9826), 1653–1664.

Centers for Disease Control and Prevention. (2012). *Youth risk behaviour surveillance—United States 2011. Morbidity and Mortality Weekly Report*. Atlanta, GA: Office of Surveillance, Epidemiology, and Laboratory Services, CDC.

Chassin, L., Hussong, A., & Beltran, I. (2009). Adolescent substance use. In R. M. Lerner & L. Steinberg (Eds.), *Handbook of adolescent psychology* (3rd ed., pp. 723–765). Hoboken, NJ: John Wiley & Sons.

Chatman, C. M., Malanchuk, O., & Eccles, J. S. (2001). *Ethnic identity typologies among African American early adolescents.* Paper presented at the biennual meetings of the Society for Research on Child Development, Minneapolis, Minnesota, April 19–22.

Chavous, T. M., Bernat, D. H., Schmeelk-Cone, K., Caldwell, C. H., Kohn-Wood, L., & Zimmerman, M. A. (2003). Racial identity and academic attainment among African American adolescents. *Child Development*, **74**(4), 1076–1090.

Chen, P., & Jacobson, K. C. (2012). Developmental trajectories of substance use from early adolescence to young adulthood: Gender and racial/ethnic differences. *Journal of Adolescent Health*, **50**(2), 154–163.

Cheung, G. W., & Rensvold, R. B. (2002). Evaluating goodness-of-fit indexes for testing measurement invariance. *Structural Equation Modeling*, **9**(2), 233–255.

Choe, D. E., Stoddard, S. A., & Zimmerman, M. A. (2014). Developmental trajectories of African American adolescents' family conflict: Differences in mental health problems in young adulthood. *Developmental Psychology*, **50**(4), 1226–1232.

Chumlea, W. C., Schubert, C. M., Roche, A. F., Kulin, H. E., Lee, P. A., Himes, J. H., et al. (2003). Age at menarche and racial comparisons in US girls. *Pediatrics*, **111**(1), 110–113.

Clark, D. B., Thatcher, D. L., & Tapert, S. F. (2008). Alcohol, psychological dysregulation, and adolescent brain development. *Alcoholism: Clinical and Experimental Research*, **32**(3), 375–385.

Clausen, J. A. (1993). *American lives: Looking back at the children of the Great Depression.* Berkley: University of California Press.

Cogburn, C. D., Chavous, T. M., & Griffin, T. M. (2011). School-based racial and gender discrimination among African American adolescents: Exploring gender variation in frequency and implications for adjustment. *Race and Social Problems*, **3**(1), 25–37.

Cohen, J. (1988). *Statistical power analysis for the behavioral sciences* (2nd ed.). Hillsdale, NJ: Erlbaum.

Cohen, J., Cohen, P., West, S. G., & Aiken, L. S. (2003). *Applied multiple regression/correlation analysis for the behavioral sciences* (3rd ed.). Mahwah, NJ: Erlbaum.

Cohen, J. S., & Smerdon, B. A. (2009). Tightening the dropout tourniquet: Easing the transition from middle to high school. *Preventing School Failure: Alternative Education for Children and Youth*, **53**(3), 177–184.

Cohen, P., Cohen, J., Kasen, S., Velez, C. N., Hartmark, C., Johnson, J., et al. (1993). An epidemiological study of disorders in late childhood and adolescence: I. Age- and gender-specific prevalence. *Journal of Child Psychology and Psychiatry*, **34**(6), 851–867.

Coie, J. D., Watt, N. F., West, S. G., Hawkins, J. D., Asarnow, J. R., Markman, H. J., et al. (1993). The science of prevention: A conceptual framework and some directions for a national research program. *American Psychologist*, **48**(10), 1013–1022.

Colarossi, L. G., & Eccles, J. S. (2000). A prospective study of adolescents' peer support: Gender differences and the influence of parental relationships. *Journal of Youth and Adolescence*, **29**(6), 661–678.

Colarossi, L. G., & Eccles, J. S. (2003). Differential effects of support providers on adolescents' mental health. *Social Work Research*, **27**(1), 19–30.

Cole, D. A., Tram, J. M., Martin, J. M., Hoffman, K. B., Ruiz, M. D., Jacquez, F. M., et al. (2002). Individual differences in the emergence of depressive symptoms in children and adolescents: A longitudinal investigation of parent and child reports. *Journal of Abnormal Psychology*, **111**(1), 156.

Collins, W. A. (1995). *Relationships and development: Family adaptation to individual change.* Westport, CT: Ablex.

Collins, W. A., & Laursen, B. (2004). Changing relationships, changing youth: Interpersonal contexts of adolescent development. *The Journal of Early Adolescence, 24*(1), 55–62.

Conger, R. D., & Ge, X. (1999). Conflict and cohesion in parent–adolescent relations: Changes in emotional expression from early to mid-adolescence. In M. J. Cox & J. Brooks-Gunn (Eds.), *Conflict and cohesion in families: Causes and consequences* (pp. 185–206). Mahwah, NJ: Erlbaum.

Conger, R. D., Ge, X., Elder, G. H., Lorenz, F. O., & Simons, R. L. (1994). Economic stress, coercive family process, and developmental problems of adolescents. *Child Development, 65*(2), 541–561.

Conger, R. D., Lorenz, F. O., Elder, G. H., Melby, J. N., Simons, R. L., & Conger, K. J. (1991). A process model of family economic pressure and early adolescent alcohol use. *The Journal of Early Adolescence, 11*(4), 430–449.

Cook, T. D., Herman, M. R., Phillips, M., & Settersten, R. A., Jr. (2002). Some ways in which neighborhoods, nuclear families, friendship groups, and schools jointly affect changes in early adolescent development. *Child Development, 73*(4), 1283–1309.

Cooper, S. M., Brown, C., Metzger, I., Clinton, Y., & Guthrie, B. (2013). Racial discrimination and African American adolescents' adjustment: Gender variation in family and community social support, promotive and protective factors. *Journal of Child and Family Studies, 22*(1), 15–29.

Costello, D. M., Swendsen, J., Rose, J. S., & Dierker, L. C. (2008). Risk and protective factors associated with trajectories of depressed mood from adolescence to early adulthood. *Journal of Consulting and Clinical Psychology, 76*(2), 173.

Côté, J. E. (2009). Identity formation and self-development in adolescence. In R. M. Lerner & L. Steinberg (Eds.), *Handbook of adolescent psychology* (3rd ed., pp. 266–304). Hoboken, NJ: John Wiley & Sons.

Crews, F., He, J., & Hodge, C. (2007). Adolescent cortical development: A critical period of vulnerability for addiction. *Pharmacology Biochemistry and Behavior, 86*(2), 189–199.

Crocker, J., & Luhtanen, R. (1990). Collective self-esteem and ingroup bias. *Journal of Personality and Social Psychology, 58*(1), 60–67.

Crosnoe, R., Cavanagh, S., & Elder, G. H. (2003). Adolescent friendships as academic resources: The intersection of friendship, race, and school disadvantage. *Sociological Perspectives, 46*(3), 331–352.

Cross, W. E., Jr. (1991). *Shades of black: Diversity in African-American identity.* Philadelphia, PA: Temple University Press.

Daddis, C., & Smetana, J. (2005). Middle-class African American families' expectations for adolescents' behavioral autonomy. *International Journal of Behavioral Development, 29*(5), 371–381.

Davidson, R. J., Jackson, D. C., & Kalin, N. H. (2000). Emotion, plasticity, context, and regulation: Perspectives from affective neuroscience. *Psychological Bulletin, 126*, 890–909.

Davis-Kean, P. E. (2005). The influence of parent education and family income on child achievement: The indirect role of parental expectations and the home environment. *Journal of Family Psychology, 19*(2), 294–304.

De Fraine, B., Van Damme, J., & Onghena, P. (2007). A longitudinal analysis of gender differences in academic self-concept and language achievement: A multivariate multilevel latent growth approach. *Contemporary Educational Psychology, 32*(1), 132–150.

De Goede, I. H. A., Branje, S. J. T., Delsing, M. J. M. H., & Meeus, W. H. J. (2009). Linkages over time between adolescents' relationships with parents and friends. *Journal of Youth and Adolescence*, **38**(10), 1304–1315.

De Goede, I. H. A., Branje, S. J. T., & Meeus, W. H. J. (2009). Developmental changes in adolescents' perceptions of relationships with their parents. *Journal of Youth and Adolescence*, **38**, 75–88.

Değirmencioğlu, S. M., Urberg, K. A., Tolson, J. M., & Richard, P. (1998). Adolescent friendship networks: Continuity and change over the school year. *Merrill-Palmer Quarterly-Journal of Developmental Psychology*, **44**(3), 313–337.

Deković, M. (1999). Risk and protective factors in the development of problem behavior during adolescence. *Journal of Youth and Adolescence*, **28**(6), 667–685.

DeVore, E. R., & Ginsburg, K. R. (2005). The protective effects of good parenting on adolescents. *Current Opinion in Pediatrics*, **17**(4), 460–465.

Denissen, J. J., Zarrett, N. R., & Eccles, J. S. (2007). I like to do it, I'm able, and I know I am: Longitudinal couplings between domain-specific achievement, self-concept, and interest. *Child Development*, **78**(2), 430–447.

Derogatis, L. R. (1996). *SCL-90-R: Symptom Checklist-90-R: Administration, scoring, and procedures manual*. NCS Pearson.

DeWit, D. J., Adlaf, E. M., Offord, D. R., & Ogborne, A. C. (2000). Age at first alcohol use: A risk factor for the development of alcohol disorders. *American Journal of Psychiatry*, **157**(5), 745–750.

Diemer, M. A., Marchand, A. D., McKellar, S. E., Malanchuk, O. (2016). Promotive and corrosive factors in African American students' math beliefs and achievement. *Journal of Youth and Adolescence*, **45**(6), 1208–1225.

Dishion, T. J. (2000). Cross-setting consistency in early adolescent psychopathology: Deviant friendships and problem behavior sequelae. *Journal of Personality*, **68**(6), 1109–1126.

Dodge, K. A., Dishion, T. J., & Lansford, J. E. (2006). Deviant peer influences in intervention and public policy for youth. Social Policy Report. Volume 20, Number 1. *Society for Research in Child Development*.

Dornbusch, S. M., Ritter, P. L., Leiderman, P. H., Roberts, D. F., & Fraleigh, M. J. (1987). The relation of parenting style to adolescent school performance. *Child Development*, **58**(5), 1244–1257.

Dotterer, A. M., Lowe, K., & McHale, S. M. (2014). Academic growth trajectories and family relationships among African American youth. *Journal of Research on Adolescence*, **24**(4), 734–747.

Dougherty, K., & Kienzl, G. (2006). It's not enough to get through the open door: Inequalities by social background in transfer from community colleges to four-year colleges. *The Teachers College Record*, **108**(3), 452–487.

Duckworth, A. L., Peterson, C., Matthews, M. D., & Kelly, D. R. (2007). Grit: Perseverance and passion for long-term goals. *Journal of Personality and Social Psychology*, **92**(6), 1087–1101.

Durik, A. M., Vida, M., & Eccles, J. S. (2006). Task values and ability beliefs as predictors of high school literacy choices: A developmental analysis. *Journal of Educational Psychology*, **98**(2), 382–393.

Eccles (Parsons), J. E., Adler, T., & Meece, J. L. (1984). Sex differences in achievement: A test of alternate theories. *Journal of Personality and Social Psychology*, **46**(1), 26.

Eccles, J. S. (1994). Understanding women's educational and occupational choices. *Psychology of Women Quarterly*, **18**(4), 585–609.

Eccles, J. S. (2012). Supporting America's children and adolescents. *Macalester International*, **29**(1), 1–23.

Eccles, J. S., Early, D., Fraser, K., Belansky, E., & McCarthy, K. (1997). The relation of connection, regulation, and support for autonomy to adolescents' functioning. *Journal of Adolescent Research*, **12**(2), 263–286.

Eccles, J. S., Jacobs, J. E., & Harold, R. D. (1990). Gender role stereotypes, expectancy effects, and parents' socialization of gender differences. *Journal of Social Issues*, **46**(2), 183–201.

Eccles, J. S., Lord, S. E., Roeser, R. W., Barber, B. L., & Jozefowicz, D. M. H. (1999). The association of school transitions in early adolescence with developmental trajectories through high school. In J. Schulenberg, J. Maggs, & K. Hurrelman (Eds.), *Health risks and developmental transitions during adolescence* (pp. 283–320). Cambridge: Cambridge University Press.

Eccles, J. S., & Midgley, C. (1989). Stage-environment fit: Developmentally appropriate classrooms for young adolescents. *Research on Motivation in Education*, **3**, 139–186.

Eccles, J. S., Midgley, C., Buchanan, C. M., Wigfield, A., Reuman, D., & MacIver, D. (1993). Development during adolescence: The impact of stage/environment fit. *American Psychologist*, **48**, 90–101.

Eccles, J. S., & Roeser, R. W. (2010). An ecological view of schools and development. In J. L. Meece & J. S. Eccles (Eds.), *Handbook of research on schools, schooling, and human development* (pp. 6–21). Abingdon, UK: Routledge.

Eccles, J. S., & Roeser, R. W. (2011). Schools as developmental contexts during adolescence. *Journal of Research on Adolescence*, **21**(1), 225–241.

Eccles, J. S., Vida, M. N., & Barber, B. (2004). The relation of early adolescents' college plans and both academic ability and task-value beliefs to subsequent college enrollment. *The Journal of Early Adolescence*, **24**(1), 63–77.

Eccles, J. S., & Wigfield, A. (1995). In the mind of the achiever: The structure of adolescents' academic achievement related-beliefs and self-perceptions. *Personality and Social Psychology Bulletin*, **21**(3), 215–225.

Eccles, J. S., Wong, C. A., & Peck, S. C. (2006). Ethnicity as a social context for the development of African-American adolescents. *Journal of School Psychology*, **44**, 407–426.

Elliott, D., Huizinga, D., & Menard, S. (1989). *Multiple problem youth: Delinquency, substance use, and mental health problems*. New York, NY: Springer-Verlag.

Elmore, R. F. (2009). Schooling adolescents. In R. M. Lerner & L. Steinberg (Eds.), *Handbook of adolescent psychology* (3rd ed., pp. 193–227). Hoboken, NJ: John Wiley & Sons.

Epstein, J. L. (1989). The selection of friends: Changes across the grades and in different school environments. In T. J. Berndt & G. W. Ladd (Eds.), *Peer relationships in child development* (pp. 158–187). New York, NY: John Wiley & Sons.

Erikson, E. H. (1950). *Childhood and society*. New York, NY: W. W. Norton & Co.

Erikson, E. H. (1959). Identity and the life cycle. *Psychological Issues*, **1**, 18–164.

Erol, R. Y., & Orth, U. (2011). Self-esteem development from age 14 to 30 years: A longitudinal study. *Journal of Personality and Social Psychology*, **101**(3), 607–619.

Euling, S. Y., Herman-Giddens, M. E., Lee, P. A., Selevan, S. G., Juul, A., Sørensen, T. I., et al. (2008). Examination of US puberty-timing data from 1940 to 1994 for secular trends: Panel findings. *Pediatrics*, **121**(Supplement 3), S172–S191.

Farrington, D. P. (2009). Conduct disorder, aggression, and delinquency. In R. M. Lerner & L. Steinberg (Eds.), *Handbook of adolescent psychology* (3rd ed., pp. 683–722). Hoboken, NJ: John Wiley & Sons.

Fergus, S., & Zimmerman, M. A. (2005). Adolescent resilience: A framework for understanding healthy development in the face of risk. *Annual Review of Public Health*, **26**, 399–419.

Fergusson, D. M., Horwood, L.J., & Lynskey, M.T. (1994). Parental separation, adolescent psychopathology, and problem behaviors. *Journal of the American Academy of Child Adolescent Psychiatry*, **33**, 1122–1131

Fine, M. (1986). Why urban adolescents drop into and out of public high school. *The Teachers College Record*, **87**(3), 393–409.

Finn, J. D. (1989). Withdrawing from school. *Review of Educational Research*, **59**(2), 117–142.

Ford, D. H., & Lerner, R. M. (1992). *Developmental systems theory: An integrative approach.* Thousand Oaks, CA: Sage Publications.

Fredricks, J. A., Blumenfeld, P. C., & Paris, A. H. (2004). School engagement: Potential of the concept, state of the evidence. *Review of Educational Research*, **74**(1), 59–109.

Fredricks, J. A., & Eccles, J. S. (2002). Children's competence and value beliefs from childhood through adolescence: Growth trajectories in two male-sex-typed domains. *Developmental Psychology*, **38**(4), 519–533.

Fredricks, J. A., & Eccles, J. S. (2010). Breadth of extracurricular participation and adolescent adjustment among Africa-American and European-American youth. *Journal of Research on Adolescence*, **29**(2), 307–333.

French, S. E., Seidman, E., Allen, L., & Aber, J. L. (2006). The development of ethnic identity during adolescence. *Developmental Psychology*, **42**, 1–10.

Fuligni, A. (1998). Authority, autonomy, and parent-adolescent relationships: A study of adolescents from Mexican, Chinese, Filipino, and European backgrounds. *Developmental Psychology*, **34**, 782–792.

Fuligni, A. J. (2007). Family obligation, college enrollment, and emerging adulthood in Asian and Latin American families. *Child Development Perspectives*, **1**(2), 96–100.

Fuligni, A.J., & Eccles, J. S. (1993). Perceived parent-child relationships and early adolescents' orientation towards peers. *Developmental Psychology*, **29**, 622–632.

Fuligni, A. J., Eccles, J. S., Barber, B. L., & Clements, P. (2001). Early adolescent peer orientation and adjustment during high school. *Developmental Psychology*, **37**(1), 28.

Fuligni, A.J., Hughes, D. L., & Way, N. (2009). Ethnicity and immigration. In R. M. Lerner & L. Steinberg (Eds.), *Handbook of adolescent psychology* (3rd ed., pp. 527–569). Hoboken, NJ: John Wiley & Sons.

Furman, W., & Buhrmester, D. (1992). Age and sex differences in perceptions of networks of personal relationships. *Child Development*, **63**(1), 103–115.

Furstenberg, F. F., Cook, T. D., Eccles, J., Elder, G. H., & Sameroff, A. (1999). *Managing to make it: Urban families and adolescent success.* Chicago, IL: University of Chicago Press.

Galambos, N. L., Barker, E. T., & Krahn, H. J. (2006). Depression, self-esteem, and anger in emerging adulthood: Seven-year trajectories. *Developmental Psychology*, **42**(2), 350.

Galambos, N. L., & Krahn, H. J. (2008). Depression and anger trajectories during the transition to adulthood. *Journal of Marriage and Family*, **70**, 15–27.

Garber, J., Keiley, M. K., & Martin, N. C. (2002). Developmental trajectories of adolescents' depressive symptoms: Predictors of change. *Journal of Consulting and Clinical Psychology*, **70**(1), 79.

Garcia-Coll, C. Crnic, K., Lamberty, G., Wasik, B. H., Jenkins, R., Garcia, H. V., et al. (1996). An integrative model for the study of developmental competencies in minority children. *Child Development*, **67**(5), 1891–1914.

Garmezy, N., Masten, A. S., & Tellegen, A. (1984). The study of stress and competence in children: A building block for developmental psychopathology. *Child Development*, **55**(1), 97–111.

Garner, D. M., Olmstead, M. P., & Polivy, J. (1983). Development and validation of a multidimensional eating disorder inventory for anorexia nervosa and bulimia. *International Journal of Eating Disorders*, **2**(2), 15–34.

Garrett, J. L., & Eccles, J. S. (2009). Transition to adulthood: Linking late-adolescent lifestyles to family and work status in the mid-twenties. In I. Schoon & R. K. Silberseisen (Eds.), *Transitions from school to work: Globalization, individualization, and patterns of diversity* (pp. 243–264). New York, NY: Cambridge University Press.

Ge, X., Conger, R. D., & Elder, G. H., Jr. (2001). Pubertal transition, stressful life events, and the emergence of gender differences in adolescent depressive symptoms. *Developmental Psychology*, **37**(3), 404–417.

Ge, X., Lorenz, F. O., Conger, R. D., Elder, G. H., & Simons, R. L. (1994). Trajectories of stressful life events and depressive symptoms during adolescence. *Developmental Psychology*, **30**(4), 467–483.

Ge, X., Natsuaki, M. N., & Conger, R. D. (2006). Trajectories of depressive symptoms and stressful life events among male and female adolescents in divorced and nondivorced families. *Development and Psychopathology*, **18**(01), 253–273.

Geuzaine, C., Debry, M., & Liesens, V. (2000). Separation from parents in late adolescence: The same for boys and girls? *Journal of Youth and Adolescence*, **29**, 79–91.

Gilligan, C. (1982). *In a different voice*. Cambridge, MA: Harvard University Press.

Gilligan, C., Lyons, N., & Hammer, T. (1990). *Making connections*. Cambridge, MA: Harvard University Press.

Gniewosz, B., Eccles, J. S., & Noack, P. (2012). Secondary school transition and the use of different sources of information for the construction of the academic self-concept. *Social Development*, **21**(3), 537–557.

Goldbaum, S., Craig, W. M., Pepler, D., & Connolly, J. (2003). Developmental trajectories of victimization: Identifying risk and protective factors. *Journal of Applied School Psychology*, **19**(2), 139–156.

Goldstein, S. E., Davis-Kean, P. E., & Eccles, J. S. (2005). Parents, peers, and problem behavior: A longitudinal investigation of the impact of relationship perceptions and characteristics on the development of adolescent problem behavior. *Developmental Psychology*, **41**(2), 401–413.

Goldstein, S. E., Malanchuk, O., Davis-Kean, P., & Eccles, J.S. (2007). Risk factors of sexual harassment by peers: A longitudinal investigation of African American and European American adolescents. *Journal of Research on Adolescence*, **17**(2), 285–300.

Gootman, J. A., & Eccles, J. (Eds.). (2002). *Community programs to promote youth development*. Washington, DC: National Academies Press.

Gore, S., & Aseltine, R. H., Jr. (2003). Race and ethnic differences in depressed mood following the transition from high school. *Journal of Health and Social Behavior*, **44**, 370–389.

Gottfried, A. E., Fleming, J. S., & Gottfried, A. W. (2001). Continuity of academic intrinsic motivation from childhood through late adolescence: A longitudinal study. *Journal of Educational Psychology*, **93**(1), 3–13.

Graber, J. A. (2004). *Internalizing problems during adolescence*. Hoboken, NJ: John Wiley & Sons.

Graber, J. A., & Sontag, L. M. (2004). Internalizing problems during adolescence. In R. M. Lerner & L. Steinberg (Eds.), *Handbook of adolescent psychology* (3rd ed., pp. 305–357). Hoboken, NJ: John Wiley & Sons.

Graham, J. W. (2009). Missing data analysis: Making it work in the real world. *Annual Review of Psychology*, **60**, 549–576.

Graham, S., Munniksma, A., & Juvonen, J. (2014). Psychosocial benefits of cross-ethnic friendships in urban middle schools. *Child Development*, **85**(2), 469–483.

Grant, B. F., & Dawson, D. A. (1997). Age at onset of alcohol use and its association with DSM-IV alcohol abuse and dependence: Results from the National Longitudinal Alcohol Epidemiologic Survey. *Journal of Substance Abuse*, **9**, 103–110.

Gray, M. R., & Steinberg, L. (1999). Unpacking authoritative parenting: Reassessing a multidimensional construct. *Journal of Marriage and the Family*, **61**(3), 574–587.

Greene, M. L., & Way, N. (2005). Self-esteem trajectories among ethnic minority adolescents: A growth curve analysis of the patterns and predictors of change. *Journal of Research on Adolescence*, **15**, 151–178.

Greene, M. L., Way, N., & Pahl, K. (2006). Trajectories of perceived adult and peer discrimination among Black, Latino, and Asian American adolescents: patterns and psychological correlates. *Developmental Psychology*, **42**, 218.

Gutman, L. M. (2006). How student and parent goal orientations and classroom goal structures influence the math achievement of African Americans during the high school transition. *Contemporary Educational Psychology*, **31**(1), 44–63.

Gutman, L. M., & Eccles, J. S. (1999). Financial strain, parenting behaviors, and adolescents' achievement: Testing model equivalence between African American and European American single- and two-parent families. *Child Development*, **70**(6), 1464–1476.

Gutman, L. M., & Eccles, J. S. (2007). Stage-environment fit during adolescence: Trajectories of family relations and adolescent outcomes. *Developmental Psychology*, **43**(2), 522–537.

Gutman, L. M., Eccles, J. S., Peck, S., & Malanchuk, O. (2011). The influence of family relations on trajectories of cigarette and alcohol use from early to late adolescence. *Journal of Adolescence*, **34**(1), 119–128.

Gutman, L. M., & Midgley, C. (2000). The role of protective factors in supporting the academic achievement of poor African American students during the middle school transition. *Journal of Youth and Adolescence*, **29**(2), 223–249.

Gutman, L. M., & Sameroff, A. J. (2004). Continuities in depression from adolescence to young adulthood: Contrasting ecological influences. *Development and Psychopathology*, **16**(04), 967–984.

Gutman, L. M., Sameroff, A. J., & Cole, R. (2003). Academic growth curve trajectories from 1st grade to 12th grade: Effects of multiple social risk factors and preschool child factors. *Developmental Psychology*, **39**(4), 777.

Gutman, L. M., Sameroff, A. J., & Eccles, J. S. (2002). The academic achievement of African American students during early adolescence: An examination of multiple risk, promotive, and protective factors. *American Journal of Community Psychology*, **30**(3), 367–399.

Gutman, L. M., & Schoon, I. (2012). Correlates and consequences of uncertainty in career aspirations: Gender differences among adolescents in England. *Journal of Vocational Behavior*, **80**(3), 608–618.

Hagen, J. W., Nelson M. J., & Velissaris, N. (2004). *Comparison of research in two major journals on adolescence.* Presented at Biennial Meeting of the Society of Research in Adolescence, Baltimore, M.D.

Hamm, J. V., Brown, B., & Heck, D. J. (2005). Bridging the ethnic divide: Student and school characteristics in African American, Asian-descent, Latino, and White adolescents' cross-ethnic friend nominations. *Journal of Research on Adolescence*, **15**(1), 21–46.

Hankin, B. L., Abramson, L. Y., Moffitt, T. E., Silva, P. A., McGee, R., & Angell, K. E. (1998). Development of depression from preadolescence to young adulthood: Emerging gender differences in a 10-year longitudinal study. *Journal of Abnormal Psychology*, **107**(1), 128–140.

Harkness, S., & Super, C. M. (2002). Culture and parenting. *Handbook of Parenting*, **2**, 253–280.

Harris, A. L. (2008). Optimism in the face of despair: Black-White differences in beliefs about school as a means for upward social mobility. *Social Science Quarterly*, **89**(3), 608–630.

Harris-Britt, A., Valrie, C. R., Kurtz-Costes, B., & Rowley, S. J. (2007). Perceived racial discrimination and self-esteem in African American youth: Racial socialization as a protective factor. *Journal of Research On Adolescence*, **17**(4), 669–682.

Harter, S. (1985). Competence as a dimension of self-evaluation: Toward a comprehensive model of self-worth. In R. Leahy (Ed.), *The development of the self*. New York, NY: Academic Press.

Hartup, W. W. (1996). The company they keep: Friendships and their developmental significance. *Child Development*, **67**(1), 1–13.

Hawkins, J. D., Catalano, R. F., & Miller, J. Y. (1992). Risk and protective factors for alcohol and other drug problems in adolescence and early adulthood: Implications for substance abuse prevention. *Psychological Bulletin*, **112**(1), 64–105.

Henry, K. L., Knight, K. E., & Thornberry, T. P. (2012). School disengagement as a predictor of dropout, delinquency, and problem substance use during adolescence and early adulthood. *Journal of Youth and Adolescence*, **41**(2), 156–166.

Hill, J. P., & Lynch, M. E. (1983). The intensification of gender-related role expectations during early adolescence. In *Girls at puberty* (pp. 201–228). New York, NY: Springer.

Hirschi, T., & Gottfredson, M. (1983). Age and the explanation of crime. *American Journal of Sociology*, **89**(3), 552–584.

Hoek, H. W. (2006). Incidence, prevalence and mortality of anorexia nervosa and other eating disorders. *Current Opinion in Psychiatry*, **19**(4), 389–394.

Hox, J. J. (2000). Multilevel analysis of grouped and longitudinal data. In T. D. Little, K. U. Schnabel, & J. Baumert (Eds.), *Modeling longitudinal and multiple-group data: Practical issues, applied approaches, and specific examples* (pp. 1–15). Hillsdale, NJ: Erlbaum.

Huang, C. (2012). Discriminant and criterion-related validity of achievement goals in predicting academic achievement: A meta-analysis. *Journal of Educational Psychology*, **104**(1), 48.

Hudson, J. I., Hiripi, E., Pope, H. G., & Kessler, R. C. (2007). The prevalence and correlates of eating disorders in the National Comorbidity Survey Replication. *Biological Psychiatry*, **61**(3), 348–358.

Hughes, D., Rodriguez, J., Smith, E. P., Johnson, D. J., Stevenson, H. C., & Spicer, P. (2006). Parents' ethnic-racial socialization practices: A review of research and directions for future study. *Developmental Psychology*, **42**(5), 747–770.

Huynh, V. W., & Fuligni, A. J. (2010). Discrimination hurts: The academic, psychological, and physical well-being of adolescents. *Journal of Research on Adolescence*, **20**(4), 916–941.

Jacobs, J. E., Lanza, S., Osgood, D. W., Eccles, J. S., & Wigfield, A. (2002). Changes in children's self-competence and values: Gender and domain differences across grades one through twelve. *Child Development*, **73**(2), 509–527.

James, S. A. (1994). John Henryism and the health of African-Americans. *Culture, Medicine and Psychiatry,* **18**(2), 163–182.

Jodl, K. M., Michael, A., Malanchuk, O., Eccles, J. S., & Sameroff, A. (2001). Parents' role in shaping early adolescents' occupational aspirations. *Child Development,* **72**(4), 1247–1265.

Johnson, M. K., Crosnoe, R., & Elder, G. H., Jr. (2001). Students' attachment and academic engagement: The role of race and ethnicity. *Sociology of Education,* **74**(4), 318–340.

Johnston, L. D., O'Malley, P. M., & Bachman, J. G., (1987). *National trends in drug use and related factors among American high school students and young adults, 1975–1986.* Rockville, MD: National Institute on Drug Abuse.

Johnston, L. D., O'Malley, P. M., Bachman, J. G., & Schulenberg, J. E. (2011). *Monitoring the future national survey results on drug use, 1975–2010.* Ann Arbor: Institute for Social Research, University of Michigan.

Juang, L. P., & Silbereisen, R. K. (2002). The relationship between adolescent academic capability beliefs, parenting and school grades. *Journal of Adolescence,* **25**(1), 3–18.

Juvonen, J., Le, V. N., Kaganoff, T., Augustine, C. H., & Constant, L. (2004). *Focus on the wonder years: Challenges facing the American middle school.* Santa Monica, CA: RAND.

Kandel, D. B., & Yamaguchi, K. (2002). Stages of drug involvement in the US population. In D. B. Kandel (Ed.), *Stages and pathways of drug involvement: Examining the gateway hypothesis* (pp. 65–89). Cambridge: Cambridge University Press.

Kao, G., & Joyner, K. (2004). Do race and ethnicity matter among friends? *The Sociological Quarterly,* **45**(3), 557–573.

Kao, G., & Thompson, J. (2003). Racial and ethnic stratification in educational achievement and attainment. *Annual Review of Sociology,* **29**, 417–442.

Kao, G., & Tienda, M. (1998). Educational aspirations among minority youth. *American Journal of Education,* **106**, 349–384.

Kawabata, Y., & Crick, N. R. (2011). The significance of cross-racial/ethnic friendships: Associations with peer victimization, peer support, sociometric status, and classroom diversity. *Developmental Psychology,* **47**(6), 1763–1775.

Keijsers, L., & Poulin, F. (2013). Developmental changes in parent-child communication throughout adolescence. *Developmental Psychology,* **49**, 2301–2308.

Kia-Keating, M., Dowdy, E., Morgan, M. L., & Noam, G. G. (2011). Protecting and promoting: An integrative conceptual model for healthy development of adolescents. *Journal of Adolescent Health,* **48**(3), 220–228.

Kim, B. E., Oesterle, S., Catalano, R. F., & Hawkins, J. D. (2015). Change in protective factors across adolescent development. *Journal of Applied Developmental Psychology,* **40**, 26–37.

Kim, S., Kamphaus, R. W., Orpinas, P., & Kelder, S. H. (2010). Change in the manifestation of overt aggression during early adolescence: Gender and ethnicity. *School Psychology International,* **31**(1), 95–111.

Kim-Cohen, J., Caspi, A., Taylor, A., Williams, B., Newcombe, R., Craig, I. W., et al. (2006). MAOA, maltreatment, and gene-environment interaction predicting children's mental health: New evidence and a meta-analysis. *Molecular Psychiatry,* **11**(10), 903–913.

Kling, K. C., Hyde, J. S., Showers, C. J., & Buswell, B. N. (1999). Gender differences in self-esteem: A meta-analysis. *Psychological Bulletin,* **125**(4), 470–500.

Kochhar, R., & Fry, R. (2014). Wealth inequality has widened along racial, ethnic lines since end of Great Recession. *Pew Research Center,* **12**. http://www.pewresearch.org/fact-tank/2014/12/12/racial-wealth-gaps-great-recession/

Kovacs, M. (1992). *Children's depression inventory manual.* North Tonawanda, NY: Multi-Health Systems.

Lansford, J. E., Dodge, K. A., Fontaine, R. G., Bates, J. E., & Pettit, G. S. (2014). Peer rejection, affiliation with deviant peers, delinquency, and risky sexual behavior. *Journal of Youth and Adolescence,* **43**(10), 1742–1751.

Lansford, J. E., Malone, P. S., Castellino, D. R., Dodge, K. A., Pettit, G. S., & Bates, J. E. (2006). Trajectories of internalizing, externalizing, and grades for children who have and have not experienced their parent's divorce or separation. *Journal of Family Psychology,* **20**, 292–301.

Larson, R. W. (2000). Toward a psychology of positive youth development. *American Psychologist,* **55**(1), 170–183.

Larson, R. W., Richards, M. H., Moneta, G., Holmbeck, G., & Duckett, E. (1996). Changes in adolescents' daily interactions with their families from ages 10 to 18: Disengagement and transformation. *Developmental Psychology,* **32**(4), 744–754.

Laursen, B., & Collins, W. A. (2009). Parent-child relationships during adolescence. In R. M. Lerner & L. Steinberg (Eds.), *Handbook of adolescent psychology.* (3rd ed., pp. 723–765). Hoboken, NJ: John Wiley & Sons.

Laursen, B., Coy, K. C., & Collins, W. A. (1998). Reconsidering changes in parent–child conflict across adolescence: A meta-analysis. *Child Development,* **69**, 817–832.

Lent, R. W., Brown, S. D., & Hackett, G. (1994). Toward a unifying social cognitive theory of career and academic interest, choice, and performance. *Journal of Vocational Behavior,* **45**(1), 79–122.

Lerner, R. M. (2005). Promoting positive youth development: Theoretical and empirical bases. In *White paper prepared for the Workshop on the Science of Adolescent Health and Development, National Research Council/Institute of Medicine.* Washington, DC: National Academies of Science.

Lerner, R. M. (2006). Developmental science, developmental systems, and contemporary theories of human development. In R. M. Lerner (Ed.), *Theoretical models of human development. Vol. 1 of Handbook of child psychology* (6th ed., pp. 1–17). Editors-in-chief: W. Damon & R. M. Lerner. Hoboken, NJ: Wiley.

Lerner, R. M. (2007). *The good teen: Rescuing adolescence from the myths of the storm and stress years.* New York, NY: Crown Publishing Group.

Lerner, J. V., Phelps, E., Forman, Y., & Bowers, E. P. (2009). Positive youth development. In R. M. Lerner & L. Steinberg (Eds.), *Handbook of adolescent psychology* (3rd ed., pp. 524–558). Hoboken, NJ: Wiley.

Lerner, R. M., Schwartz, S. J., & Phelps, E. (2009). Problematics of time and timing in the longitudinal study of human development: Theoretical and methodological issues. *Human Development,* **52**(1), 44–68.

Lewinsohn, P. M., Hops, H., Roberts, R. E., Seeley, J. R., & Andrews, J. A. (1993). Adolescent psychopathology: I. Prevalence and incidence of depression and other DSM-III—R disorders in high school students. *Journal of Abnormal Psychology,* **102**(1), 133–144.

Levitt, M. J., Guacci-Franco, N., & Levitt, J. L. (1993). Convoys of social support in childhood and early adolescence: Structure and function. *Developmental Psychology,* **29**(5), 811–818.

Levpušček, M. P. (2006). Adolescent individuation in relation to parents and friends: Age and gender differences. *European Journal of Developmental Psychology,* **3**(3), 238–264.

Li, Y., & Lerner, R. M. (2011). Trajectories of school engagement during adolescence: Implications for grades, depression, delinquency, and substance use. *Developmental Psychology,* **47**(1), 233.

Little, R. J., & Rubin, D. B. (1989). The analysis of social science data with missing values. *Sociological Methods & Research*, **18**(2–3), 292–326.

Lloyd-Richardson, E. E., Papandonatos, G., Kazura, A., Stanton, C., & Niaura, R. (2002). Differentiating stages of smoking intensity among adolescents: Stage-specific psychological and social influences. *Journal of Consulting and Clinical Psychology*, **70**(4), 998–1009.

Lösel, F., & Farrington, D. P. (2012). Direct protective and buffering protective factors in the development of youth violence. *American Journal of Preventive Medicine*, **43**(2), S8–S23.

Ludden, A. B., & Eccles, J. S. (2007). Psychosocial, motivational, and contextual profiles of youth reporting different patterns of substance use during adolescence. *Journal of Research on Adolescence*, **17**(1), 51–88.

Lynam, D. R., Caspi, A., Moffitt, T. E., Loeber, R., & Stouthamer-Loeber, M. (2007). Longitudinal evidence that psychopathy scores in early adolescence predict adult psychopathy. *Journal of Abnormal Psychology*, **116**(1), 155.

Lynne-Landsman, S. D., Graber, J. A., Nichols, T. R., & Botvin, G. J. (2011). Trajectories of aggression, delinquency, and substance use across middle school among urban, minority adolescents. *Aggressive Behavior*, **37**(2), 161–176.

Magnuson, K., & Waldfogel, J. (Eds.). (2008). *Steady gains and stalled progress: Inequality and the Black-White test score gap*. New York, NY: Russell Sage Foundation New York.

Magnusson, D. (1985). Implications of an interactional paradigm for research on human development. *International Journal of Behavioral Development*, **8**(2), 115–137.

Magnusson, D. (2003). The person approach: Concepts, measurement models, and research strategy. In W. Damon (Series Ed.), S. C. Peck, & R. W. Roeser (Vol. Eds.), *New directions for child and adolescent development: Vol. 101. Person-centered approaches to studying human development in context* (pp. 3–24). San Francisco, CA: Jossey-Bass.

Major, B., Barr, L., Zubek, J., & Babey, S. H. (1999). Gender and self-esteem: A meta-analysis. In W. B. Swann, Jr., J. H. Langlois, & L. A. Gilbert (Eds.), *Sexism and stereotypes in modern society: The gender science of Janet Taylor Spence* (pp. 223–253). Washington DC: American Psychological Association.

Malanchuk, O., Ross, L., & Davis-Kean, P. (2010). *The influence of race in predicting occupational prestige and gendered aspirations*. Paper presented at the annual meeting of the Pathways to Adulthood International Conference, London, England, July 12–13.

Marsh, H. W. (1992). Content specificity of relations between academic achievement and academic self-concept. *Journal of Educational Psychology*, **84**(1), 35–42.

Marsh, H. W., & Craven, R. (2006). Reciprocal effects of self-concept and performance from a multidimensional perspective. *Perspectives on Psychological Science*, **1**, 95–180.

Marsh, H. W., & Shavelson, R. (1985). Self-concept: Its multifaceted, hierarchical structure. *Educational Psychologist*, **20**, 107–123.

Martino, S. C., Ellickson, P. L., & McCaffrey, D. F. (2009). Multiple trajectories of peer and parental influence and their association with the development of adolescent heavy drinking. *Addictive Behaviors*, **34**(8), 693–700.

Mason, M. J., Mennis, J., Linker, J., Bares, C., & Zaharakis, N. (2014). Peer attitudes effects on adolescent substance use: The moderating role of race and gender. *Prevention Science*, **15**(1), 56–64.

Masten, A. S. (2001). Ordinary magic: Resilience processes in development. *American Psychologist*, **56**(3), 227–238.

McAdoo, H. (Ed.). (1993). *Family ethnicity: Strength in diversity*. Thousand Oaks, CA: Sage.

McDade, T. W., Chyu, L., Duncan, G. J., Hoyt, L. T., Doane, L. D., & Adam, E. K. (2011). Adolescents' expectations for the future predict health behaviors in early adulthood. *Social Science & Medicine*, **73**(3), 391–398.

McElhaney, K. B., Allen, J. P., Stephenson, J. C., & Hare, A. L. (2009). Attachment and autonomy during adolescence. In R. M. Lerner & L. Steinberg (Eds.), *Handbook of adolescent psychology* (3rd ed., pp. 358–403). Hoboken, NJ: John Wiley & Sons.

McGill, R. K., Way, N., & Hughes, D. (2012). Intra- and interracial best friendships during middle school: Links to social and emotional well-being. *Journal of Research on Adolescence*, **22**(4), 722–738.

McLeod, G. F., Horwood, L. J., & Fergusson, D. M. (2016). Adolescent depression, adult mental health and psychosocial outcomes at 30 and 35 years. *Psychological Medicine*, **46**(7), 1–12.

McLoyd, V. C. (1990). Minority children: Introduction to the special issue. *Child Development*, **61**(2), 263–266.

McLoyd, V. C. (1998). Socioeconomic disadvantage and child development. *American Psychologist*, **53**(2), 185–204.

McLoyd, V. C., & Steinberg, L. (Eds.). (1998). *Studying minority adolescents: Conceptual, methodological, and theoretical issues*. Mahwah, NJ: Erlbaum.

McNelles, L. R., & Connolly, J. A. (1999). Intimacy between adolescent friends: Age and gender differences in intimate affect and intimate behaviors. *Journal of Research on Adolescence*, **9**(2), 143–159.

Measelle, J. R., Stice, E., & Hogansen, J. M. (2006). Developmental trajectories of co-occurring depressive, eating, antisocial, and substance abuse problems in female adolescents. *Journal of Abnormal Psychology*, **115**(3), 524.

Meece, J. L., Eccles-Parsons, J., Kaczala, C. M., Goff, S. E., & Futterman, R. (1982). Sex differences in math achievement: Toward a model of academic choice. *Psychological Bulletin*, **91**, 324–348.

Meeus, W., Iedema, J., Maassen, G., & Engels, R. (2005). Separation-individuation revisited: On the interplay of parent-adolescent relations, identity and emotional adjustment in adolescence. *Journal of Adolescence*, **28**(1), 89–106.

Meeus, W., Van De Schoot, R., Keijsers, L., Schwartz, S. J., & Branje, S. (2010). On the progression and stability of adolescent identity formation: A five-wave longitudinal study in early-to-middle and middle-to-late adolescence. *Child Development*, **81**(5), 1565–1581.

Mello, Z. R. (2008). Gender variation in developmental trajectories of educational and occupational expectations and attainment from adolescence to adulthood. *Developmental Psychology*, **44**(4), 1069–1080.

Mello, Z. R. (2009). Racial/ethnic group and socioeconomic status variation in educational and occupational expectations from adolescence to adulthood. *Journal of Applied Developmental Psychology*, **30**(4), 494–504.

Meredith, W. (1993). MI, factor analysis and factorial invariance. *Psychometrika*, **58**, 525–43.

Merikangas, K. R., He, J. P., Burstein, M., Swanson, S. A., Avenevoli, S., Cui, L., et al. (2010). Lifetime prevalence of mental disorders in US adolescents: Results from the National Comorbidity Survey Replication–Adolescent Supplement (NCS-A). *Journal of the American Academy of Child & Adolescent Psychiatry*, **49**(10), 980–989.

Mickelson, R. A. (1990). The attitude-achievement paradox among Black adolescents. *Sociology of Education*, **63**(1): 44–61.

Miller, D. B., & MacIntosh, R. (1999). Promoting resilience in urban African American adolescents: Racial socialization and identity as protective factors. *Social Work Research*, **23**(3), 159–169.

Miller, S., Malone, P. S., Dodge, K. A., & Conduct Problems Prevention Research Group. (2010). Developmental trajectories of boys' and girls' delinquency: Sex differences and links to later adolescent outcomes. *Journal of Abnormal Child Psychology*, **38**(7), 1021–1032.

Moffitt, T. E. (1993). Adolescence-limited and life-course-persistent antisocial behavior: A developmental taxonomy. *Psychological Review*, **100**(4), 674.

Moffitt, T. E. (2003). Life-course-persistent and adolescence-limited antisocial behavior: A 10-year research review and a research agenda. In B. Lahey, T. Moffitt, & A. Caspi, (Eds.), *Causes of conduct disorder and juvenile delinquency* (pp. 49–75). New York, NY: Guilford Press.

Moffitt, T. E., Caspi, A., Harrington, H., & Milne, B. J. (2002). Males on the life-course-persistent and adolescence-limited antisocial pathways: Follow-up at age 26 years. *Development and Psychopathology*, **14**(01), 179–207.

Molloy, B. L., & Herzberger, S. D. (1998). Body image and self-esteem: A comparison of African-American and Caucasian women. *Sex Roles*, **38**(7–8), 631–643.

Montgomery, C., Montgomery, C., Fisk, J. E., Montgomery, C., Fisk, J. E., Craig, L., et al. (2008). The effects of perceived parenting style on the propensity for illicit drug use: The importance of parental warmth and control. *Drug and Alcohol Review*, **27**(6), 640–649.

Morgan, P. L., Farkas, G., & Wu, Q. (2009). Five-year growth trajectories of kindergarten children with learning difficulties in mathematics. *Journal of Learning Disabilities*. **42**(4), 306–321.

Muthén, L. K., & Muthén, B. O. (1998–2010): *Mplus: Statistical analyses with latent variables: User's guide*. Los Angeles, CA: Muthén & Muthén.

Nam, C. B., & Powers, M. G. (1983). *The socioeconomic approach to status measurement: With a guide to occupational and socioeconomic status scores*. Houston, TX: Cap and Gown.

National Educational Longitudinal Study of 1988. (1988). Washington, DC: National Center for Educational Statistics.

Nesselroade, J. R., Gerstorf, D., Hardy, S. A., & Ram, N. (2007). Focus article: Idiographic filters for psychological constructs. *Measurement: Interdisciplinary Research and Perspectives*, **5**(4), 217–235.

Nesselroade, J. R., & Molenaar, P. C. M. (2010). Emphasizing intraindividual variability in the study of development over the life span: Concepts and issues. In W. F. Overton (Ed.) & Richard M. Lerner (Editor-in-Chief), *Handbook of life-span development: Cognition, biology, and methods across the lifespan* (Vol. 1, pp. 30–54). Hoboken, NJ: Wiley.

Neumark-Sztainer, D., Wall, M., Larson, N. I., Eisenberg, M. E., & Loth, K. (2011). Dieting and disordered eating behaviors from adolescence to young adulthood: Findings from a 10-year longitudinal study. *Journal of the American Dietetic Association*, **111**(7), 1004–1011.

Newes-Adeyi, G. M., Chen, C. M., Williams, G. D., & Faden, V. B. (2007). Surveillance Report# 81: Trends in underage drinking in the United States, 1991–2005. Rockville, MD: National Institute on Alcohol Abuse and Alcoholism.

Niwa, E. Y., Way, N., & Hughes, D. L. (2014). Trajectories of ethnic-racial discrimination among ethnically diverse early adolescents: Associations with psychological and social adjustment. *Child Development*, **85**(6), 2339–2354.

Noguera, P. A. (2003). The trouble with Black boys: The role and influence of environmental and cultural factors on the academic performance of African American males. *Urban Education*, **38**(4), 431–459.

Noller, P., & Callan, V. J. (1990). Adolescents' perceptions of the nature of their communication with parents. *Journal of Youth and Adolescence*, **19**(4), 349–362.

Ogbu, J. U. (2003). *Black American students in an affluent suburb: A study of academic disengagement.* Mahwah, NJ: Erlbaum.

Ong, A. D., Bergeman, C. S., Bisconti, T. L., & Wallace, K. A. (2006). Psychological resilience, positive emotions, and successful adaptation to stress in later life. *Journal of Personality and Social Psychology*, **91**(4), 730–749.

Orth, U., & Robins, R. W. (2014). The development of self-esteem. *Current Directions in Psychological Science*, **23**(5), 381–387.

Orth, U., Robins, R. W., & Roberts, B. W. (2008). Low self-esteem prospectively predicts depression in adolescence and young adulthood. *Journal of Personality and Social Psychology*, **95**(3), 695–708.

Pahl, K., & Way, N. (2006). Longitudinal trajectories of ethnic identity among urban Black and Latino adolescents. *Child Development*, **77**(5), 1403–1415.

Paikoff, R. L., Collins, W. A., & Laursen, B. (1988). Perceptions of efficacy and legitimacy of parental influence techniques by children and early adolescents. *Journal of Early Adolescence*, **8**, 37–52.

Parke, R. D., & Buriel, R. (1998). Socialization in the family: Ethnic and ecological perspectives. In N. Eisenberg (Ed.), *Handbook of child psychology, 5th ed.: Vol 3. Social, emotional, and personality development* (pp. 463–552). Hoboken, NJ: John Wiley & Sons.

Parker, S., Nichter, M., Nichter, M., Vuckovic, N., Sims, C., & Ritenbaugh, C. (1995). Body image and weight concerns among African American and White adolescent females: Differences that make a difference. *Human Organization*, **54**(2), 103–114.

Patterson, G. R., Dishion, T. J., & Yoerger, K. (2000). Adolescent growth in new forms of problem behavior: Macro-and micro-peer dynamics. *Prevention Science*, **1**(1), 3–13.

Peck, S. C., Brodish, A. B., Malanchuk, O., Banerjee, M., & Eccles, J. S. (2014). Racial/ethnic socialization and identity development in Black families: The role of parent and youth reports. *Developmental Psychology*, **50**(7), 1897–1909.

Peck, S. C., Feinstein, L., & Eccles, J. S. (Eds.). (2008). Unexpected educational pathways. *Journal of Social Issues* **64**(1), 135–156.

Peck, S. C., & Roeser, R. W. (Eds.). (2003). Person-centered approaches to studying development in context. In W. Damon (Series Ed.), *New directions for child and adolescent development* (Vol. 101). San Francisco, CA: Jossey-Bass.

Pellmar, T. C., Brandt, E. N., Jr., & Baird, M. A. (2002). Health and behavior: The interplay of biological, behavioral, and social influences: Summary of an Institute of Medicine report. *American Journal of Health Promotion*, **16**(4), 206–219.

Perkins, S. A., & Turiel, E. (2007). To lie or not to lie: To whom and under what circumstances. *Child Development*, **78**(2), 609–621.

Pfoertner, T. K., Rathmann, K., Elgar, F. J., de Looze, M., Hofmann, F., Ottova-Jordan, V., et al. (2014). Adolescents' psychological health complaints and the economic recession in late 2007: A multilevel study in 31 countries. *The European Journal of Public Health*, **6**, 961–967.

Phinney, J. S. (1990). Ethnic identity in adolescents and adults: Review of research. *Psychological Bulletin*, **108**(3), 499–514.

Phinney, J. S. (1992). The multigroup ethnic identity measure: A new scale for diverse groups. *Journal of Adolescence, 13*, 171–183.

Phinney, J. S., & Ong, A. D. (2007). Conceptualization and measurement of ethnic identity: Current status and future directions. *Journal of Counseling Psychology, 54*(3), 271.

Pincus, F. L. (1996). Discrimination comes in many forms: Individual, institutional and structural. *American Behavioral Scientist, 40*(2), 186–194.

Piquero, A. R. (2007). Taking stock of developmental trajectories on criminal activity over the life course. In A. Liberman (Ed.), *The long view of crime: A synthesis of longitudinal research* (pp. 23–78). New York, NY: Springer.

Powers, S. I. (2011). *Genes, hormones, and family behavior: What makes adolescence unique?* New York, NY: Springer Science Business Media.

Quillian, L., & Campbell, M. E. (2003). Beyond black and white: The present and future of multiracial friendship segregation. *American Sociological Review, 68*(4), 540–566.

Raudenbush, S., Bryk, A., Cheon, Y. F., & Congdon, R. (2000). *HLM 5: Hierarchical linear and nonlinear modeling.* Lincolnwood, IL: Scientific Software International.

Resnick, M. D., Bearman, P. S., Blum, R. W., Bauman, K. E., Harris, K. M., Jones, J., et al. (1997). Protecting adolescents from harm: Findings from the National Longitudinal Study on Adolescent Health. *Jama, 278*(10), 823–832.

Richman, C., Clark, M., & Brown, K. (1985). General and specific self-esteem in late adolescent students: Race x gender x SES effects. *Adolescence, 20*, 555–566.

Risch, S. C., Jodl, K. M., & Eccles, J. S. (2004). The role of the father-adolescent relationship in shaping adolescents' attitudes toward divorce. *Journal of Marriage and Family, 66*(1), 46–58.

Roderick, M. (2003). What's happening to the boys? Early high school experiences and school outcomes among African American male adolescents in Chicago. *Urban Education, 38*(5), 538–607.

Roeser, R. W., & Eccles, J. S. (1998). Adolescents' perceptions of middle school: Relation to longitudinal changes in academic and psychological adjustment. *Journal of Research on Adolescence, 8*(1), 123–158.

Roeser, R. W., Eccles, J. S., & Freedman-Doan, C. (1999). Academic functioning and mental health in adolescence patterns, progressions, and routes from childhood. *Journal of Adolescent Research, 14*(2), 135–174.

Roeser, R. W., Eccles, J. S., & Sameroff, A. J. (2000). School as a context of early adolescents' academic and social-emotional development: A summary of research findings. *The Elementary School Journal, 100*(5), 443–471.

Rose, A. J. (2002). Co-rumination in the friendships of girls and boys. *Child Development, 73*(6), 1830–1843.

Rose, A. J., & Rudolph, K. D. (2006). A review of sex differences in peer relationship processes: Potential trade-offs for the emotional and behavioral development of girls and boys. *Psychological Bulletin, 132*(1), 98.

Rubin, K. H., Bukowski, W. M., & Laursen, B. (Eds.). (2011). *Handbook of peer interactions, relationships, and groups.* New York, NY: Guilford Press.

Ruble, D. N., & Seidman, E. (1996). Social transitions: Windows into social psychological processes. In E. T. Higgins & A. W. Kruglanski (Eds.), *Social psychology: Handbook of basic principles* (pp. 830–856). New York, NY: Guilford Press.

Rude, J., & Herda, D. (2010). Best friends forever? Race and the stability of adolescent friendships. *Social Forces, 89*(2), 585–607.

Rumberger, R. W. (2001). *Why students drop out of school and what can be done.* Cambridge, MA: Civil Rights Project, Harvard University.

Rumberger, R. W. (1987). High school dropouts: A review of issues and evidence. *Review of Educational Research,* **57**(2), 101–121.

Rutter, M. (1987). Psychosocial resilience and protective mechanisms. *American Journal of Orthopsychiatry,* **57** (3), 316–331.

Sameroff, A. J. (2000). Ecological perspectives on developmental risk. *WAIMH Handbook of Infant Mental Health,* **4**, 3–33.

Sameroff, A. J., & Gutman, L. M. (2004). Contributions of risk research to the designs of successful interventions. In P. Allen-Meares & M. W. Fraser (Eds.), *Intervention with children and adolescents: An interdisciplinary perspective* (pp. 9–26). Boston, MA: Allyn-Bacon.

Savickas, M. L. (2005). The theory and practice of career construction. In S. D. Brown & R. W. Lent (Eds.), *Career development and counseling: Putting theory and research to work* (pp. 42–70). Hoboken, NJ: Wiley.

Schaefer, E. S. (1965). A configurational analysis of children's reports of parent behavior. *Journal of Consulting Psychology,* **29**(6), 552.

Schafer, J. L., & Graham, J. W. (2002). Missing data: Our view of the state of the art. *Psychological Methods,* **7**(2), 147–177.

Schneider, B. H., Dixon, K., & Udvari, S. (2007). Closeness and competition in the inter-ethnic and co-ethnic friendships of early adolescents in Toronto and Montreal. *The Journal of Early Adolescence,* **27**(1), 115–138.

Schoon, I., Martin, P., & Ross, A. (2007). Career transitions in times of social change: His and her story. *Journal of Vocational Behavior,* **70**(1), 78–96.

Schulenberg, J. E., & Maggs, J. L. (2002). A developmental perspective on alcohol use and heavy drinking during adolescence and the transition to young adulthood. *Journal of Studies on Alcohol, Supplement,* **14**, 54–70.

Schwartz, S. J., Montgomery, M. J., & Briones, E. (2006). The role of identity in acculturation among immigrant people: Theoretical propositions, empirical questions, and applied recommendations. *Human Development,* **49**(1), 1–30.

Schwartz, S. J., Pantin, H., Coatsworth, J. D., & Szapocznik, J. (2007). Addressing the challenges and opportunities for today's youth: Toward an integrative model and its implications for research and intervention. *The Journal of Primary Prevention,* **28**(2), 117–144.

Seaton, E. K., Neblett, E. W., Upton, R. D., Hammond, W. P., & Sellers, R. M. (2011). The moderating capacity of racial identity between perceived discrimination and psychological well-being over time among African American youth. *Child Development,* **82**(6), 1850–1867. https://doi.org/10.1111/j.1467-8624. 2011.01651.x

Seaton, E. K., Scottham, K. M., & Sellers, R. M. (2006). The status model of racial identity development in African American adolescents: Evidence of structure, trajectories, and well-being. *Child Development,* **77**(5), 1416–1426.

Seaton, E. K., Yip, T., & Sellers, R. M. (2009). A longitudinal examination of racial identity and racial discrimination among African American adolescents. *Child Development,* **80**(2), 406–417.

Sellers, R. M., Copeland-Linder, N., Martin, P. P., & Lewis, R. L. (2006). Racial identity matters: The relationship between racial discrimination and psychological functioning in African American adolescents. *Journal of Research on Adolescence,* **16**(2), 187–216.

Sellers, R. M., Smith, M. A., Shelton, J. N., Rowley, S. A., & Chavous, T. M. (1998). Multidimensional model of racial identity: A reconceptualization of African American racial identity. *Personality and Social Psychology Review*, **2**(1), 18–39.

Shanahan, L., McHale, S. M., Crouter, A. C., & Osgood, D. W. (2007). Warmth with mothers and fathers from middle childhood to late adolescence: Within-and between-families comparisons. *Developmental Psychology*, **43**(3), 551–563.

Shrum, W., Cheek, N. H., Jr, & MacD, S. (1988). Friendship in school: Gender and racial homophily. *Sociology of Education*, **61**(4), 227–239.

Simmons, R. G., & Blyth, D. A. (1987). *Moving into adolescence: The impact of pubertal chance and school context.* Hawthorne, NY: Aldine de Gruyter.

Simons-Morton, B., & Chen, R. (2009). Peer and parent influences on school engagement among early adolescents. *Youth & Society*, **41**, 3–25.

Simpkins, S. D., Davis-Kean, P. E., & Eccles, J. S. (2006). Math and Science motivation: A longitudinal examination of the links between choices and beliefs. *Developmental Psychology*, **42**(1), 70–83.

Smetana, J. G. (1988). Adolescents' and parents' conceptions of parental authority. *Child Development*, **59**, 321–335.

Smetana, J. G. (1989). Adolescents' and parents' reasoning about actual family conflict. *Child Development*, **60**, 1052–1067.

Smetana, J. G. (1995). Parenting styles and conceptions of parental authority during adolescence. *Child Development*, **66**, 299–316.

Smetana, J. G. (2000). Middle-class African American adolescents' and parents' conceptions of parental authority and parenting practices: A longitudinal investigation. *Child Development*, **71**, 1672–1686.

Smetana, J. G., Campione-Barr, N., & Daddis, C. (2004). Longitudinal development of family decision-making: Defining healthy behavioral autonomy for middle-class African American adolescents. *Child Development*, **75**, 1418–1434.

Smetana, J. G., Campione-Barr, N., & Metzger, A. (2006). Adolescent development in interpersonal and societal contexts. *Annual Review of Psychology*, **57**, 255–284.

Smetana, J. G., Daddis, C., & Chuang, S. S. (2003). "Clean your room!" A longitudinal investigation of adolescent-parent conflict and conflict resolution in middle-class African American families. *Journal of Adolescent Research*, **18**(6), 631–650.

Smink, F. R., Van Hoeken, D., & Hoek, H. W. (2012). Epidemiology of eating disorders: Incidence, prevalence and mortality rates. *Current Psychiatry Reports*, **14**(4), 406–414.

Smith-Bynum, M. A., Lambert, S. F., English, D., & Ialongo, N. S. (2014). Associations between trajectories of perceived racial discrimination and psychological symptoms among African American adolescents. *Development and Psychopathology*, **26**(4), 1049–1065.

Smollar, J., & Youniss, J. (1989). Transformations in adolescents' perceptions of parents. *International Journal of Behavioral Development*, **12**(1), 71–84.

Spoth, R., Trudeau, L., Guyll, M., Shin, C., & Redmond, C. (2009). Universal intervention effects on substance use among young adults mediated by delayed adolescent substance initiation. *Journal of Consulting and Clinical Psychology*, **77**(4), 620.

Squeglia, L. M., Jacobus, J., & Tapert, S. F. (2009). The influence of substance use on adolescent brain development. *Clinical EEG and Neuroscience*, **40**(1), 31–38.

Steele, C. M., & Aronson, J. (1995). Stereotype threat and the intellectual test performance of African Americans. *Journal of Personality and Social Psychology*, **69**(5), 797.

Steinberg, L. (1988). Reciprocal relation between parent-child distance and pubertal maturation. *Developmental Psychology*, **24**(1), 122.

Steinberg, L. (1990). Interdependence in the family: Autonomy, conflict, and harmony in the parent–adolescent relationship. In S. S. Feldman & G. R. Elliot (Eds.), *At the threshold: The developing adolescent* (pp. 255–276). Cambridge, MA: Harvard University Press.

Steinberg, L. (2001). We know some things: Parent–adolescent relationships in retrospect and prospect. *Journal of Research on Adolescence*, **11**(1), 1–19.

Steinberg, L. (2005). Cognitive and affective development in adolescence. *Trends in Cognitive Sciences*, **9**(2), 69–74.

Steinberg, L. (2008). A social neuroscience perspective on adolescent risk-taking. *Developmental Review*, **28**(1), 78–106.

Steinberg, L., & Morris, A. S. (2001). Adolescent development. *Journal of Cognitive Education and Psychology*, **2**(1), 55–87.

Steinberg, L., Mounts, N. S., Lamborn, S. D., & Dornbusch, S. M. (1991). Authoritative parenting and adolescent adjustment across varied ecological niches. *Journal of Research on Adolescence*, **1**(1), 19–36.

Steinberg, L., & Silverberg, S. B. (1986). The vicissitudes of autonomy in early adolescence. *Child Development*, **57**(4), 841–851.

Stice, E. (2002). Risk and maintenance factors for eating pathology: A meta-analytic review. *Psychological Bulletin*, **128**(5), 825–848.

Stiglbauer, B., Gnambs, T., Gamsjäger, M., & Batinic, B. (2013). The upward spiral of adolescents' positive school experiences and happiness: Investigating reciprocal effects over time. *Journal of School Psychology*, **51**(2), 231–242.

Stoddard, S. A., Zimmerman, M. A., & Bauermeister, J. A. (2011). Thinking about the future as a way to succeed in the present: A longitudinal study of future orientation and violent behaviors among African American youth. *American Journal of Community Psychology*, **48**(3–4), 238–246.

Swanson, S. A., Crow, S. J., Le Grange, D., Swendsen, J., & Merikangas, K. R. (2011). Prevalence and correlates of eating disorders in adolescents: Results from the national comorbidity survey replication adolescent supplement. *Archives of General Psychiatry*, **68**(7), 714.

Syed, M., & Azmitia, M. (2009). Longitudinal trajectories of ethnic identity during the college years. *Journal of Research on Adolescence*, **19**(4), 601–624.

Tang, S., McLoyd, V. C., & Hallman, S. K. (2016). Racial socialization, racial identity, and academic attitudes among African Amerian adolescents: Examining the moderating influence of parent-adolescent communication. *Journal of Youth and Adolescence*, **45**, 1141–1155.

Tangney, J. P., Baumeister, R. F., & Boone, A. L. (2004). High self-control predicts good adjustment, less pathology, better grades, and interpersonal success. *Journal of Personality*, **72**(2), 271–324.

Tilson, E. C., McBride, C. M., Lipkus, I. M., & Catalano, R. F. (2004). Testing the interaction between parent–child relationship factors and parent smoking to predict youth smoking. *Journal of Adolescent Health*, **35**(3), 182–189.

Touchette, E., Henegar, A., Godart, N. T., Pryor, L., Falissard, B., Tremblay, R. E., et al. (2011). Subclinical eating disorders and their comorbidity with mood and anxiety disorders in adolescent girls. *Psychiatry Research*, **185**(1), 185–192.

Trzesniewski, K. H., Donnellan, M. B., Moffitt, T. E., Robins, R. W., Poulton, R., & Caspi, A. (2006). Low self-esteem during adolescence predicts poor health, criminal behavior, and limited economic prospects during adulthood. *Developmental Psychology, 42*(2), 381–390.

Twenge, J. M., & Nolen-Hoeksema, S. (2002). Age, gender, race, socioeconomic status, and birth cohort difference on the children's depression inventory: A meta-analysis. *Journal of Abnormal Psychology, 111*(4), 578.

Tynes, B. M., Umaña-Taylor, A. J., Rose, C. A., Lin, J., & Anderson, C. J. (2012). Online racial discrimination and the protective function of ethnic identity and self-esteem for African American adolescents. *Developmental Psychology, 48*(2), 343–355.

Van Der Put, C. E., Deković, M., Stams, G. J. J., Van Der Laan, P. H., Hoeve, M., & Van Amelsfort, L. (2011). Changes in risk factors during adolescence implications for risk assessment. *Criminal Justice and Behavior, 38*(3), 248–262.

Vecchione, M., Alessandri, G., Barbaranelli, C., & Gerbino, M. (2010). Stability and change of ego resiliency from late adolescence to young adulthood: A multiperspective study using the ER89-R Scale. *Journal of Personality Assessment, 92*(3), 212–221.

Verboom, C. E., Sijtsema, J. J., Verhulst, F. C., Penninx, B. W., & Ormel, J. (2014). Longitudinal associations between depressive problems, academic performance, and social functioning in adolescent boys and girls. *Developmental Psychology, 50*(1), 247.

Viner, R. M., Ozer, E. M., Denny, S., Marmot, M., Resnick, M., Fatusi, A., et al. (2012). Adolescence and the social determinants of health. *The Lancet, 379*(9826), 1641–1652.

Voelkl, K. E. (1997). Identification with school. *American Journal of Education, 105*, 294–318.

Voyer, D., & Voyer, S. D. (2014). Gender differences in scholastic achievement: A meta-analysis. *Psychological Bulletin, 140*(4), 1174–1204.

Wallace, J. M., Bachman, J. G., O'Malley, P. M., Johnston, L. D., Schulenberg, J. G., & Cooper, S. M. (2002). Tobacco, alcohol, and illicit drug use: Racial and ethnic differences among high school seniors. *Public Health Report, 117*, 67–75.

Wang, M. T., & Dishion, T. J. (2012). The trajectories of adolescents' perceptions of school climate, deviant peer affiliation, and behavioral problems during the middle school years. *Journal of Research on Adolescence, 22*(1), 40–53.

Wang, M. T., Dishion, T. J., Stormshak, E. A., & Willett, J. B. (2011). Trajectories of family management practices and early adolescent behavioral outcomes. *Developmental Psychology, 47*(5), 1324.

Wang, M. T., & Eccles, J. S. (2012). Social support matters: Longitudinal effects of social support on three dimensions of school engagement from middle to high school. *Child Development, 83*(3), 877–895.

Wang, M. T., & Fredricks, J. A. (2014). The reciprocal links between school engagement, youth problem behaviors, and school dropout during adolescence. *Child Development, 85*(2), 722–737.

Wang, M. T., & Huguley, J. P. (2012). Parental racial socialization as a moderator of the effects of racial discrimination on educational success among African American adolescents. *Child Development, 83*(5), 1716–1731.

Way, N., & Chen, L. (2000). Close and general friendships among African American, Latino, and Asian American adolescents from low-income families. *Journal of Adolescent Research, 15*(2), 274–301.

Way, N., & Greene, M. L. (2006). Trajectories of perceived friendship quality during adolescence: The patterns and contextual predictors. *Journal of Research on Adolescence*, 16(2), 293–320.

Webb, J., Bray, J. H., Adams, G., & Getz, J. G. (2002). Gender differences in adolescent alcohol use, externalizing and internalizing behavior problems, and peer influence. *American Journal of Orthopsychiatry*, 72, 392–400.

Welsh, B. C., & Farrington, D. P. (2007). *Preventing crime*. New York, NY: Springer Science+Business Media.

Wigfield, A., Byrnes, J. P., & Eccles, J. S. (2006). Development during early and middle adolescence. *Handbook of Educational Psychology*, 2, 87–113.

Wigfield, A., & Eccles, J. S. (2002). The development of competence beliefs, expectancies for success, and achievement values from childhood through adolescence. In A. Wigfield & J. S. Eccles (Eds.), *Development of achievement motivation* (pp. 91–120). San Diego, CA: Academic Press.

Wigfield, A., Eccles, J. S., Mac Iver, D., Reuman, D. A., & Midgley, C. (1991). Transitions during early adolescence: Changes in children's domain-specific self-perceptions and general self-esteem across the transition to junior high school. *Developmental Psychology*, 27(4), 552.

Wigfield, A., Eccles, J. S., & Pintrich, P. (1996). Development between the ages of 11 and 25. In D. Berliner & R. Calfee (Eds.), *Handbook of educational psychology*. New York, NY: Macmillan.

Wilkinson, R. B. (2004). The role of parental and peer attachment in the psychological health and self-esteem of adolescents. *Journal of Youth and Adolescence*, 33, 479–493.

Williams, D. R., Neighbors, H. W., & Jackson, J. S. (2003). Racial/ethnic discrimination and health: Findings from community studies. *American Journal of Public Health*, 93(2), 200–208.

Williams, J. L., Aiyer, S. M., Durkee, M. I., & Tolan, P. H. (2014). The protective role of ethnic identity for urban adolescent males facing multiple stressors. *Journal of Youth and Adolescence*, 43(10), 1728–1741.

Windle, M., & Windle, R. C. (2012). Early onset problem behaviors and alcohol, tobacco, and other substance use disorders in young adulthood. *Drug and Alcohol Dependence*, 121(1), 152–158.

Wong, C. A., Eccles, J. S., & Sameroff, A. (2003). The influence of ethnic discrimination and ethnic identification on African American adolescents' school and socioemotional adjustment. *Journal of Personality*, 71(6), 1197–1232.

Wong, M. M., Nigg, J. T., Zucker, R. A., Puttler, L. I., Fitzgerald, H. E., Jester, J. M., et al. (2006). Behavioral control and resiliency in the onset of alcohol and illicit drug use: A prospective study from preschool to adolescence. *Child Development*, 77(4), 1016–1033.

Zahn-Waxler, C., Shirtcliff, E. A., & Marceau, K. (2008). Disorders of childhood and adolescence: Gender and psychopathology. *Annual Review of Clinical Psychology*, 4, 275–303.

Zhang, Z., Browne, M. W., & Nesselroade, J. R. (2011). Higher-order factor invariance and idiographic mapping of constructs to observables. *Applied Developmental Science*, 15(4), 186–200.

Zimmerman, M. A., Copeland, L. A., Shope, J. T., & Dielman, T. E. (1997). A longitudinal study of self-esteem: Implications for adolescent development. *Journal of Youth and Adolescence*, 26(2), 117–141.

ACKNOWLEDGMENTS

This article is part of the issue "Moving Through Adolescence: Developmental Trajectories of African American and European American Youth" Gutman, Peck, Malanchuk, Sameroff, and Eccles (Issue Authors). For a full listing of articles in this issue, see: http://onlinelibrary.wiley.com/doi/10.1111/mono.v82.4/issuetoc.

- The original data were funded by the MacArthur Network on Successful Adolescent Development in High Risk Settings (Chair: R. Jessor). [Waves 1–3].
- Waves 4 and 5 were partially funded by: NICHD Grant no. R01 HD33437 to Jacquelynne S. Eccles and Arnold J. Sameroff and a W.T. Grant Foundation no. 2143 awarded to Jacquelynne S. Eccles.
- Wave 6 was funded by the Spencer Foundation Grant MG no. 200000275 to Tabbye Chavous and Jacquelynne S. Eccles.
- Waves 7 and 8 were partially funded by NICHD Grant no. R01 HD048970 to Jacquelynne S. Eccles and Stephen C. Peck and Wave 8 biomarker data by NIA Grant no. RC2AG03678001 to Jacquelynne S. Eccles and Stephen C. Peck with subcontracts to Emma Adam, Margaret Kemeny, and Wendy Berry-Mendes.

We thank the following people for their support of this project (listed alphabetically): Todd Bartko, Elaine Belansky, Heather Bouchey, Amanda Brodish, Nick Butler, Celina Chatman, Courtney Cogburn, Diane Early, Kari Fraser, Thomas Fuller-Rowell, Katie Jodl, Ariel Kalil, Linda Kuhn, Sarah Lord, Karen McCarthy, Alice Michael, Melanie Overby, Robert Roeser, Sherri Steele, Erika Taylor, Janice Templeton, Cindy Winston, and Carol Wong. The data are archived at the Henry A. Murray Research Archive at Harvard University: http://www.murray.harvard.edu/contact-us

DOI: 10.1111/mono.12338

COMMENTARY

COMMENTARY ON "MOVING THROUGH ADOLESCENCE: DEVELOPMENTAL TRAJECTORIES OF AFRICAN AMERICAN AND EUROPEAN AMERICAN YOUTH"

Judith G. Smetana

> This article is part of the issue "Moving Through Adolescence: Developmental Trajectories of African American and European American Youth" Gutman, Peck, Malanchuk, Sameroff, and Eccles (Issue Authors). For a full listing of articles in this issue, see: http://onlinelibrary.wiley.com/doi/10.1111/mono.v82.4/issuetoc.

This commentary discusses Gutman et al.'s monograph on developmental trajectories of African American and European American youth. Conceptual and methodological strengths of the monograph are highlighted, and the historical context of the study, including societal and technological changes that have altered the experience of adolescence and advances in developmental science that have occurred since the MADICS was conducted, are discussed. Finally, several suggestions are offered for ways Gutman et al.'s analyses could be elaborated to address further questions about adolescent development in context.

This monograph, written by Gutman, Peck, Malanchuk, Sameroff, and Eccles, presents analyses of longitudinal data from the Maryland Adolescent Development in Context Study (MADICS). The eight waves of MADICS have yielded numerous groundbreaking publications over the past 25 years that have furthered our understanding of adolescent development. This monograph, employing four waves of data following adolescents from age 12 to 20 years, takes a broader look. It provides a detailed, comprehensive

Corresponding author: Judith G. Smetana, Department of Clinical and Social Sciences in Psychology, Meliora Hall, RC 270266, University of Rochester, Rochester, NY 14627, email: judith.smetana@rochester.edu

DOI: 10.1111/mono.12339

picture of normative developmental trajectories for a range of psychological characteristics during adolescence, as moderated by adolescents' gender, socioeconomic status (SES), family marital status, and race/ethnicity. The authors employed a social-ecological framework to consider risk and protective factors in the development of and variations in psychological well-being, ethnic/racial identity and discrimination, academic functioning, problem behaviors, and family and peer relationships. Integrating both resilience and positive youth development frameworks, the overarching question addressed in this monograph is whether adolescence is a developmental period of heightened risk. Based on their analyses, Gutman et al. concluded emphatically that it is not and that the youth sampled here reported relatively stable and developmentally healthy pathways through adolescence, with some variations according to content domain. In this commentary, I first highlight some of the important strengths of this monograph. Then, in keeping with its social-ecological perspective, I consider the historical context in which the study was conducted. I discuss some of the societal and technological changes that have altered the experience of adolescence, as well as conceptual and methodological advances in our science that have occurred since the MADICS data were collected. Finally, I offer some suggestions for further ways the analyses presented here could be elaborated to address central questions about adolescent development.

CONTRIBUTIONS TO THE LITERATURE

This monograph makes several unique contributions to the literature. First, as the monograph notes, racial and ethnic minorities in the United States are underrepresented in studies of normative development. The analyses reported here address this significant gap in the literature by comparing African American and European American adolescents on multiple dimensions of normative development while carefully controlling for sociodemographic background. MADICS was conducted in Prince George County, Maryland, USA, and this county was selected for its unique characteristics. It is diverse in terms of its mix of rural, urban, and suburban environs, and it is unusual not only in having a very closely matched SES distribution of African American and European Americans, but also a high proportion of middle-class African American families. Although the monograph authors found significant differences in SES (as well as family marital status) between African American and European American families, these differences were much smaller than is typically observed and were carefully covaried in the analyses. Indeed, as the authors noted in Chapter 1, they chose to sample teens living in the same geographical area and attending the same schools to overcome the confounds between race/ethnicity and family SES that have often plagued past research. Furthermore, as I have noted elsewhere (Smetana, 2011a, 2011b), middle-class African Americans have been underrepresented in developmental science research, particularly in studies of normative development. Thus, the use of an African American sample that is largely middle class and the detailed ethnic/racial comparisons across many areas of adolescent functioning in this carefully selected sample make a particularly welcome and valuable contribution to the literature.

Moreover, the monograph shows impressive attention to methodological detail. There were high rates of retention in this large longitudinal sample (as well as detailed attention to sources of attrition), the items were carefully matched across the study waves, construct and measurement invariance were demonstrated, and cross-wave correlations were examined to provide evidence of convergent validity. These are significant strengths of the study that increase our confidence in the findings. The results of this monograph offer many insights into normative development across time and multiple domains and will inform future research on adolescent development.

CONSIDERING THE FINDINGS IN CONTEXT

In interpreting the results of this monograph, there are several caveats common to the use of large survey data that should be noted. First, more than a quarter of a century has passed since collection of the MADICS data commenced and two decades since it was completed. The social ecological framework of the present monograph, with its focus on lives in context, also demands a consideration of cohort effects, which link age and historical time (Elder, 1998; Elder, Johnson, & Crosnoe, 2003). Thus, readers should keep in mind the historical context in which these data were collected. Youth who participated in this study were born in the late 1970s. The larger political and social context of their adolescence included renewed ethnic conflicts around the world (the Gulf War, the Bosnian war, and the Rwandan and Bosnian genocides), as well as new political alliances, such as the creation of the European Union. As some of these events suggest, the 1990s were marked by a worldwide rise in ethnic nationalism, also accompanied by enormous economic expansion in the United States (the term "irrational exuberance" was coined during this decade in response to the "dot-com" bubble). Although difficult to estimate without comparisons to other age cohorts, these events likely had implications for study participants' views, particularly of race relations and their beliefs and optimism about their educational, economic, and social prospects.

Furthermore, the last decade of the 20th century saw enormous sea changes in technology. The World Wide Web as a public Internet service began in 1991, and ownership of personal computers increased dramatically during the decade. Although these events occurred during the period in which the MADICS data were collected, their impact was not felt until later. The omnipresence of the Internet in daily life, the proliferation of and reliance on different forms of social media, and the constant use of cell phones that are essential aspects of the adolescent experience today most likely were not part of the MADICS cohort's—nor their parents'—lives.

In addition, although the measures examined in this monograph are generally robust, developmental science has progressed over the decades since MADICS was initiated. The monograph authors were able to avail themselves of the best current thinking about adolescent risk and preventive factors in framing the study, but their choice of measures was constrained by the decisions made when the study began. Overall, the measures hold up remarkably well; most of the constructs (at least those that were chosen for this monograph) are relevant and important. Like many large-scale surveys assessing functioning across multiple domains, however, key constructs in MADICS were sometimes assessed using one- or two-item measures, often developed for this study, limiting the ability to make comparisons to other well-established measures.

And as one might expect, there are some gaps. As is noted in the monograph, better measures of racial/ethnic identity were being developed or have emerged since the study began, and conceptualizations of racial/ethnic identity have become more integrated and elaborated (Umaña-Taylor et al., 2014). Additionally, more granular approaches to studying the racial/ethnic context have been developed. For instance, recent research has shown the value of considering adolescent adjustment as a function of racial/ethnic youths' numerical representation in classrooms and schools (Benner & Graham, 2007; Graham, 2006), referred to as Simpson's diversity index (Graham, 2016). The measures of family functioning cover central constructs but miss nuances that have become important in the current literature. For instance, research over the past 20 years has fruitfully unpacked parental knowledge from monitoring and behavioral control (Kerr, Stattin, & Burk, 2010)—neither of which were examined here; expanding on this distinction, recent research has shown the importance of considering adolescent disclosure and secrecy with parents (Darling, Cumsille, Caldwell, & Dowdy, 2006; Marshall, Tilton-Weaver, & Bosdet, 2005), as well as adolescents' beliefs about parental authority legitimacy (Kuhn & Laird, 2011; Smetana, Metzger, Gettman, & Campione-Barr, 2006) as significant protective and risk factors in adolescent development. Likewise, the measures of peer relationships, which were selected to parallel some of the parent measures, provide useful information about how much adolescents communicate with peers and whether their friends are academically oriented or engage in delinquent behaviors. Newer research, however, has focused on the quality of adolescent friendships and even, whether conversations skew positive or negative (Granic & Dishion, 2003), which have been found to be as important as whether or not they have friends (Rubin, Bukowski, & Bowker, 2015).

WHAT IS HOT AND WHAT IS NOT

Furthermore, interest in some topics has waned, while other topics have become much more prominent. For example, in recent years, research on peer relationships has focused heavily on peer harassment and victimization (including cyberbullying, an unfortunate consequence of the technological advances of the 1990s). We now know that such behaviors are all too common and that they have detrimental effects on adolescent development. Interest has also increased over the past decades in studying adolescents' romantic relationships, including the experiences of LGBTQI youth—a topic that also intersects with research on bullying, victimization, and schooling (e.g., Russell & Horn, 2017). Given that these topics have emerged more recently as issues of intense scholarly interest, the authors cannot be faulted for not including them here. It is more surprising, however, that the authors did not include assessments of adolescents' sexual behavior and involvement, which was viewed primarily in terms of risk in earlier research and has come to be viewed within a more normative developmental framework today and risky only when involvement commences at young ages (Diamond, Bonner, & Dickenson, 2015). Finally, given that the study is viewed through the lens of a positive youth development (PYD) framework, it is surprising that the measures of well-being largely focus on the presence or absence of negative conditions (e.g., depression, eating disorders) rather than measures of positive development (e.g., civic engagement or developmental assets).

One other general concern can be raised. In an *Annual Review of Psychology* chapter written a decade ago, my colleagues and I noted that research on adolescent development has become increasingly contextual and much less developmental. By that we meant that interest in intra-individual processes such as autonomy, identity, intimacy, self-understanding, and moral development (all typically seen as critical developmental tasks of adolescence) has waned and has been replaced by an emphasis on individual differences in adjustment (Smetana, Campione-Barr, & Metzger, 2006). These concerns are relevant here. The focus here is undeniably on development, as analyzed by developmental trajectories, but development of what? Although the authors describe the selection of study measures as based on the developmental tasks of adolescence, I remain unclear as to precisely how those developmental tasks were conceptualized here. All of the domains studied here are interesting, central, and worthy of study, and the comparisons of European and African American youth on these dimensions yield valuable findings. But it can be argued that part of the utility of studying changes over time in, say, parent and peer relationships is in identifying the patterns and trajectories of these relationships that facilitate or undermine the development of other intrapersonal processes. Thus, for instance, intrusive parenting and low levels of support are problematic *because* they undermine adolescent autonomy development. Similarly, concerns with adolescents' peer relationships are in part because they impact other important tasks of adolescence, such as the development of identity and intimacy; they may also, perhaps, facilitate too-early autonomy, which is dysfunctional for development (Dishion, Nelson, & Bullock, 2004). Thus, more conceptual clarification of how the authors view these developmental tasks would have enhanced the monograph. These concerns also raise questions about the analyses.

MODELING GROWTH

Hierarchical linear growth models were performed on each measure, as grouped within content domains (e.g., well-being, parents, peers, etc.). Needless to say, these analyses yielded a wealth of findings to ponder, but overall, the developmental trends were largely consistent with results from past research (which is not surprising, given that past research using these data were sometimes used in formulating hypotheses). Overall, the authors concluded that there was stronger evidence of positive than problematic development and that the ages associated with the greatest risks varied according to the particular outcome studied. Experimentation with different substances and involvement in problem behavior peaked in middle adolescence, having friends who are negative influences increased over time, beliefs about academic ability and school motivation decreased over time, and racial/ethnic identity and relationships with parents remained relatively stable across this developmental period. Furthermore, SES and marital status had relatively few effects (although marital status may have had more of an impact if it had been modeled as a time-varying covariate rather than as a static variable). Gender, race/ethnicity, and their interaction moderated the developmental trends. These findings are interesting and important to document, and they were also mostly as anticipated. Are there any big surprises in the findings? Not so much. They largely confirm our current understanding of normative adolescent development while highlighting some variations among this largely middle-class European American and African American sample of males and females.

This does not diminish the value of the current analyses. The results provide a detailed, comprehensive picture of change over time during adolescence across multiple dimensions, as well as their sociodemographic correlates. The integrative summaries both at the end of each chapter and at the end of the monograph demonstrate admirable breadth and help to contextualize the findings in the broader developmental literature. The results have archival value, but because of the sheer number of analyses performed on such a large variety of measures, the findings resist easy assimilation. Readers may want to dip into the findings and focus on particular content domains of interest to get a descriptive picture of various developmental trends.

The authors of this monograph accomplished what they set out to do, and their agenda—and the methodological underpinnings involved in conducting these analyses—were undeniably ambitious, but they left me wanting more. By restricting the analyses to individual items and measures and focusing on individual content domains in isolation, many interesting and important questions—indeed, ones raised by the authors themselves—were left unanswered and instead were posed here as directions and hypotheses for further research. In interpreting their findings in particular areas, the authors offer many speculations on how these findings are linked to constructs in other domains—interpretations that could have been empirically tested with the data at hand. For instance, the authors noted in the introduction that there has been a longstanding interest among researchers in how changes in adolescents' interactions and relationships with parents influence changes in interactions with peers (and vice versa) and that although these two systems are often connected conceptually, they are rarely linked empirically. Making those connections was described as one of the main goals of this monograph. Indeed, as noted previously, the specific measures of peer and parent relationships were selected to provide parallels across these two contexts. Yet, although the present data afforded opportunities to elucidate precisely such issues, the analyses, with growth in parent and peer relationships modeled separately, do not provide insight into this issue. Such analyses have been conducted with other samples (De Goede, Branje, Delsing, & Meeus, 2009; Van Doorn, Branje, VanderValk, De Goede, & Meeus, 2011), and conducting similar analyses here would have a permitted useful comparison, as well as addressing important developmental questions. Likewise, recent research has linked ethnic/racial identity with academic functioning, psychological well-being, and health (Rivas-Drake et al., 2014) and some might argue for the centrality of making such connections. Numerous other questions raised in the monograph, such as whether trajectories of psychological well-being and academic aspirations and motivations are linked with different dimensions of relationships with parents or peers, were not addressed. Thus, the monograph largely leaves to future research a consideration of links across processes, content domains, and contexts over time. Such analyses are the essence of an ecological approach (Bronfenbrenner, 2009), and thus it is surprising that such links were not made here.

In saying this, I recognize that the authors argued against aggregating their measures into latent constructs, but doing so would have permitted a more focused set of analyses linking trajectories of psychological well-being and academic achievement, aspirations, and motivations with other developmental processes and contexts. The questions the authors raise in attempting to interpret their analyses beg for greater consideration of transactional processes within and across different interpersonal contexts (family, school, and peers; Sameroff, 2009; Sameroff & MacKenzie, 2003), as well as an examination of the links between the different growth trajectories modeled separately here. For instance, multivariate growth models, which estimate associations between growth factors across constructs (Curran, Obeidat, & Losardo, 2010), would have allowed explicit tests of the types of associations across domains mentioned previously (e.g., whether declines in the quality of relationships with parents over time are systematically associated with over-time increases in associations with deviant peers). Methods for analyzing longitudinal data have exploded in recent years (Little, 2013), offering many opportunities to investigate the data in new and exciting ways. The authors acknowledged these issues in their conclusions, viewing the results of the current monograph as a basis for future analyses examining "multivariate heterogeneity in adolescents' profiles and developmental trajectories" (p. 139). Admittedly, a different set of analyses would have addressed different questions and led to a very different monograph from the present one, but the questions raised in this commentary (and in the monograph) hopefully will intrigue other scholars and encourage them to extend the work presented here, either through further analyses of these data or as a springboard for new studies. For instance, there also has been an explosion of research in the neuroscience of adolescence (Casey, Jones, & Somerville, 2011), and the results of this monograph could inform further investigations of how neurological changes impact social and affective processing (Crone & Dahl, 2012).

The authors close, as do I, by stating that the MADICS data are available; hopefully others will take on this challenge, as there are numerous interesting questions from this very important data set that remain to be addressed. In summary, the authors have done the field a great service by bringing together a wealth of findings from this large, unique, and very valuable data set, allowing readers to compare and contrast both the sociodemographic variations in the findings as well as the different developmental trajectories illuminated here. And although the notion that adolescence is a time of "storm and stress" has been largely discarded (but see Arnett, 1999), the detailed analyses of trajectories of change across different domains of adolescent functioning provide a great deal of specificity to our understanding of positive youth development. They also highlight the developmental periods that pose specific risks in different domains for particular groups. This is a notable contribution to our conceptual understanding, as well as having enormous practical significance for promoting healthy development and protecting youth during vulnerable periods. The broad scope of the monograph provides novel information regarding similarities and differences in normative changes across adolescence for a relatively comparable sample of European American and African American males and females and demonstrates that adolescence is a period of vulnerability but also provides opportunity for positive growth and development.

REFERENCES

Arnett, J. J. (1999). Adolescent storm and stress, reconsidered. *American Psychologist,* **54,** 317–326.

Benner, A. D., & Graham, S. (2007). Navigating the transition to multi-ethnic urban high schools: Changing ethnic congruence and adolescents' school-related affect. *Journal of Research on Adolescence,* **17,** 207–220. https://doi.org/10.1111/j.1532-7795.2007.00519.x

Bronfenbrenner, U. (2009). *The ecology of human development.* Cambridge, MA: Harvard University Press.

Casey, B. J., Jones, R. M., & Somerville, L. H. (2011). Braking and accelerating of the adolescent brain. *Journal of Research on Adolescence,* **21,** 21–33. https://doi.org/10.1111/j.1532-7795.2010.00712.x

Crone, E. A., & Dahl, R. E. (2012). Understanding adolescence as a period of social-affective engagement and goal flexibility. *Nature Reviews Neuroscience,* **13,** 636–650. https://doi. org/10.1038/nrn3313

Curran, P. J., Obeidat, K., & Losardo, D. (2010). Twelve frequently asked questions about growth curve modeling. *Journal of Cognition and Development,* **11,** 121–136. https://doi.org/10.1080/15248371003699969

Darling, N., Cumsille, P., Caldwell, L. L., & Dowdy, B. (2006). Predictors of adolescents' disclosure to parents and perceived parental knowledge: Between- and within-person differences. *Journal of Youth and Adolescence,* **35,** 667–678. https://doi.org/10.1007/s10964-006-9058-1

De Goede, I. H. A., Branje, S. J. T., Delsing, M. J. M. H., & Meeus, W. H. J. (2009). Linkages over time between adolescents' relationships with parents and friends. *Journal of Youth and Adolescence,* **38,** 1304–1315. https://doi.org/10.1007/s10964-009-9403-2

Diamond, L. M., Bonner, S. B., & Dickenson, J. (2015). The development of sexuality. In R. M. Lerner (Series Ed.) & M. E. Lamb (Volume Ed.), *Handbook of child psychology and developmental science* (Vol. 3, pp. 888–931). New York, NY: Wiley.

Dishion, T. J., Nelson, S. E., & Bullock, B. M. (2004). Premature adolescent autonomy: Parent disengagement and deviant peer process in the amplification of problem behaviour. *Journal of Adolescence,* **27,** 515–530.

Elder, G. H. (1998). The life course as developmental theory. *Child Development,* **69,** 1–12. https://doi.org/10.1111/j.1467-8624.1998.tb06128.x

Elder, G. H., Jr., Johnson, M. K., & Crosnoe, R. (2003). The emergence and development of life course theory. In J. T. Mortimer & M. Shanahan (Eds.), *Handbook of the life course* (pp. 3–19). New York, NY: Springer.

Graham, S. (2006). Peer victimization in school: Exploring the ethnic context. *Current Directions in Psychological Science, 15*, 317–321. https://doi.org/10.1111/j.1467-8721.2006.00460.x

Graham, S. (2016). Commentary: The role of race/ethnicity in a developmental science of equity and justice. *Child Development, 8*, 1493–1504. https://doi.org/10.1111/cdev.12602

Granic, I., & Dishion, T. J. (2003). Deviant talk in adolescent friendships: A step toward measuring a pathogenic attractor process. *Social Development, 12*, 314–334. https://doi.org/10.1111/1467-9507.00236

Kerr, M., Stattin, H., & Burk, W. J. (2010). A reinterpretation of parental monitoring in longitudinal perspective. *Journal of Research on Adolescence, 20*, 39–64. https://doi.org/10.1111/j.1532-7795.2009.00623.x

Kuhn, E. S., & Laird, R. D. (2011). Individual differences in early adolescents' beliefs in the legitimacy of parental authority. *Developmental Psychology, 47*, 1353–1365. https://doi.org/10.1037/a0024050

Little, T. D. (2013). *Longitudinal structural equation modeling.* New York, NY: Guilford Press.

Marshall, S. K., Tilton-Weaver, L. C., & Bosdet, L. (2005). Information management: Considering adolescents' regulation of parental knowledge. *Journal of Adolescence, 28*, 633–647. https://doi.org/10.1016/j.adolescence.2005.08.008

Rivas-Drake, D., Seaton, E. K., Markstrom, C., Quintana, S., Syed, M., Lee, R. M., et al. (2014). Ethnic and racial identity in adolescence: Implications for psychosocial, academic, and health outcomes. *Child Development, 85*, 40–57. https://doi.org/10.1111/cdev.12200

Rubin, K. H., Bukowski, W. M., & Bowker, J. C. (2015). Children in peer groups. In R. M. Lerner (Series Ed.) & M. C. Bornstein & T. Leventhal (Volume Eds.), *Handbook of child psychology and developmental science* (Vol. 4, pp. 175–222). New York, NY: Wiley.

Russell, S. T., & Horn, S. S. (Eds.). (2017). *Sexual orientation, gender identity, and schooling.* New York, NY: Oxford University Press.

Sameroff, A. (2009). The transactional model. In A. Sameroff (Ed.), *The transactional model of development: How children and contexts shape each other* (pp. 3–21). Washington DC: American Psychological Association.

Sameroff, A. J., & MacKenzie, M. J. (2003). Research strategies for capturing transactional models of development: The limits of the possible. *Development and Psychopathology, 15*, 613–640. https://doi.org/10.1017/S0954579403000312

Smetana, J. (2011a). *Adolescents, families, and social development: How teens construct their worlds.* West Sussex, England: Wiley-Blackwell.

Smetana, J. G. (2011b). Parenting beliefs, parenting, and parent-adolescent communication in African American families. In N. E. Hill, T. Mann, & H. Fitzgerald (Eds.), *African American children's mental health: Development and context* (Vol. 1, pp. 173–197). New York, NY: Praeger Press.

Smetana, J. G., Campione-Barr, N., & Metzger, A. (2006). Adolescent development in interpersonal and societal contexts. *Annual Review of Psychology, 57*, 255–284. https://doi.org/10.1146/annurev.psych.57.102904.190124

Smetana, J. G., Metzger, A., Gettman, D. C., & Campione-Barr, N. (2006). Disclosure and secrecy in adolescent-parent relationships. *Child Development, 77*, 201–217.

Umaña-Taylor, A. J., Quintana, S. M., Lee, R. M., Cross, W. E., Rivas-Drake, D., Schwartz, S. J., et al. (2014). Ethnic and racial identity during adolescence and into young adulthood: An integrated conceptualization. *Child Development*, **85**, 21–39. https://doi.org/10.1111/cdev.12196

Van Doorn, M. D., Branje, S. J., VanderValk, I. E., De Goede, I. H., & Meeus, W. H. (2011). Longitudinal spillover effects of conflict resolution styles between adolescent-parent relationships and adolescent friendships. *Journal of Family Psychology*, **25**, 157–161. https://doi.org/10.1037/a0022289

CONTRIBUTORS

This article is part of the issue "Moving Through Adolescence: Developmental Trajectories of African American and European American Youth" Gutman, Peck, Malanchuk, Sameroff, and Eccles (Issue Authors). For a full listing of articles in this issue, see: http://onlinelibrary.wiley.com/doi/10.1111/mono.v82.4/issuetoc.

Leslie M. Gutman is Associate Professor of Psychology and Director of the Masters Program in Behavior Change at University College London. She is also a Senior Associate of the Early Intervention Foundation and Associate Editor of the *Journal of Adolescence*. Her research focuses on mental health and well-being, aspirations and achievement, and risk and resilience in children and adolescents.

Stephen C. Peck is a Senior Research Fellow at the David P. Weikart Center for Youth Program Quality. During work on this monograph, he was an Assistant Research Scientist in the Achievement Research Lab at the University of Michigan. His research focuses on lifespan development in context, or the study of self/identity/personality as a multilevel information processing system designed to regulate human experience and behavior in relation to contextual opportunities and constraints.

Oksana Malanchuk received her PhD in Social Psychology from the University of Michigan. She served as the Project Manager of the MADICS study from 1994 to 2016, contributing to the questionnaire design, data collection and analysis of Waves 3 through Wave 8. Her research has focused on social identities, including racial/ethnic identity, their development and their outcomes.

DOI: 10.1111/mono.12340

Arnold J. Sameroff is Professor Emeritus of Psychology and Research Professor Emeritus at the Center for Human Growth and Development at the University of Michigan. His research focus has been on pathways to competence and mental health from infancy to adulthood.

Jacquelynne Eccles, Distinguished University Professor of Education at University of California, Irvine and Distinguished Professor of Psychology and Education Emeritus at the University of Michigan, Ann Arbor, got her PhD at UCLA in 1974. She is past president of the Society for Research on Adolescence, and both Division 7 (Development Psychology) and 35 (Psychology of Women) of the American Psychological Association. She studies social development in the context of schools, families, and peer groups.

Judith Smetana is Professor of Psychology, Director of the Developmental Psychology PhD program, and past Frederica Warner Chair at the University of Rochester. Her research focuses on adolescent–parent relationships and parenting in different ethnic and cultural contexts and on the development of children's moral and social reasoning. In addition to numerous articles and chapters, she is the author of *Adolescents, families, and social development: How teens construct their worlds* (Wiley-Blackwell, 2011).

STATEMENT OF EDITORIAL POLICY

The SRCD *Monographs* series aims to publish major reports of developmental research that generates authoritative new findings and that foster a fresh perspective and/or integration of data/research on conceptually significant issues. Submissions may consist of individually or group-authored reports of findings from some single large-scale investigation or from a series of experiments centering on a particular question. Multiauthored sets of independent studies concerning the same underlying question also may be appropriate. A critical requirement in such instances is that the individual authors address common issues and that the contribution arising from the set as a whole be unique, substantial, and well integrated. Manuscripts reporting interdisciplinary or multidisciplinary research on significant developmental questions and those including evidence from diverse cultural, racial, and ethnic groups are of particular interest. Also of special interest are manuscripts that bridge basic and applied developmental science, and that reflect the international perspective of the Society. Because the aim of the *Monographs* series is to enhance cross-fertilization among disciplines or subfields as well as advance knowledge on specialized topics, the links between the specific issues under study and larger questions relating to developmental processes should emerge clearly and be apparent for both general readers and specialists on the topic. In short, irrespective of how it may be framed, work that contributes significant data and/or extends a developmental perspective will be considered.

Potential authors who may be unsure whether the manuscript they are planning wouldmake an appropriate submission to the SRCD *Monographs* are invited to draft an outline or prospectus of what they propose and send it to the incoming editor for review and comment.

Potential authors are not required to be members of the Society for Research in Child Development nor affiliated with the academic discipline of psychology to submit a manuscript for consideration by the *Monographs*. The significance of the work in extending developmental theory and in contributing new empirical information is the crucial consideration.

Submissions should contain a minimum of 80 manuscript pages (including tables and references). The upper boundary of 150–175 pages is more flexible, but authors should try to keep within this limit. Manuscripts must be double-spaced, 12pt Times New Roman font, with 1-inch margins. If color artwork is submitted, and the authors believe color art is necessary to the presentation of their work, the submissions letter should indicate that one or more authors or their institutions are prepared to pay the substantial costs associated with color art reproduction. Please submit manuscripts electronically to the SRCD *Monographs* Online Submissions and Review Site (Scholar One) at http://mc.manuscriptcentral.com/mono. Please contact the *Monographs* office with any questions at monographs@srcd.org.

The corresponding author for any manuscript must, in the submission letter, warrant that all coauthors are in agreement with the content of the manuscript. The corresponding author also is responsible for informing all coauthors, in a timely manner, of manuscript submission, editorial decisions, reviews received, and any revisions recommended. Before publication, the corresponding author must warrant in the submissions letter that the study has been conducted according to the ethical guidelines of the Society for Research in Child Development.

A more detailed description of all editorial policies, evaluation processes, and format requirements can be found under the "Submission Guidelines" link at http://srcd.org/publications/monographs.

Monographs Editorial Office
e-mail: monographs@srcd.org

Editor, Patricia J. Bauer
Department of Psychology, Emory University
36 Eagle Row
Atlanta, GA 30322
e-mail: pjbauer@emory.edu

Note to NIH Grantees

Pursuant to NIH mandate, Society through Wiley-Blackwell will post the accepted version of Contributions authored by NIH grantholders to PubMed Central upon acceptance. This accepted version will be made publicly available 12 months after publication. For further information, see http://www.wiley.com/go/nihmandate.

SUBJECT INDEX

Page numbers in *italics* represent tables and figures.

A

academic functioning

achievement/motivation, 8, 18, 92, 101–103, 104, 134, 137, 171, 172, 173–174

alcohol use, 111

correlational analyses, 59–60

covariate, *37–38*, 49–50

developmental trajectories, 7, 9, 18–20, 134

educational aspiration, 12, 18, *37, 38, 43,* 49, 68, *96–98,* 99–101, 104–105, 135

educational expectation 12, 18, *37, 38, 43,* 49, 65, 68–69, 78, *96, 97,* 101, 104, 105, 134

gender by race/ethnicity, 20

gender differences, 19–20, 59, 99, 104, 135

GPA, *37, 43,* 49, 59, *96, 97,* 97, 99, *98,* 104–105, 135, 137

growth models/curves, *96, 98*

importance, *38, 43,* 50, *96–98,* 101, 104

measures, 34, 91, 95–105

peer characteristics, 26, 173

positive school identification, 18, *38, 44,* 50, *96, 98,* 103, 105, 134

promotive/protective factor, 12

race/ethnic differences, 59, 65, 99, 104, 136, 173

residual variance, *97*

risky behavior and —, 20–21

school problems, *39, 44,* 50, 59, 60, 106, *108, 109* (*see also* behavior, risky/problem)

self-belief/self-concept, 7, 8, 12, 19–20, *38, 43,* 50, 60, *96–98,* 102–103, 104, 133, 134

socioeconomic status, 99, 102, 105, 137

transitions, 18–19

adolescent development, 7, 8–9. *See also* developmental trajectories
African American youth
  academic functioning, 99, 104
  academic importance, 101–102, 136
  academic motivation, 104
  alcohol use, 112, 113
  anger, 75–76, 81, 135
  cigarette use, 110, 112
  correlational analyses, 57, 59–62, 92
  cross racial/ethnic friends, 89, 135
  depression, 15
  developmental trajectories, 7–28
  eating disorders, 77–78, 81
  educational/occupational aspirations, 19–20, 65, 136
  expected racial/ethnic discrimination, 89–91, 93
  family characteristics, 24, 61, 123
  gender differences, 32, 56, 59–60, 61, 81, 90, 93
  GPA, 99, 105, 135
  intrusive parenting, 118
  John Henryism, 90–91
  marijuana use, 112
  negative relationship with parents, 118–119
  occupational aspirations, 32, 100–101, 135
  parents' worries, 91, 135
  peer characteristics, 62
  peer drug norms, 130
  positive identification with parents, 120–121, 136
  positive peers, 129, 132, 136
  research models, 67
  resilience, 16
  risky behavior, 21–22, 136
  same racial/ethnic friends, 89
  self-esteem, 15, 74, 81
  socioeconomic status differences, 32, 75, 99, 168–169
  strict parenting, 119
  study demographics, 31
  study distribution, 30
age-related changes
  academic functioning, 95–105
  developmental trajectories, 7–28
  family characteristics, 114–123
  modeling, 66–68
  peer characteristics, 124–132

psychological well-being, 70–82
race/ethnic differences, 17–18, 83–94
risky behavior, 106–113
aggression, 14–15, 21
alcohol use, 8, 11, 13, 14, 20–21
  correlational analyses, 60
  covariate, *39*, *44*, 51, 111
  family characteristics, 23, 113
  gender differences, 112
  gender and race/ethnicity, 21, *109*
  growth models, *107*
  peer characteristics, 25, 130, 131
  race/ethnicity, 112, 136
  residual variance, *108*
  socioeconomic status, 113
  See also behavior, risky/problem

B
behaviors, healthy, 7
behavior, risky/problem
  antisocial, 13
  control, 115, 116, 118
  correlational analyses, 59, 60–61
  covariates, *38–39*, 50–51
  delinquent behavior, *44*, 50–51, 60–62, 78–79, *107*, *108*, *109*, 110–111, 171
  developmental trajectories, 7, 13, 9, 20–22, 34, 172, 174
  family characteristics, 23, 106, 111, 113
  gender, 21–22, 106, 110, 112
  gender by race/ethnic interaction, 110
  growth models/curves, *107*, *109*
  measures, 106–113, 133
  media portrayal, 8
  peer characteristics, 12, 25, 26, 136
  race/ethnicity, 21–22, 106, 110
  residual variance, *108*
  risk factors, 12
  socioeconomic status, 106, 110, 113, 137
  theoretical framework, 9–10
  types of, 8, 11
  See also academic functioning, school problems; alcohol use; cigarette smoking; marijuana use

beliefs. *See* self-worth, concept of
brain maturation, 12, 20

C
Children's Depression Inventory, 47
cigarette smoking, 8, 20–21
  correlational analyses, 60
  covariate, *39, 44,* 50, 110
  family characteristics, 23
  gender differences, 112
  gender and race/ethnicity, 21, *109*
  growth models, *107*
  peer characteristics, 25, 130
  race/ethnicity, 110, 112, 136
  residual variance, *108*
  See also behavior, risky/problem
construct invariance, 54, 65
construct validity, 54
convergent validity, 54, 59–62
criminal behavior, 14, 21

D
developmental trajectories
  academic functioning, 95–105
  adolescent development, 12–13, 134
  African American youth, 7–28
  analyses and analytic plan, 54–69
  assets, 10
  European American youth, 7–28
  family characteristics, 114–123
  gender and race/ethnic differences, 134–137
  integrative summary, 133–142
  method, 29–53
  peer characteristics, 124–132
  problem behaviors, 106–113
  psychological well-being, 70–82
  race/ethnic identity and discrimination, 83–94
  research study methods, 29–53
  research study preliminary analyses and analytic plan, 54–69
  risk/protective factor, 11
  theoretical framework, 9–12

See also academic functioning; behavior, risky/problem; family characteristics; peer characteristics; psychological well-being; race/ethnic variation
discriminant validity, 54, 56, 59–62
drug use. *See* substance abuse

E
Eating Disorder Inventory (EDI) for Anorexia Nervosa and Bulimia, 47
economic prospect, 14
EDI. *See* Eating Disorder Inventory
emotional functioning, 8
European American youth
  academic functioning, 99, 136
  academic importance, 102
  academic motivation, 104
  alcohol use, 111, 112, 113
  anger, 75, 81, 135
  cigarette use, 110, 112
  correlational analyses, *58*, 59–62, 92
  cross racial/ethnic friends, 89, 135
  developmental trajectories, 7–28
  eating disorders, 77–78, 81
  educational/occupational aspirations, 19–20
  expected racial/ethnic discrimination, 89–91
  family characteristics, 61, 65, 123
  gender differences, 32, 56, 59–60, 61, 81, 90, 102
  GPA, 99, 105, 135
  intrusive parenting, 118
  John Henryism, 90–91
  marijuana use, 111–112, 136–137
  peers, 131
  negative relationship with parents, 118–119
  occupational aspirations, 32, 100–101, 135
  parent's worries, 91, 135
  characteristics, 62, 136–137
  positive identification with parents, 120–121, 122, 136
  positive peers, 129
  research models, 67
  risky behavior, 21, 136
  same racial/ethnic friends, 89
  self-esteem, 74, 81
  socioeconomic status differences, 32, 75, 99, 168–169

strict parenting, 119
study demographics, 31
study distribution, 30
Expectancy-Value Theory, 99

F
family characteristics
  authoritative parenting, 22–23
  climate, 10
  communication, 22, *40*, *45*, 52, 61, *115*, *116*, 119–120, 123, 127–128, 137
  conflict, 22
  correlational analyses, 61
  covariates, *39–40*, 51–52, 114–123
  developmental trajectories, 7, 9, 22–25
  gender by race/ethnic interaction, 121
  gender differences, 23–24 119, 122, 136
  growth models/curves, *115*, *117*
  intrusive/negative parenting, 22, *39*, *44*, 51, 61, *115–117*, 118, 122
  measures, 34, 170
  negative relationship with parents, 7, 12, *39*, *44*, 51, 61, *115–117*, 118–119, 122, 123, 133, 172
  parental control, 11, 12, 24, 114, 116–119, 122
  parental warmth/support/close relationship, 7, 8, 12, 22–24, *115–117*, 119–121, 122–123
  parents' marital status, 28, 31, 46, 66, 67, 68, 74, 75, 77, 78, 82, *84–87*, 88, 100, 101, 101, 105, 106, 110, 113, 120, 123, 128, 130, 137, 138–139, 168, 172
  positive identification with parents, 22, *40*, *45*, 52, 61, *115*, *116*, 120–123, 133, 134, 136, 172, 174
  promotive/protective parenting, 22
  race/ethnic differences, 24, 65, 89–91, 122–123, 136
  relationship shifts, 11, 173
  residual variance, *116*
  risky parenting, 22
  social support, 22, *40*, *45*, 51–52
  socioeconomic status, 24, 123
  status, 10
  strict parenting, 22, *40*, *44*, 51, 61, *115–117*, 119
  study demographics, 31
five Cs, 11
friends. *See* peer characteristics

G

gender by race/ethnic interaction, 7, 8, *84–87*
  academic functioning, 20, *98*, 99, 104–105, 135
  academic importance, 102
  academic self-concept, 102–103
  alcohol use, 112, 113
  anger, 75
  behavioral involvement, 88, *109*, 112
  cigarette use, 112
  delinquent behavior, 110–111
  developmental trajectories, 134–137, 172
  eating disorders, 77–78, 136
  educational aspirations, 99–100
  educational expectations, 100
  expected negative life chances, 78
  family characteristics, *117*
  marijuana use, 111–112
  occupational aspirations, 101
  peer characteristics, *127*, 136
  peer support, 128, 136
  positive identification with parents, 121, 122–123
  positive school identification, 103
  research models, 67
  resiliency, 75
  risky behavior, 106
  self-esteem, 74, 136
  theoretical framework, 10
gender variation, 7, 8
  academic functioning, 19
  aggression, 14–15
  anger, 75–76
  correlational analyses, 59–62, 66
  covariate, 46
  cross racial/ethnic friends, 89
  delinquent behavior, 110–111
  depressive affect, 14, 77, 80–81
  eating disorders, 14, 77–78, 81, 136
  educational aspirations, 99–101
  educational expectations, 100
  expected negative life chances, 78
  expected racial/ethnic discrimination, 90
  family characteristics, 23–24, 61
  invariance tests, 62–63, *63–64*, 64–65

missing data, 33
negative peers, 130
occupational aspirations, 101
parent–adolescent communication, 120
peer characteristics, 26, 128, 131–132
peer drug norms, 130
positive peers, 129
positive school identification, 103
psychological well-being, 14–15, 168
race/ethnic differences, 17–18, 26, 56, *84–87*, 88–94
research models, 67
resiliency, 75
risk/protective factor, 11
risky behavior, 21–22, 106, 136
same racial/ethnic friends, 89
self-esteem, 14, 74–75, 81, 136
study differences, 32
theoretical framework, 10
See also gender by race/ethnic interaction

H
hierarchical linear modeling (HLM), 27, 33, 65, 83
HLM. *See* hierarchical linear modeling

I
ICC. *See* intraclass correlation
identity formation, 11
intraclass correlation (ICC), 68
invariance tests, 62–63, *63–64*, 64–65
Iowa Youth and Family Study, 51, 52

M
MADICS. *See* Maryland Adolescent Development in Context Study
marijuana use, *39, 44,* 51, 60, *107, 108, 109,* 111–112, 130, 131, 136. *See also*
behavior, risky/problem; substance abuse
Maryland Adolescent Development in Context Study (MADICS), 9, 29,
48, 49, 52, 167, 168–169
measurement invariance, 54
MEIM. *See* Multigroup Ethnic Identity Measure
mental health. *See* psychological well-being

MIBI. *See* Multidimensional Inventory of Black Identity
Michigan Study of Adolescent Life Transitions (MSALT), 50, 52
Monitoring the Future, 50, 51
mood disorder, 13
moodiness, 76, 80
MSALT. *See* Michigan Study of Adolescent Life Transitions
Multidimensional Inventory of Black Identity (MIBI), 83
Multigroup Ethnic Identity Measure (MEIM), 83

N
National Educational Longitudinal Study, 49
neighborhood influences, 24, 75, 78
nicotine use. *See* cigarette smoking

O
occupational aspiration, 99–101, 104, 134
  covariate, *38, 43*, 49
  growth aspirations/curves, *96, 98*
  promotive/protective factor, 12
  race/ethnic differences, 65, 101, 104–105, 135
  residual variance, *97*
  socioeconomic status, 101, 105
  study differences, 32, 68

P
parent relationship. *See* family characteristics
parenting styles, 51. *See also* family characteristics
peer characteristics
  academic functioning, 26, 173
  communication, 26, *40, 45*, 52, 61, 124, *125–127*, 128, 131, 170
  correlational analyses, 56, 59–62
  covariates, *40–41*, 52–53
  depression, 26
  developmental trajectories, 7, 9, 25, 134, 174
  drug norms/substance abuse, 25, 26, *41, 45*, 53, 60, 124, *125–127*, 130, 131, 134, 136–137, 172
  family characteristics, 128, 130
  gender, 26, 62, 128, 131, 136
  gender by race/ethnic interaction, 128, 130
  growth models, *125*

measures, 34, 124–132, 170–171

negative peers, 7, *41, 45,* 53, 60, 61, 124, *125–127,* 129, 130, 133, 136, 172

positive peers, *41, 45,* 52, 60, 62, 124, *125–127,* 129, 131, 133, 137

race/ethnicity, 128, 129, 130, 173

relationship shifts, 11, 173

residual variance, *126*

risky behaviors, 12, 25, 26

socioeconomic status, 128, 129, 130, 132, 137

supportive relationship, 7, 8, 12, *41, 45,* 52, 124, *125–127,* 128

Philadelphia Family Management Study, 47, 50, 51

problem behavior. *See* behavior, risky/problem

promotive/protective factor, 9–12, 13, 16. *See also specific promotive/ protective factor*

psychological well-being

  anger, 7, 13, 14, *35, 42,* 47, 70, *71, 72,* 75–76, 79–82, 133, 135

  control, 115, 118

  correlational analyses, 56, 59–62

  depressive affect, 7, 13, 14, 15, 23, 26, *35, 42,* 47, 70, *71, 72,* 76–78, 79–82, 133

  developmental trajectories, 7, 8, 9, 13–15, 70, 79–82, 133, 134

  eating disorders, 13, 14, *35, 42,* 47, 61, 70, *71, 72,* 77–78, 79, 81–82, 137

  expected negative life chances, 13, *36, 42,* 47, 70, *71, 72,* 78–79, 82

  family characteristics, 168

  gender differences, 14–15, 79, 168

  growth curves, *73*

  growth models, *71*

  maintenance, 11

  measures, 34, *35–36, 42,* 70–82, 91

  promotive/protective factor, 12

  race/ethnicity, 15, 135, 168

  resilience, 10–11, 13, 14, 16, *35, 42,* 47, 59, 60, 70, *71, 72,* 74–75, 76, 79–82

  residual variance, *72*

  risk factors, 12, 20–21 (*see also specific factor*)

  self-esteem, 8, 13–15, 47, *35, 42,* 59, 60, 70, *71, 72,* 72, 74, 76–77, 79–82, 139

  socioeconomic status, 15, 168

R

race/ethnic (R/E) variation, 7, 8, 9, 134

  academic functioning, 99, 135, 136, 173

academic self-concept, 102–103
age-related changes, 17–18
anger, 75–76
behavioral involvement, *36*, *42*, 48, *84–86*, 88
correlational analysis, 56, 59–62, 66
covariate, 46
cross R/E friendship, 16, *36*, *43*, 48, *84–87*, 89, 92–93, 135
delinquent behavior, 110–111
eating disorders, 77–78, 136
educational/occupational aspirations, 19–20, 101
expected discrimination, *37*, *43*, 49, *84–86*, 89–91, 92, 93
educational expectations, 100
expected negative life chances, 78, 79
family characteristics, 24, 90–91, 172
gender differences, 17–18, 26–27, 56, 88–93 (*see also* gender by race/ ethnic interaction)
growth models, *84–85*
identity and discrimination, 15–18, 34, *36–37*, *42–43*, 48–49
importance, *36*, *42*, 48, *84–87*, 88–89
intrusive parenting, 118
invariance tests, 62–63, *63–64*, 64–65
John Henryism, *37*, *43*, 49, *84–87*, 90–91, 92
measures, 83–94, 170
negative relationship with parents, 118–119
occupational aspirations, 101, 104–105, 135
parent's worries, *37*, *43*, 49, *84–87*, 91, 94, 135
peer characteristics, 26–27, 127–128, 129, 130, 131–132, 136–137
peer drug norms, 130
positive identification with parents, 121
positive school identification, 103
prejudice, 24
promotive/protective factor, 12
psychological well-being, 15, 168, 173
racism, 24, 76
research models, 67
residual variance, *86*
resiliency, 74–75
risk/protective factor, 11, 12, 16
risky behavior, 21, 106
same R/E friendship, 17, *36*, *42*, 48, *84–87*, 88–89, 92–93, 135
self-esteem, 74, 136
stigma, 75–76
strict parenting, 119

theoretical framework, 10
See also gender by race/ethnic interaction
research study
  attrition patterns, 32–33, 68, 169
  commentary, 167–175
  correlational analyses, 55–56
  covariates, 46–48 (*see also specific covariates*)
  data collection, 30–31, 68
  demographics, 30
  described, 11–12, 27–28
  developmental trajectories, 7–28
  future studies, 140–141
  integrative summary, 133–142
  interview formats, 33–34
  limitations, 137–140
  measures, 34, *35–41*, 41, *42–45*, 45–46
  method, 29–53, 169
  missing data, 32–33
  models, 65–68
  participants, 27, 29–31
  preliminary analyses and analytic plan, 54–69
  procedure, 33–34
  retention patterns, 32–33, 68, 169
  study location, 29–30
  waves, 32, 63–69
risk factors, 11. *See also specific factors*
risk prevention, 10
risky behavior. *See* behavior, risky/problem

S

SAMC. *See* Study of Adolescents in Multiple Contexts
school, 11. *See also* academic functioning
self-worth, concept of, 47
SES. *See* socioeconomic status
socioeconomic status (SES)
  academic functioning, 99, 105, 137
  academic importance, 101–102
  academic self-concept, 102–103
  anger, 75–76, 81
  behavior, risky, 112–113, 137
  behavioral involvement, 88
  correlational analyses, 66

covariate, 46
delinquent behavior, 110–111
depressive affect, 15, 76–77, 81
eating disorders, 77
educational aspirations, 100
educational expectations, 100
expected negative life chances, 78, 79
family characteristics, 24, 123
GPA, 102
missing data, 33
modeling growth, 172
occupational aspirations, 101, 105
parent's worries, 91, 94, 135
peer characteristics, 127–128, 129, 132, 137
peer drug norms, 130
positive school identification, 103
psychological well-being, 15, 137, 168
race/ethnicity, *84–87*, 88, 168–169
research models, 67, 68
resiliency, 74–75, 81
risk/protective factor, 11
school problems, 106
self-esteem, 74
study differences, 32
study distribution, 30, 31
study limitations, 137–140
theoretical framework, 10
variation, 7, 8
Study of Adolescents in Multiple Contexts (SAMC), 30
substance abuse, 8, 13, 20–21 23. *See also* marijuana use; peer characteristics, drug norms/substance abuse
Symptom Check List (anger), 47

V
victimization, 16, 26, 171

CURRENT

Moving Through Adolescence: Developmental Trajectories of African American and European American Youth— *Leslie Morrison Gutman, Stephen C. Peck, Oksana Malanchuk, Arnold J. Sameroff and Jacquelynne S. Eccles* (SERIAL NO. 327, 2017)

Developmental Trajectories of Children's Adjustment across the Transition to Siblinghood: Pre-Birth Predictors and Sibling Outcomes at One Year— *Brenda L. Volling, Richard Gonzalez, Wonjung Oh, Ju-Hyun Song, Tianyi Yu, Lauren Rosenberg, Patty X. Kuo, Elizabeth Thomason, Emma Beyers-Carlson, Paige Safyer and Matthew M. Stevenson* (SERIAL NO. 326, 2017)

Developmental Methodology— *Noel A. Card* (SERIAL NO. 325, 2017)

Links Between Spatial and Mathematical Skills Across the Preschool Years— *Brian N. Verdine, Roberta Michnick Golinkoff, Kathy Hirsh-Pasek, and Nora S. Newcombe* (SERIAL NO. 324, 2017)

The Changing Nature of Executive Control in Preschool— *Kimberly Andrews Espy* (SERIAL NO. 323, 2016)

Working Memory Capacity in Context: Modeling Dynamic Processes of Behavior, Memory, and Development— *Vanessa R. Simmering* (SERIAL NO. 322, 2016)

Quality Thresholds, Features, and Dosage in Early Care and Education: Secondary Data Analyses of Child Outcomes— *Margaret Burchinal, Martha Zaslow, and Louisa Tarullo* (SERIAL NO. 321, 2016)

Gender in Low- and Middle-Income Countries— *Marc H. Bornstein, Diane L. Putnick, Jennifer E. Lansford, Kirby Deater-Deckard, and Robert H. Bradley* (SERIAL NO. 320, 2016)

A Longitudinal Study of Infant Cortisol Response During Learning Events— *Laura A. Thompson, Gin Morgan, and Kellie A. Jurado* (SERIAL NO. 319, 2015)

Studies in Fetal Behavior: Revisited, Renewed, and Reimagined— *Janet A. DiPietro, Kathleen A. Costigan and Kristin M. Voegtline* (SERIAL NO. 318, 2015)

The Role of Parents in The Ontogeny of Achievement-Related Motivation and Behavioral Choices— *Sandra D. Simpkins Jennifer A. Fredricks and Jacquelynne S. Eccles* (SERIAL NO. 317, 2015)

Sleep and Development: Advancing Theory and Research— *Mona El-Sheikh and Avi Sadeh* (SERIAL NO. 316, 2015)

The Relation of Childhood Physical Activity to Brain Health, Cognition, and Scholastic Achievement— *Charles H. Hillman* (SERIAL NO. 315, 2014)

The Adult Attachment Interview: Psychometrics, Stability and Change From Infancy, and Developmental Origins— *Cathryn Booth-LaForce and Glenn I. Roisman* (SERIAL NO. 314, 2014)

The Emergent Executive: A Dynamic Field Theory of the Development of Executive Function— *Aaron T. Buss and John P. Spencer* (SERIAL NO. 313, 2014)

Children's Understanding of Death: Toward a Contextualized and Integrated Account— *Karl S. Rosengren, Peggy J. Miller, Isabel T. Gutiérrez, Philip I. Chow, Stevie S. Schein, and Kathy N. Anderson* (SERIAL NO. 312, 2014)

Physical Attractiveness and the Accumulation of Social and Human Capital in Adolescence and Young Adulthood: Assets and Distractions— *Rachel A. Gordon, Robert Crosnoe, and Xue Wang* (SERIAL NO. 311, 2013)

The Family Life Project: An Epidemiological and Developmental Study of Young Children Living in Poor Rural Communities— *Lynne Vernon-Feagans, Martha Cox, and FLP Key Investigators* (SERIAL NO. 310, 2013)

National Institutes of Health Toolbox Cognition Battery (NIH Toolbox CB): Validation for Children Between 3 and 15 Years— *Philip David Zelazo and Patricia J. Bauer* (SERIAL NO. 309, 2013)

Resilience in Children With Incarcerated Parents— *Julie Poehlmann and J. Mark Eddy* (SERIAL NO. 308, 2013)

The Emergence of a Temporally Extended Self and Factors That Contribute to Its Development: From Theoretical and Empirical Perspectives— *Mary Lazaridis* (SERIAL NO. 307, 2013)

What Makes a Difference: Early Head Start Evaluation Findings in a Developmental Context— *John M. Love, Rachel Chazan-Cohen, Helen Raikes, and Jeanne Brooks-Gunn* (SERIAL NO. 306, 2013)

The Development of Mirror Self-Recognition in Different Sociocultural Contexts— *Joscha Kärtner, Heidi Keller, Nandita Chaudhary, and Relindis D. Yovsi* (SERIAL NO. 305, 2012)

"Emotions Are a Window Into One's Heart": A Qualitative Analysis of Parental Beliefs About Children's Emotions Across Three Ethnic Groups— *Alison E. Parker, Amy G. Halberstadt, Julie C. Dunsmore, Greg Townley, Alfred Bryant, Jr., Julie A. Thompson, and Karen S. Beale* (SERIAL NO. 304, 2012)

Physiological Measures of Emotion From a Developmental Perspective: State of the Science— *Tracy A. Dennis, Kristin A. Buss, and Paul D. Hastings* (SERIAL NO. 303, 2012)

How Socialization Happens on the Ground: Narrative Practices as Alternate Socializing Pathways in Taiwanese and European-American Families— *Peggy J. Miller, Heidi Fung, Shumin Lin, Eva Chian-Hui Chen, and Benjamin R. Boldt* (SERIAL NO. 302, 2012)

Children Without Permanent Parents: Research, Practice, and Policy— *Robert B. McCall, Marinus H. van IJzendoorn, Femmie Juffer, Christina J. Groark, and Victor K. Groza* (SERIAL NO. 301, 2011)

I Remember Me: Mnemonic Self-Reference Effects in Preschool Children— *Josephine Ross, James R. Anderson, and Robin N. Campbell* (SERIAL NO. 300, 2011)